PROJECTS AS BUSINESS CONSTITUENTS
AND GUIDING MOTIVES

PROJECTS AS BUSINESS CONSTITUENTS AND GUIDING MOTIVES

edited by

Rolf A. Lundin
Umeå University

and

Francis Hartman
The University of Calgary

KLUWER ACADEMIC PUBLISHERS
BOSTON/DORDRECHT/LONDON

Distributors for North, Central and South America:
Kluwer Academic Publishers
101 Philip Drive
Assinippi Park
Norwell, Massachusetts 02061 USA
Telephone (781) 871-6600
Fax (781) 871-6528
E-Mail <kluwer@wkap.com>

Distributors for all other countries:
Kluwer Academic Publishers Group
Distribution Centre
Post Office Box 322
3300 AH Dordrecht, THE NETHERLANDS
Telephone 31 78 6392 392
Fax 31 78 6546 474
E-Mail <orderdept@wkap.nl>

 Electronic Services <http://www.wkap.nl>

Library of Congress Cataloging-in-Publication Data
Projects as business constituents and guiding motives / edited by Rolf A. Lundin and
Francis Hartman.
     p.cm.
   A collection of 18 papers contributed by the editors and other North American and
European scholars.
   Includes bibliographical references and index.
   ISBN 0-7923-7834-2 (HB : alk.paper)
   1. Industrial project management. I. Lundin, Rolf A. II. Hartman, Francis T., 1950-

HD69.P75 P7635 2000
658.4'04--dc21   00-035653

Printed on acid-free paper.

Printed in the United States of America

Anell, Barbro, Umeå School of Business and Economics, Department of Business Administration, SE-901 87 Umeå, Sweden, Tel: +46 90 786 7649, Fax: +46 90 786 7764, E-mail: barbro.anell@fek.umu.se

Charue-Duboc, Florence, Centre de Recherche en Gestion, Ecole polytechnique, 1 Rue Descartes, F-75 005 Paris, France, Tel: +33 155 55 84 43, Fax: +33 155 55 84 44, E-mail: charie@poly.polytechnique.fr

Gustafsson, Magnus, Research Group for Project Based Industry, Åbo Akademi University, Biskopsgatan 10, FIN-20500 Åbo, Finland, Tel: +358 2 265 4311, Fax: +358 2 233 0494, E-mail: magnus.gustafsson@abo.fi

Hartman, Francis, University of Calgary, Room ENF 230, 2500 University Drive N.W., Calgary, Alberta T2N 1N4, Canada, Tel: +1 403 220 7178, Fax: +1 403 282 7026, E-mail: fhartman@acs.ucalgary.ca

Jugdev, Kam, IBM, Integration Services, 7th floor, 144-4 Ave SW, Calgary, Alberta T2P 3N5, Canada, Tel: +1 403 267 4136, Fax: +1 403 267 4321, E-mail: kjugdev@ca.ibm.com

Kidd, John B. Aston Business School, Aston University, B4 7ET Birmingham, United Kingdom, Fax: +44 121 359 5271, E-mail: johnkidd@compuserve.com

Kumar, Kuldeep, Erasmus University, Rotterdam School of Management, P.O. Box 1738, NL-3000 DR Rotterdam, The Netherlands, Tel: +31 10 408 2798, Fax: +31 10 452 3595, E-mail: kkumar@fac.fbk.eur.nl

Larson, Maria, European Tourism Research Institute, SE-831 25 Östersund, Sweden, Tel: +46 63 195 807, Fax: +46 63 195 810, and School of Economics and Commercial Law, Göteborg University, Department of Business Administration, Box 610, SE-405 30 Gothenburg, Sweden, Tel: +46 31 773 1894, Fax: +46 31 773 4410, E-mail: maria.larson@mgmt.gu.se

Lechler, Thomas, IBU, Karlsruhe University of Technology, Waldhornstr. 27, DE-76131 Karlsruhe, Germany, Tel: +49 721 608 7694, Fax: +49 721 608 6046, E-mail: thomas.lechler@wiwi.uni-karlsruhe.de

Lundin, Rolf A., Umeå School of Business and Economics, Department of Business Administration, SE-901 87 Umeå, Sweden, Tel: +46 90 786 6153, Fax: +46 90 786 7764, E-mail: rolf.a.lundin@fek.umu.se

Mahmoud-Jouini, Sihem Ben, University of Paris XI and CRG-Ecole Polytechnique, 1 Rue Descartes, F-75005 Paris, France, Tel: +33 1 5555 8662, Fax: +33 1 5555 8444, E-mail: sihem@poly.polytechnique.fr

Pinto, Jeffrey K., School of Business, Penn State Erie, Station Road, Erie, A 16563 USA, Tel: 814 898 6430, Fax: 814 898 6223, E-mail: jkp4@psu.edu

Robins, Paul C. Aston Business School, Aston University, B4 7ET Birmingham, United Kingdom, Tel: +44 121 359 3611, Fax: +44 121 359 5271, E-mail: p.c.robins@aston.ac.uk

Rouhiainen, Pekka, Aker Rauma Offshore, 11757 Katy Highway, Suite 500, Houston TX 77079 USA, Tel: 281 679 4882, Fax: 281 558 9299, E-mail: PJRouhiainen@sparsintl.com

Seidle, Marcia, Clarion University, Marketing Department, Clarion, Pennsylvania, 15701, U.S.A, Fax: +1 814 226 1910, E-mail: seidle@mail.clarion.edu

Söderlund, Jonas, IMIE, Linköping University, SE-58183 Linköping, Sweden. Tel. +46 13 28 40 65, Fax: +46 13 28 18 73. E-mail: jonso@eki.liu.se.

Thomas, Janice, Assistant Professor, Joint Management and Engineering Project Management Specialization, University of Calgary, 2500 University Drive N.W., Calgary, Alberta, Canada, T2N 1N4, Phone 403-220-4382, Fax 403-282-0095, Email: jthomas@mgmt.ucalgary,ca.

Trailer, Jeffrey W., School of Business, Penn State Erie, Station Road, Erie, PA 16563 USA, Tel: 814 898 6268, Fax: 814 898 6223, E-mail: jwt5@psu.edu

Turner, J. Rodney, Erasmus University Rotterdam, P.O. Box 1738, NL-3000 DR Rotterdam, The Netherlands, Tel: +31 1040 82723, E-mail: jrodneyturner@compuserve.com

van Fenema, Paul C. Erasmus University, Rotterdam School of Management, P.O. Box 1738, NL-3000 DR Rotterdam, The Netherlands, Tel: +31 10 4081757, Fax: +31 10 4089010, E-mail: pfenema@fac.fbk.eur.nl

Whittaker, John, Department of Mechanical Engineering, University of Alberta, Edmonton, Alberta T6G-2G8, Canada, Tel: +1 403 492 443, Fax: +1 403 492 2200, E-mail: john.whittaker@ualberta.ca

Wilson, Tim, Clarion University, Department of Marketing, Clarion, Pennsylvania 15701, U.S.A., Tel: +1 814 226 1894, Fax: +1 814 226 1910, E-mail: twilson@mail.clarion.edu

Winch, Graham M. Bartlett School of Graduate Studies, University College London, Gower Street, London WC1E 6BT, England, United Kingdom, Tel: +44 171 504 5921, Fax: +44 171 916 1887, E-mail: g.winch@ucl.ac.uk

PREFACE AND ACKNOWLEDGMENTS

As the title states, this book is about "Projects as Business Constituents and Guiding Motives". As editors, authors and researchers we are convinced that projects are of significant importance at virtually every level of society even though companies are the focus of this book. And projects are not merely conspicuous components of businesses, they in fact signal what the businesses are all about. As you will see from some of the contributions to this book, these signals come in different forms. They have different effects. Thus, the various contributions to this book also mirror a kind of uncertainty as to what this phenomenon that we call *project* is all about. Rather than trying to define what it "really is", we have settled for the alternative, namely to let some of the variation be replicated in the different contributions. One important reason for the variations is that each author wants to stress a different aspect of projectization. Rather than providing the final definition of a project, we illustrate some of the variations as they appear in the minds of researchers and in the minds of those who work with projects every day. We believe that we do greater justice to the field by taking this stance at this stage in the evolution of project management.

However, we are well aware that in the future there will be strong demands on settling for a lasting definition of the phenomenon in question. The scientific and practical debate that is bound to emerge from the evolving definition will doubtless provide provocation and impetus for a continued development of the field. We would like such a debate to be part of the work in the IRNOP network of researchers and practitioners (IRNOP = International Research Network on Organizing by Projects).

As editors of the book we have learned the hard way that editing in fact is hard work. We are pleased that the contributors have been so patient with us over this prolonged editing process, and we do hope that potential readers will find the effort worth while. As editors we have enjoyed the hard work and wish to thank the authors for bearing with us.

We also acknowledge the support we have received from Umeå School of Business and Economics and from the University of Calgary. The publisher, Kluwer Academic Publishers, in the person of the Acquisition Editor Allard Winterink, has provided us with a lot of support needed for this kind of work.

Finally, the Calgary secretary, Janine Revay did put in a lot of work during the initial phases of this book project. Katarina Pousette, the Umeå secretary, did take on a heavy responsibility for editing the multitude of final versions of the various chapters. We acknowledge their assistance at the same time as we extend our thanks to all other persons who have assisted us in our work in one way of the other (including each other).

Rolf A. Lundin
Umeå School of Business and Economics

Francis Hartman
University of Calgary

CHAPTER 1

PERVASIVENESS OF PROJECTS IN BUSINESS

Rolf A. Lundin, Umeå School of Business and Economics, Umeå, Sweden
Francis Hartman, University of Calgary, Canada

PREVALENCE OF PROJECTS ON THE RISE?

The purpose of this book is to describe and analyze the roles that projects play in business. What are the mechanisms involved? Implicitly our suggestion is that projects are important for a variety of reasons, one of them being that there is an abundance of them. In fact, there also seems to be wide agreement in the business world and among researchers that projects are much more prevalent now than they used to be (Ekstedt *et al.* 1999, Lundin and Midler 1998). This agreement appears to have been around for quite some time which should mean that there is in fact a positive trend. The agreement is not based on sufficiently hard facts or impeccable data, though. One reason for this is of course that there are very little, if any hard data available. Economic activities are registered almost exclusively with companies as the important units, seldom or never with projects. Another reason is that there is not one agreed upon definition of projects, but there are several. And most definition efforts have flaws in one way or the other. Projects come in such a variety of shapes and under such a variety of circumstances that efforts to find an overall and strong definition appear if not futile, at least very difficult. However, there have been some seemingly promising attempts to instigate order in this diversity of project definitions by trying to find characteristic project patterns aligning with various sets of parameters (like business, tools, size, complexity etc.). These efforts to characterize projects are mainly made in order to identify how to manage them more effectively. At that, there is a way to go before results of these attempts are both successful and useful, in particular for the statistical purposes we have in mind here.

However, one tentative definition of projects that might be a particularly useful one in the context of the present book focusing on projects as building blocks of business activities is the following: "any activity that sustains or enhances shareholder value". This definition is useful for business decision making purposes since it refers to the profit making imperative and since such well known things as product development, marketing campaigns and other well known types of business projects would be included. Unfortunately, the definition just given has flaws as well. Considering the well documented failure rates of projects in business (cf. examples from the Information Systems area given by Pinto 1999: 31-32, and from the IT area Romberg 1998, as well as from other fields) most projects, in some case up to 95% of them in fact were failures. This means that they should have a negative value for shareholders. Adhering to the "shareholder value" definition would imply that a meager 5% should be included if the definition provided above were to be used. This means that we were to loose 95% of the efforts, and these 95% failures might even constitute the most interesting part – if learning from failures is important. And we would not want that to happen in our treatise of projects in business. One way out of that difficulty might be to specify that projects "intended" to add to shareholder value should be included. But then there would be a need to define "intended" which is possibly more difficult than it sounds. At that, the "shareholder" definition provided above has an implicit, normative argument imbedded in itself.

There is absolutely no reason to believe that projects in businesses are undertaken with the precise and only goal to enhance "shareholder value". If you ask a CEO concerning the business he is in charge of, he is most likely to refute any statement that not all projects hosted by his company are intended to promote shareholder value. It is his job to do so! But there are few reasons to believe him since there are so many different rationales at work when projects are initiated and very few of them in fact have anything to do with shareholder value. Under norms of rationality, the project rhetoric in any particular case is likely to refer to shareholder value, but it is unlikely that the rhetoric tells the entire project story. Projects possibly prove their usefulness to the members of the organization also in other ways, which means that even projects quite far away from being useful for shareholders have sponsors. Thus, under these circumstances we have refrained from trying to find any precise definition or delimitation of what a project is. Since we are interested in the role that projects play in business, no matter if they are in line with shareholder expectations or not, the temptation to exclude ventures that do not adhere to one of the more stringent definitions of what a project is should be avoided. We believe that one should keep an open mind concerning the matter and we prefer to do so, at least at the present time.

Notwithstanding definition problems, attempts have been made to measure the prevalence of projects at a generalized level. But since direct data are not available, the measurement has been through indirect indicators. Eriksson (1997) has scrutinized in total seven different indicators ranging from the number of papers presented at professional conferences (arranged by the professional organizations PMI and IPMA) over the years to the frequency of newspaper ads about project related jobs. All seven indicators demonstrate a rising trend in support of the conjecture that the prevalence of projects is on the rise. And there is no reason to believe that the trend has been broken since the study of these indicators was made. Rather, the speed of change seems to be even higher than it was at the time. The current membership to the PMI – the professional organization most heavily represented in the US - is now an impressive 50 000, which means that its membership count has doubled in a couple of years only. The change in job ads might not be all that conspicuous but the trend is highly positive.

Most trends, if not all, have a tendency to reach saturation, but thus far there seems to be no sign of a saturation point or saturation level for the indicators on project phenomena in society. Logically though, there has to be a level beyond which the trend cannot continue. The indicator named *frequency of newspaper ads about project related jobs* cannot indeed surpass 100% of all ads and an entire population is not likely to join a professional organization in the project area just to mention a couple of obvious examples. But thus far, no general saturation supported by data can be discerned. So, the prevalence of projects as defined implicitly through the indicators seems to be on the rise still. Indeed we seem to be on our way towards a projectized society.

MECHANISMS AT WORK

If there is an increasing prevalence of projects overall, what are the reasons? And what are the implications? Our intuition tells us that in certain areas there simply cannot be too much of an increase, or at least the increase cannot be sustained over very long periods of time. To take one example, the construction of dwellings might go up temporarily, but in the long run we would expect that kind of project activity to be more or less stable. And similar examples can be found and similar arguments can be made in other areas than construction as well. So if prevalence is going up, the expansion story that the indicators tell has to be explained in a different manner, not by sheer and uniform expansion. In essence, this should leave us with a suspicion that the project as a form for work organization is expanding into new application areas.

It seems in fact quite plausible that we are witnessing a spread of project ideas into other application areas rather than an outright expansion in traditional project fields. One thing that supports such a contention is that the project terminology tends to surface in professions and in fields where it was previously unheard of. To take one example that appears extreme in the present context, family therapists have been overheard talking about their projects and thus referring to the families they were currently working with. That kind of application is a far cry from the construction and engineering activities where projects in their modern forms seem to have originated but the example serves as an illustration to how the use of a project terminology has expanded. The entire project terminology is current being integrated into the professional languages of many different fields. One might even argue that there is a social or an institutional reconstruction going on, where many well established truths in a variety of professional fields get confronted with a project way of thinking and where the project terminology seems to get integrated into the general activities of that professional field. Broader uses of project management approaches are made overall and in that development we tend to see an upsurge of "soft projects" as the project idea drifts further afield!

There might be different ways to understand the spread into new fields. Possibly, one might talk about a "push effect" or a "pull effect". The push effect is supposed to illustrate the notion that project ideas and terminology get "marketed" so efficiently by consultants, teachers and others with particular reference to useful effects in other fields that people simply buy in to applications also in their own. You might say that people's minds get invaded by project notions. Ideas from the project management field get more or less pushed onto potential adopters.

Alternatively, people for some reason come to realize that the project way of thinking and acting solves problems for them in their daily work, so they tend to use that kind of thinking which means that there is some sort of pull effect in the spreading mechanism. The pull effect does not necessarily have anything to do with projects as a fad, even though the spreading of project ideas seems so fast at present. Adopters in general should be considered as rational since adoption is likely to be based on an underlying usefulness to them. No matter push or pull: At the heart of the spreading is exposure. People increasingly get exposed to the project ideas and adapt their private and public rhetoric as a result of that exposure. Presumably they also alter their way of work in the process.

This overview of possible mechanisms, all indicating in one way or the other that the fields of application for project ideas is on the move, implies one additional reason for not adopting any stringent definition of the focal concept "project" at the present time. There are changing definitions of what a project is and should be. Some of the original, intentionally precise definitions are presently giving way to more generalized notions of appropriate ways to work with projects. For research reasons and maybe also for business reasons we should let that happen and be open to a broad use of project approaches.

PROJECT MAN?

Up till now, we have referred to projects as work related procedures. Projects are seen as a general form for organizing work activities rather than something else. However, we should as well be open to another possibility, namely that projects have something to do with personal life styles. Implicit in the discussion above, concerning the kind of mechanisms that might be at work is a suggestion that mechanisms might be of the "people" type. Some of us are simply more susceptible to the project rhetoric and to the habit of organizing by project than others because it is closely related to the way we want to organize and handle our own lives, i.e. in a sequence of project-like activities. Lindgren and Packendorff (1997) who also found gender differences when it comes to attitudes to, and actions in, projects have pursued this line of reasoning. Related to that are the notions of boundary-less careers and career portfolios that might be a current manifestation of project aptness at the individual level (Arthur and Rousseau 1996). The personal experience of one of the authors from some 3 000+ oral exams with MBA students is that these fairly well educated youngsters do not talk of their future careers and of their plans in terms of attaining a certain, specified position. Rather, they tend to talk about the sequence of work related experiences they want to get in the near future. And their explicit plans never seem to cover more than five years.

The denomination "project man" has been coined (Lundin and Söderholm 1995) as a prototype role that people inclined to work in projects might play. The role is a parallel to the constructs "economic man" and "administrative man" used and elaborated upon by Simon (1997) in making an extensive review of the differences between economics and the administrative sciences when it comes to how the two areas tend to regard the human actor. In essence, the project man denomination should be taken as a similar construct in the sense that it is supposed to describe how persons working in a project environment tend to think and behave. It is different in the sense that it is supposed to be generated empirically rather than theoretically (as in the Simon case), so it should also have a bearing on the real world. Whether we can find project men as a widespread phenomenon in society remains to be seen, but the alternative is there.

Let us continue this kind of reasoning in order to widen the perspectives a bit further. History tells us that the physical environment of man has shaped him as a human being in his view of what is important in life in general and to survive in his habitat in particular. Collectors, hunters and farmers are examples based on historical evidence. Sequentially, collectors and hunters became farmers, then became the industrial proletariat. What is the next step going to be? Will there be any next step? The physical environments of the industrial worker, of collectors and of farmers are certainly different from the present habitat, i.e. the environment in something that resembles a projectized society. Will the human being be shaped in a uniform way in a projectized society as well? Or will the human being shape society and take the lead in societal change into something that resembles a project direction? Taking the lead or not taking the lead, this entire line of speculative and superficial reasoning serves to demonstrate that there is more to projects in business than merely a way to organize work. Project thinking in its modern version seems to have started with technical applications and most recently it has spilled over to encompass also business issues and needs. Social issues ranging all the way from teams to broad societal problems are currently finding their way into the project field of applications. There is a strong indication that we should be open to a wide range of possibilities and thinking when it comes to the present and the future role of projects in business.

PROJECT WORK IN BUSINESS

As has been discussed above there is a wide variety of trends (or viewpoints) concerning projects in society and in business. And business management needs to see and to control them all in the business arena. Along with traditional ways of working with project, we have thus far explicitly covered inventiveness when it comes to new and less traditional application areas. Businesses abound with "soft projects" carrying a lot less structure than the traditional ones. We have also covered some of the human aspects of projects in the "project man" discussion. Businesses might be recruiting a new breed of human actors as compared to previously with effects on project work.

One trend that has not been covered so far is the standardization movement which is sweeping the business world and which has now reached the project area on a grand scale (cf. Eskerod and Östergren 1998). The trend has two forms in relation to projects: 1) It is high fashion among major companies to subscribe to a standardized form for how to run projects in their particular companies. The sentence "This is the way we run projects in our company" illustrates that this form of standardization is more of a hierarchical expression than a generalized standardization. 2) The second form of standardization efforts is now coming of age. It was launched by the professional organizations in the field (PMI and IPMA alluded to previously). Essentially, the form of standardization they are providing consists of promoting "cook books" concerning how to run projects in general. They also promote certification of the project manager as a professional person. Even though Twyford (1999) expresses serious doubts whether project management ever will become a profession in the same sense as there are professions in law and medicine, certification is a strong standardization movement. Even though the two forms of standardization might have similar effects to business, they plausibly have different grounds for justification. The first form is probably born out of an effort by line management to control the projects better over their life time and to integrate their companies into a coherent whole, and the second one is supposed to provide general advice of a "best practice" type.

Anyway, there appear to be two diametrically different developments taking place simultaneously; the first kind, standardization, fosters familiarity and the second kind experimentation along novel lines. Both of them are interesting in their own right. Confrontation between them is bound to have impacts, at least when the confrontation takes place within a company.

The confrontation comment made above also has a bearing on – and illustrates – one important aspect of the so called multi-project problem existing in several companies. Most of the time multi-project refers to the multitude of similar projects hosted within a company competing for the same types of scarce resources and where the (optimality) problems concern how to prioritize between the projects. In this case, the confrontation issue points to quite a different kind of problem, namely that many people are members of a multitude of project teams. That is one aspect of the multi-project problem that has not been discussed much, at least not in the literature. In an organization with many minor projects run simultaneously, there will not be a one-to-one relationship between man and project, but a one-to-many relationship. In other words most people are involved in several projects. In such a situation most people are unlikely to be enthusiastic and highly motivated for all projects they are involved in. If there are too many, they might even find it difficult to hold the different projects apart mentally. They can do so only by documents and under such circumstances at least some project work is likely to be a dreadful experience (cf. projects as salt-mine arguments in Lundin 1999). Social issues and personnel well-being seems to be at stake here. This is evidently a serious management problem for many companies of the kind today and the use of semi-permanent projects teams does not appear to be the solution. Maybe it is difficult to pay attention to personal goals and careers in a project environment? The task focus in projects gets all the attention.

There is a wide variety of other concerns that one might have in relation to projects in business. However, management should keep in mind that projects are important constituents in business. Projects have a potential to be profit generators and some of them constitute guiding motives for what the business is all about. And is a dynamic organization not one that responds through a continued series of projects?

PERVASIVENESS AND PURPOSE

The project area appears very much to be on the move in society at large and in business. As illustrated above the project way of doing things and project thinking is transforming not only the way businesses are managed as well as how they are conceived but also the societal context. There might be a project invasion that is going on. Projects permeate most businesses. Old traditions are giving way to new ones. One might even say that there is a redefinition of what businesses are and should be that is going on and projects play an important role in that redefinition. Especially since projects appear to play such an important role, it is tempting from a research point of view to look for a definition to adhere to so that the phenomena can be properly studied. For reasons already given we feel that one should not do so. However, from a business viewpoint we are less confident concerning a similar recommendation for businesses in general. Efficiency motives and experimentation motives exist side by side. And when efficiency motives dominate there might be a need to treat a particular class of projects in a very standardized way. This should certainly be true when survival is at stake.

This is not to say that business managers should not look out for what is happening in a world of project type experiments and project type developments. This brings us back to the purpose of this book. Its rationale is to provide the reader, be it someone from business or someone from research, with an overview of some current developments. The selection of chapters have been made so as to mirror some of the most important aspects of projects in a business context. The different chapters have been divided into four sections thus mirroring some of the reasoning above:

I.   Projects and Business Sense-Making
II.   Business Issues and Projects
III.   Projects for Innovation and Change
IV.   People's Projects

In the final chapter of the book we summarize some of our impressions from working with the selection of chapters and allude to what the future might be.

THE CONTRIBUTIONS – WHAT TO LOOK FOR?

The different chapters are self-contained and speak well for themselves. However, the following review of the chapters might serve as an introduction for the reader by outlining the main message in each of them and also by indicating some details that we have come to appreciate in process of editing.

In the first section of the book, the concentration is on projects as a main rationale and a main constituent of and for business. In that section the notion of how projects are used to make sense out of businesses in context is also alluded to. The first in this selection of four chapters has been written by J. Rodney Turner. It concentrates on how projects for profit tie in with the traditional views of what private companies are all about. How do projects contribute to the value of equity of the host companies? Shareholder value analysis is described at a generic level, where in particular the effects of delays and lowered levels of functionality is focused, and applied for the cases of Zeneca and ICI. Investment appraisals have a particular flavor to them in the project contexts described. The imperatives that projects should be finished on time and to specifications focuses the role and the obligations of the project manager. This leads us over to the chapter three written by Janice L. Thomas. In that chapter two different orientations when it comes to project management are contrasted: control and sense-making. In the past, normative versions of project management control aspects dominated and there was a continuous effort to find "the right way" to handle projects. More recent versions of a similar normative type were directed towards matching circumstances with appropriate project management models. The other orientation - sense-making - centers on organizing rather than organization and on project management as communication and not as control. The difference is that sense-making on the part of the project participants becomes integral of the organizing processes.

The next chapter of this selection is on globally distributed projects. Paul C. van Fenema and Kuldeep Kumar analyze the host of internationalizing problems connected with coordinating project work at multiple sites and time zones as compared to the case where the projects are local. Their assessment of the implications of the global distributedness encompasses how work packages (or modules) are assigned to project locations. Interdependence is a source for control demands in projects of that type. The last chapter of the first section on business sense-making and projects also focuses on control and on control forms. More specifically, type of participation is put forward as an important determinant for the relevancy of control forms. Bureaucratic control is singled out as impossible in temporary structures (i.e. projects) where professional control is deemed to be more likely to be an important one. Personnel engaged in projects might get stuck in what is called the "honey trap", meaning that they get so consumed in the project work that they are doing so that they will not be able to be attractive for new exciting projects.

The next set of four chapters concerns a related subject, i.e. projects as integral parts of business, where the fact that companies host projects is in focus. The first chapter by Barbro Anell is about the problems and the opportunities involved in multi-project management - handling portfolios of projects. Managing the totality of projects is different as compared to managing one particular project "in splendid isolation". The special twitch to the multi-project problem in this case concerns the need to have a steady flow of projects into the portfolio and a flow (of a similar rate) out of the portfolio. Balancing the portfolio and having the courage to decide on terminating projects with bleak forecasts are useful in this context as well as a capacity to generate new projects. The latter capacity - for pre-project activities - is alluded to in the following chapter by Tim Wilson and Marcia Seidle where business service projects as an expanding part of business is in focus. The nature and the content of such pre-project interactions concerning business services have been studied in a variety of business segments and found to have an important impact on the outcome of the projects.

The next chapter by Jeffrey Pinto, Pekka Rouhiainen and Jeffrey Trailer relates an effort to link customer satisfaction to project success. In this chapter the efforts of one particular company to bring customer satisfaction into evaluation of projects is scrutinized by way of value chain analysis. A partnering mentality is needed in business to business projects as in the case analyzed. In the final chapter of the second part the author, Graham Winch, argues that management of projects should be regarded as a generic business process. He gives a variety of reasons for that. The main one is that management creates new value through projects. The reader is urged to pay special attention to the references to business process analysis.

One type of projects devoted exclusively to the creation of new value is the class of projects denominated as projects concerning innovation and change. In the first chapter of section III John Whittaker reminds us that the nature of projects has been changing at the same time as project purposes have developed from classical manual projects to strategic development and change projects. Management in the latter case has options that are more constrained than for traditional projects and has to be adjusted accordingly. A similar kind of adaptation has to be engineered when markets are changing. One example of that is treated in the following chapter where Sihem Ben Mahmoud-Jouini analyzes how French building contractors switch from a demand-pull logic to a supply-push one. The switch has strong implications for innovation.

In the third chapter of the section on innovation and change Florence Charue-Duboc discusses innovation in the chemical industry where the final customer is detached from product development. At the same time there is a strong overlap between basic research and innovation in new products. In the chapter a development design model is described and analyzed in terms of skills and coordination needed. The final chapter in the section, written by Maria Larson is about marketing of a mega-event. The special mega-event in this case is the World Championship in Athletics in Gothenburg. The author develops the notion of a "political market square" in an effort to grasp the mechanisms that are at work in this kind of once-in-a-lifetime kind of project. As a contrast to that notion a hierarchical project network is described. In the political market square trusting relationships are difficult to develop. On the other hand the relative chaos promotes considerable innovation.

The title of the forth section is intended to introduce the general issues concerning people and how they work in and relate to projects. The first chapter of that group is about the not so heroic aspects of project leaders. By way of a survey of the literature and a Delphi study to experienced project managers the authors, Kam Jugdev, Francis Hartman and Janice L. Thomas, have been able identify and prioritize common fears and frustrations that project leaders have in their work situation. They also make an effort to provide recommendations on how to address these critical job challenges. The problems that cross-cultural aspects add to project work are alluded to in the chapter written by John B. Kidd and Paul C. Robins. In fact, cross-cultural complications might be an important cause for project failure. The discussion centers on communication where creating so-called high context messages are suggested as a solution to cultural difficulties to communicate effectively.

In the third chapter of the forth section, written by Magnus Gustafsson, it is argued that trust plays an important role in international business projects. The author has participated in a major study concerning a multitude of international projects and ponders the meaning of culture, cultural differences and the appearance of trust in that kind of context. The author summarizes the discussion by stating that "inter-cultural differences become problems only when you think they do not exist". In the last chapter of the section the author, Thomas Lechler, presents empirical evidence of people as determinants of project success. In total 448 projects from German industries have been compared in terms of success (as measured by project team and customer satisfaction) and different success factors. By way of a Lisrel analysis the author found that people related factors are more important for success than formal arrangements.

The very last chapter of the book contains a few reflections emanating from the various chapters concerning issues, especially research related issues, that we as editors find particularly relevant for the project scene and for business in the future. We should not anticipate that description, but one contention is that there is a shift in how practitioners and researchers need to work together concerning these matters.

PROJECTS AND BUSINESS SENSE-MAKING

CHAPTER 2

PROJECTS FOR SHAREHOLDER VALUE:
THE INFLUENCE OF PROJECTS AT DIFFERENT FINANCIAL RATIOS

J. Rodney Turner, Erasmus University, Rotterdam, The Netherlands

ABSTRACT

Projects are undertaken to add value to the sponsoring organization. In the private sector, this means increasing the value of shares to holders of equity. Traditionally, projects are said to be successful if they are completed to time, cost and quality. Certainly, the earlier a project is completed, the more cheaply and the greater the functionality, the greater is its contribution to shareholder value. However, it is often not known what the relative impacts of time, cost and functionality are. This chapter uses shareholder value analysis to assess the impact of projects on the sponsoring organization. First it is necessary to enhance shareholder value analysis for the analysis of projects. It is shown that the impact of projects on their parent organization can be predicted from eight financial ratios linked to eight value drivers, and the nature of the impact is different for different industries with different ratios. It is concluded that managers need to understand these different impacts, and in their annual appraisal project managers should be judged by the contribution of their projects to the value of the organization.

LINKING PROJECT SUCCESS, PERFORMANCE AND APPRAISAL

Many people judge project success by whether a project contributes value to the sponsoring organization, (Wateridge 1995, 1996, 1998). Further, if the project team co-ordinate their efforts to deliver value to the sponsor, it increases the chance of achieving a successful outcome. The most significant contributor to project success is to agree the success criteria with the stakeholders at the start of the project, and to coordinate their efforts to deliver those agreed criteria as the project progresses (Turner 1999, 2000). This may require individual team members to sub-optimize the parameter that interests them, (time, cost or functionality), to achieve an overall optimum for the project. However, usually no guidance is given to project managers and their teams about the appropriate balance between these three parameters, the so-called *golden triangle*. Many project managers are judged in their annual performance reviews by how many of their projects were completed on cost and time, so that becomes their main focus. Perhaps they should be judged on the potential of their projects to create value for the organization, which may require greater focus on functionality.

Net present value, (NPV), has traditionally been used to assess the value of a project, (Lock 2000). It is assumed the NPV of a project represents its contribution to the value of the parent organization. However, it has not been possible to prove conclusively that NPV is correlated to shareholder value creation, (Woods and Randall 1989). The technique has other weaknesses, (Mehari 2000). Its application is independent of the financial ratios of the sponsoring organization, and it favours projects from parts of the business with high indirect costs and low direct costs, in direct contradiction to conventional management thinking. Businesses with high indirect costs are more exposed to business cycles, and are less able to control costs overall. Further, and strangely, even though it is used to appraise projects, NPV is not used as a project control tool, to compare alternative recovery strategies for projects in difficulty, (Gardiner and Stewart 2000). It is not used to determine the appropriate balance between time, cost and functionality to maximize wealth generation of the project.

A modern technique of investment appraisal analyses a project's contribution to the value of equity of the parent company, called shareholder value, (Mills 1994, Mills and Turner 1995). Shareholder Value Analysis, (SVA), calculates a company's value as the net present value of future dividends, paid out of free cash flow after profit has been used to pay tax and reinvest in the business. It estimates future free cash flow in terms of eight value drivers. SVA suggests that the contribution of a project to the value of the firm is the NPV, and so its contribution to shareholder value is NPV less new debt required to finance the project. The eight value drivers alone cannot be used to determine the performance of projects undertaken by the organization. However, the value drivers can be calculated from eight traditional financial ratios, which can in turn be used to predict the NPV of projects. Using the financial ratios, it is possible to identify a generic project for an organization, and analyze the relative impacts of variations in time, cost and functionality, to determine how these differ for different organizations, with different financial performance.

In this chapter, I introduce the financial ratios, and show how they can be used to predict the shareholder value of a company and to determine the NPV of a generic project. I use the model for net present value of a generic project to analyze the impact of changes in time, cost and functionality on the net present value, and hence the shareholder value of the organization. I use ten of the UK's top 100 companies as examples to show how the impact varies between companies with different ratios. I then do a more detailed analysis on two of the organizations to give a broader feel of the impacts, and to provide a basis for extrapolating the data for the other companies. The two organizations, Zeneca and ICI, used to be the same company until their demerger in the early 1990s. This perhaps illustrates the pressures that led to the demerger.

SHAREHOLDER VALUE ANALYSIS

Shareholder Value Analysis calculates the value of shares in a company as the net present value of future dividends. Future dividends are paid out of free cash flow, which is profit, less tax, less money reinvested in the business, (Mills 1994, Mills and Turner 1995):

$$\text{Dividends} = \text{Free cash flow}$$
$$= \text{Profit} - \text{tax} - \text{capital invested in the business}$$

In traditional shareholder value analysis, future free cash flow is calculated from eight parameters, called value drivers. There are three operational drivers used to estimate future cash generated by the business:

D1 sales growth rate
D2 operating profit margin, (or operating costs as a percentage of turnover)
D3 cash tax rate

and five investment drivers used to calculate the amount of cash invested in the business, and at what cost, and over what planning period:

D4 replacement fixed capital employed, RFCE, (assumed equal to depreciation)
D5 incremental fixed capital employed, IFCE, (required to generate sales growth)
D6 incremental working capital employed, IWCE, (also required to generate sales growth)
D7 cost of capital
D8 planning period

There is no replacement working capital investment: that is treated as revenue, paid out of operating costs. The contribution of a project to shareholder value is the NPV minus new debt required to finance the project. It is not possible to calculate the NPV of a project, and hence its influence on shareholder value, directly from the eight value drivers. However, it is possible to calculate the value drivers and the NPV of projects from the following financial ratios:

R1 direct cost to turnover   = direct costs/turnover
R2 indirect cost to turnover   = indirect cost/turnover
R3 depreciation to turnover   = depreciation/turnover
R4 rate of depreciation   = depreciation/fixed capital employed
R5 fixed capital employed to turnover = fixed capital employed/turnover
R6 working capital employed to turnover = working capital employed/turnover
R7 debt to capital employed   or debt equity ratio
R8 interest rate on debt

The value drivers D2 to D7 can be calculated from ratios R1 to R6 as follows:

$$
\begin{aligned}
\text{D2} &= 100\% - \text{R1} - \text{R2} - \text{R3} - \text{R8}*\text{R7}*(\text{R5}+\text{R6}) \\
\text{R3} &= \text{R4} / \text{R5} \\
\text{D4} &= \text{Sales} * \text{R3} \\
&= \text{Turnover} * \text{R4} \\
\text{D5} &= \text{D1} * \text{R5} \\
\text{D6} &= \text{D1} * \text{R6} \\
\text{D7} &= (1\text{-R7})*\text{RE} + \text{R7}*\text{R8} \\
\text{RE} &= \text{return on equity expected by shareholders}
\end{aligned}
$$

D1 and D8 are assumed from the company's strategic plan, and D7 is the weighted average cost of capital, calculated from R7, R8, and assumed returns expected by holders of equity, RE. The analysis takes the turnover in a base year, and an assumed rate of growth, to calculate shareholder value. Table 1 shows the calculation for a UK company from the pharmaceutical industry, Zeneca, using numbers obtained from the 1997 annual report. This calculation assumes a constant debt equity ratio. It is also possible to do the calculation assuming constant debt. The latter gives an answer about 3% smaller. Table 2 contains the ratios for ten of the UK's top 100 companies, using figures obtained from their annual reports for 1996 or 1997. This Table also includes the calculated shareholder value for each of these companies using a six year planning period. The final column shows the amount the companies were trading above or below the calculated figure in the middle of 1998, immediately before the strong rise of the stock market through to the middle of 1999, (a positive figure means the market capitalization was that percentage greater than the shareholder value calculated).

Table 1. Shareholder Value Analysis for Zeneca

SHAREHOLDER VALUE ANALYSIS FOR ZENECA

Year	Ratios	0	1	2	3	4	5	6
Sales Growth Rate, (assumed)	12.0%		12%	12%	12%	12%	12%	12%
Sales		100.00	112.00	125.44	140.49	157.35	176.23	197.38
Direct Costs, (R1)	50.5%	(50.50)	(56.56)	(63.35)	(70.95)	(79.46)	(89.00)	(99.68)
Indirect Costs, (R2)	24.5%	(24.50)	(27.44)	(30.73)	(34.42)	(38.55)	(43.18)	(48.36)
Interest, (from R7 see below)		(1.50)	(1.68)	(1.88)	(2.11)	(2.36)	(2.64)	(2.96)
Depreciation, (R3)	10.0%	(4.15)	(4.65)	(5.21)	(5.83)	(6.53)	(7.31)	(8.19)
		======	======	======	=====	=====	=====	=====
Operating Profit		19.35	21.67	24.27	27.19	30.45	34.10	38.19
Cash Tax Rate, (D3)	35.0%	6.77	7.59	8.50	9.51	10.66	11.94	13.37
		======	======	======	=====	=====	=====	=====
Profit After Tax		12.58	14.09	15.78	17.67	19.79	22.17	24.83
Add back Depreciation, (R3)		4.15	4.65	5.21	5.83	6.53	7.31	8.19
		======	======	======	=====	=====	=====	=====
Operating Cash Flow		16.73	18.73	20.98	23.50	26.32	29.48	33.02
Less RFCE, (R3)		(4.15)	(4.65)	(5.21)	(5.83)	(6.53)	(7.31)	(8.19)
Less IFCE, (R5)		(2.29)	(2.57)	(2.87)	(3.22)	(3.60)	(4.04)	(4.52)
Less IWCE, (R6)		(0.50)	(0.56)	(0.62)	(0.70)	(0.78)	(0.88)	(0.98)
		======	======	======	=====	=====	=====	=====
Free Cash Flow		9.79	10.96	12.28	13.75	15.40	17.25	19.32
Cost of Capital, (D7)	6.0%	6.0%	6.0%	6.0%	6.0%	6.0%	6.0%	6.0%
Discount Factor		1.00	0.94	0.89	0.84	0.79	0.75	0.70
PV of Free Cash Flow			10.34	10.93	11.55	12.20	12.89	13.62
Cummulative PV			10.34	21.27	32.82	45.02	57.92	71.54

Residual Free Cash	**24.83**
Residual Value	**413.77**
	=====
PV of Residual Value	**309.19**
Cummulative PV	**71.54**
	=====

CAPITALISATION

Year		0	1	2	3	4	5	6
Fixed Capital Employed, (R5)	41.5%	41.50	46.48	52.06	58.30	65.30	73.14	81.91
Incremental FCE, (R5)		4.98	5.58	6.25	7.00	7.84	8.78	9.83
IFCE paid from Equity, (1-R7)	46.0%	2.29	2.57	2.87	3.22	3.60	4.04	4.52
Working Capital Empl'd, (R6)	9.0%	9.00	10.08	11.29	12.64	14.16	15.86	17.76
Incremental WCE, (R6)		1.08	1.21	1.35	1.52	1.70	1.90	2.14
IWCE paid from equity, (1-R7)	46.0%	0.50	0.56	0.62	0.70	0.78	0.88	0.98
Total Capital Employed		50.50	56.56	63.35	70.95	79.46	89.00	99.68
Debt, (R7)	54.0%	27.27	30.54	34.21	38.31	42.91	48.06	53.83
Equity, (1-R7)	46.0%	23.23	26.02	29.14	32.64	36.55	40.94	45.85
Interest, (R8)	5.5%	1.50	1.68	1.88	2.11	2.36	2.64	2.96

Table 2. Ratios and Shareholder Value for ten UK FTSE100 companies
(Data obtained from company reports)

Sector	Name	Direct Costs R1 %T	Indirect Costs R2 %T	Depr'n R4 %FCE	FCE/ Sales R5 %T	WCE/ Sales R6 %T	Debt/ CE R7 %	SVA6 Y %T	Capit'n /SVA %
Pharm	Glaxo	33.0%	27.0%	10.5%	45.5%	5.5%	49.0%	680%	11.9%
Breweries	Guiness	40.0%	28.5%	5.0%	93.5%	51.0%	35.0%	310%	24.7%
Media	Reed Elsevier	38.5%	34.5%	3.0%	85.5%	18.0%	77.5%	394%	-17.6%
Pharm	Zeneca	50.5%	24.5%	10.0%	41.5%	9.0%	54.0%	380%	21.7%
Stores	Marks & Spencer	76.5%	8.5%	4.5%	46.0%	25.0%	18.0%	190%	11.4%
Chemicals	BOC Group	59.5%	20.0%	8.5%	90.0%	12.5%	37.0%	139%	-13.9%
Electricals	GEC	66.0%	22.5%	22.5%	16.0%	8.0%	-83.0%	148%	21.7%
Engin'ing	British Aerospace	84.0%	6.5%	8.0%	32.5%	7.5%	40.0%	104%	20.5%
Stores	Sainsbury's	91.5%	2.0%	0.0%	44.0%	7.5%	46.0%	74%	-34.6%
Chemicals	ICI	72.0%	19.0%	6.0%	54.0%	15.5%	71.0%	40%	61.9%

The direct costs include costs of sales, materials and labour where included. They also include duties for liquour sales and oil and gas products, and research and development costs. Figures in annual reports are quoted inclusive and exclusive of duty. The calculation can be performed either way. Since the model is linear, the same answer is obtained. (Elsewhere, I have performed the calculation of the Norwegian State company, Statoil, as a comparison to BP. In Statoil's annual report at least, the distinction between duty, corporation tax and owner's dividend appears somewhat unconventional.) It is usual to treat research and development as a sunk, and therefore indirect, cost. However, this distorts the investment appraisal process, favoring products with high research and low production costs over products with low research and high production costs. Some firms make R&D a direct cost by charging an internal royalty. It can be argued that as part of the investment appraisal process, research costs should be treated as a direct cost if the comparison is between making the product as opposed to licensing its production elsewhere. I also believe that it should be included as a direct cost, because in deciding to invest in a product from a part of the business with high research costs, the firm commits itself to ongoing research in that area to support that business.

THE GENERIC PROJECT

It is possible to identify a generic project for an organization, one that has the same financial ratios as the company as a whole, to perform notional investment appraisal, and to analyze the relative impact of variations in time cost and functionality of that generic project. Table 3 contains the calculation of Net Present Value, NPV, for the generic project in Zeneca. Starting with an initial fixed capital investment of 100 units, all other figures can be determined using the financial ratios. It is then also possible to calculate the contribution of the generic project to increased shareholder value assuming,

Table 3. Analysis of the generic project for Zeneca

GENERIC PROJECT ANALYSIS FOR ZENECA

	Ratios	Data	0	1	2	3	4	5	6
Year			0	1	2	3	4	5	6
Fixed Capital, (R5)	41.5%	100.00	100.00	0.00					
Working Capital, (R6)	9.0%	21.69	21.69						
			=====	=====	=====	=====	=====	=====	=====
Sales		240.96		240.96	240.96	240.96	240.96	240.96	240.96
Cost of Sales, (R1)	50.5%	121.69		121.69	121.69	121.69	121.69	121.69	121.69
			=====	=====	=====	=====	=====	=====	=====
Profit				119.28	119.28	119.28	119.28	119.28	119.28
			=====	=====	=====	=====	=====	=====	=====
Cash Flow			(121.69)	119.28	119.28	119.28	119.28	119.28	119.28
Discount Factor, (D7)	6.0%		1.00	0.94	0.89	0.84	0.79	0.75	0.70
Present Value			(121.69)	112.53	106.16	100.15	94.48	89.13	84.09
			=====	=====	=====	=====	=====	=====	=====
Net Present Value			(121.69)	(9.16)	97.00	197.14	291.62	380.75	464.84
Shareholder value, A1									464.84
Shareholder value, A2									410.84
Shareholder value, A3									364.84

A1 no new debt is required to finance the project, that is it is financed out of retained profit, in which case the increase in shareholder value is equal to the NPV

A2 new debt is required at the average rate of debt to capital employed, in which case the increase in shareholder value is NPV less R7

A3 100% new debt is required, in which case the increase in shareholder value is NPV minus 100.

Table 4. Shareholder value of the generic project, and the impact of variations in project performance

Name	ƒSV Proj A1	ƒSV Proj A2	ƒSV Proj A3	ƒSV ƒS 10% A4	ƒSV ƒS 10% A5	ƒSV ƒC 10% A6	ƒSV ƒC 10% A7	ƒSV ƒC 10% A8	ƒSV ƒT 10% A9	ƒSV ƒT 10% A10	ƒSV ƒT 10% A11	ƒSV ƒT 10% A12
Glaxo	612	563	512	73	109	10	15	20	6	18	17	20
Guinness	161	126	61	32	53	10	14	20	4	9	8	11
Reed Elsevier	232	155'	132	36	58	10	18	20	4	10	9	11
Zeneca	464	410	364	58	118	10	15	20	5	19	18	21
Marks & Spencer	97	79	(3)	25	107	10	12	20	5	18	17	19
BOC Group	94	57	(6)	13	55	10	14	20	3	10	9	11
GEC	895	978	795	104	308	10	2	20	11	49	48	50
British Aerospace	119	79	19	25	141	10	14	20	7	25	24	26
Sainsbury's	25	(21)	(75)	14	167	10	15	20	7	18	17	19
ICI	123	52	23	26	91	10	17	20	4	15	15	17

Table 4 contains the calculated contribution to shareholder value for the generic project in each of the ten companies in Table 2 for a project with initial investment of 100 units, with each of the assumptions A1 to A3. All projects have a life of six years, except Sainsbury's, which needed a life of 10 years to show positive NPV. Using the generic project, it is possible to calculate the effect of changes in time, cost and functionality on the outturn of the generic project. In all cases the change is calculated as an absolute figure. Since the model is linear, the absolute figure is independent of assumptions A1 to A3. The following assumptions are made.

Functionality
Loss of functionality either reduces sales volume, or sales price or both. Both result in a loss in turnover. If there is a loss in sales volume, then presumable it will be possible to achieve some savings in direct costs, and hence direct costs might be treated as variable. If there is a loss in sales price, then there will be no reduction in costs, and so they will need to be treated as fixed. The two extremes of treating direct costs as fixed and variable were considered. In any given case it is expected that the actual outcome will be somewhere in between. So:

A4 10% reduction in sales, all costs variable

A5 10% reduction is sales, all costs fixed

Cost

I assumed possible overspend of fixed capital only. Overspend can be paid for out of equity or new debt. I investigated paying for it out of equity only, debt only and debt and equity at the given debt:equity ratio. So:

A6 10% increase in capital cost, no additional debt

A7 10% increase in capital cost, additional debt at the standard debt to capital employed ratio

A8 10% increase in capital cost, funded entirely from debt.

Time

When a project is delayed, loss in NPV or shareholder value comes from two sources. Firstly, the delay will almost certainly lead to an increase in capital cost. Projects which are delayed usually cost more, through rework and an increase in time dependent costs. Secondly, there may be loss of sales. Here two assumptions are possible. One is that there is a loss of sales in year 1, but these are regained at the end of the project life. There will be a small loss of NPV, because the time value of sales in year 7 is less than year 1. The other is that the sales lost in year 1 are lost for all time. This will occur if there is a limited market window, or delay allows a competitor to capture market share, (in which case the loss may be even greater still). I made one of four possible assumptions when considering a delay to a project:

A9 The start of the project is delayed, but all the cost is spent in the original period, and there is no overspend. All sales lost in year 1 are regained in year 7.

A10 The start of the project is delayed, but all the cost is spent in the original period, and there is no overspend. All sales lost in year 1 are lost forever.

A11 The start of the project is delayed, and the expenditure of the project is spread over the extended time period, but there is no overspend, that is the same amount of money is spent over a longer period. All sales lost in year 1 are lost forever.

A12 The start of the project is delayed, the expenditure is spread over the longer period and there are some time dependent costs. I assumed that 25% of the costs were time dependent. The resulting overspend could be paid for out of a mixture of debt and equity, at the standard ratio. All sales lost in year 1 are lost forever.

Impact of Project Performance

Table 4 shows the impact of underperformance of functionality, cost and time on the generic projects from the ten companies. In all cases, except Sainsburys, I assumed that the project has a six year life. In high cost, high capital companies, a longer project life may be more appropriate. For Sainsburys I had to assume a ten year project life to obtain positive net present value. From this data we can conclude:

(a) Loss of sales, (functionality), always has a greater impact than time or cost. As would be expected, the impact is more severe if the sales costs are fixed.

It is absolutely essential that companies with high costs are able to control their costs if there is a loss of sales. For companies with high sales to capital employed and low costs, the impact of loss of sales is very much more severe than overspend or delay, and so it is essential to achieve the functionality. Delay or overspend may be appropriate to maintain functionality, (as long as the delay does not itself result in loss of sales). For companies with low sales to turnover, and high costs, keeping a control on costs and timescale is almost as important as maintaining functionality.

(b)   Columns A6 and A8 contain the same numbers in absolute terms for all companies, because the model is linear. The figure in column A7 lies between dependent on the debt equity ratio, (except for GEC which has a cash mountain). In low sales to turnover companies, (capital intensive companies), capital cost is almost as important as sales if they can control their costs of sales.

(c)   Comparison of columns A10 and A11 shows that delaying expenditure without losing sales actually results in an improvement of NPV and shareholder value. (One project where this was observed in practice was Thames Barrier, Morris and Hough 1987.) Comparison of columns A1 and A12 shows that for all companies, the impact of lost sales resulting from a delay is greater than the impact of any resulting overspend. Column A6 shows that the impact is less marked if the sales are delayed rather than lost, (which will be the case in the public sector where the revenues are cost savings).

(d)   The relative impact of delay and overspend is dependent on the financial ratios of the company. Delay has more impact in capital intensive companies with high costs, because sales are needed to pay for the investment.

All these results suggest that it is more important to obtain the correct functionality for a project than to finish rigidly on cost and time.

COMPARISON OF ZENECA AND ICI

Zeneca and ICI are two companies which were demerged in the early 1990s from the then one company ICI. Table 5 contains a more specific list of variations of project performance to compare the impact on the value of each company. It can be seen the impacts are quite diverse. This raises the question of how was it possible to make rational comparisons of projects from different parts of the business when they were the same company. The assumption must be that projects from the part of the business that is now Zeneca will have always won out in competition for scarce resources. The part of the business that is now ICI was being milked to invest in Zeneca, meaning it would have been gradually run down if the two businesses had not been split. In the mid 1980s I was employed by ICI to do investment appraisal of projects from the petrochemical industry. I found that my projects, with high operating costs but low indirect costs could not compete against projects from less profitable parts of the business with high indirect costs but low operating costs.

Table 5 Comparison of the Impact of Variation in the Performance of the Generic Project in Zeneca and ICI

Variation in Project Performance Parameter	Impact on Zeneca	Impact on ICI
Generic Project NPV, for initial FCE investment of 100 units	464	123
Sales down 10%, direct costs variable, A4	NPV down 13%	NPV down 21%
Sales down 10%, direct costs fixed, A5	NPV down 25%	NPV down 75%
Sales loss for break-even, direct costs variable	80%	50%
Sales loss for break-even, direct costs fixed	40%	13%
Fixed Capital Overspend 10%, A7	NPV down 02%	NPV down 09%
Fixed Capital Overspend for break-even, A7	460%	125%
Delay of 1 month, assumption A12	NPV down 05%	NPV down 14%
Delay of 1 year, A12	NPV down 53%	NPV down 159%

CONCLUSIONS AND FUTURE RESEARCH

The following conclusions can be drawn from the research:

1. It is important for project managers to understand the impact of loss of functionality on the performance of their projects, and to balance the need to obtain the appropriate functionality against a desire to finish rigorously on cost and time.

2. Project managers should be judged in their annual performance appraisal not just on how many of their project were finished on cost and time, but also on the ability of their projects to generate sales. Given the results of this chapter, greater weighting should be given to sales potential than cost or time performance, but the appropriate weightings will vary from company to company dependent on the financial ratios.

3. Understanding the impact of financial ratios on the performance of their project will help project managers weigh up conflicting demands for performance on cost, time and functionality on their projects. Perhaps project managers could be judged against their performance compared to the generic project for their organization.

4. When undertaking investment appraisal, and comparing competing projects in a portfolio, research costs, although sunk, should be treated as direct costs, because:

- in order to stay in the business, the company needs to conduct ongoing research
- without conducting future research the company will lose shareholder value
- the research cost should be treated as a lost royalty payment

5. Shareholder value analysis can provide an investment appraisal technique, which, when coupled with appropriate risk analysis, can show the risk associated with high fixed costs. It can also provide a control tool to allow constant monitoring of the impact of project decisions on shareholder value to optimize owner's wealth. This would allow comparison of the impact of project decisions on time cost and functionality, and their differential impact on shareholder value.

Research is continuing at Erasmus University Rotterdam into these areas, sponsored by the Tinbergen Institute.

CHAPTER 3

MAKING SENSE OF PROJECT MANAGEMENT

Janice Lynne Thomas, University of Calgary, Alberta

ABSTRACT

As interest in projects and project management as a way to manage the organization of the future increases, creating a comprehensive understanding and theory of effective project management is of paramount importance for both practitioners and organizational research. This is particularly important given the rate of failure of projects today.

Recent research exhibits two different orientations towards the function of project management - control versus sense-making. Conventional project management wisdom is based on the control orientation. It assumes a generic and unitary model of project management applicable in all circumstances. Contingency theory and other perspectives on project management call into question this basic underlying assumption. The sense-making orientation, adapted from the social constructionist school of thought, provides grounding and explanation for the existence of communication failures and missed expectations on projects.

This chapter delineates these research streams, and discusses how applying sense-making theories to project management can enrich our understanding of why projects might succeed or fail.

PROJECT MANAGEMENT: CREATING ORDER OUT OF CHAOS

The study of project management occurs at the intersection of theorists and practitioners, and between the fields of Technology and Business Administration. Examples of organizational projects include: setting up new technological processes; bringing out new products; starting up new ventures; consummating a merger; seeing through the completion of a contract; and supervising the construction of a new plant. For years project management existed as a technical activity of questionable value, but recently 'management by projects' has been recognized as a powerful way to manage in a business environment attempting to achieve higher levels of performance and productivity (Morris 1994). There is even a body of literature that suggests that projects and project management will be the future of organizational study (Bennis 1968, Clegg 1989, Weick 1995).

In addition, there are two other fundamental reasons why we should understand project management. First, projects are an integral structural building block of today's organizations (Hardy 1994) in almost every industry. Furthermore, increasing use of outsourcing and strategic alliances reflect the project approach to management based on contractual hierarchical relations (Stinchcombe 1985a). The second fundamental change is the increasing role change plays in organizational life. Managing this change is where project management comes into play (Cleland and Gareis 1994, Morris 1994). The project mode of operation is thought to be more flexible and adaptable to changing circumstances than the standard continuous mode of operation found in traditional organizations (e.g. Frame 1995, Morris 1994).

As interest in forms of temporary organizing has grown, there have been repeated calls for more research and theoretical development around projects in organizational theory (Bryman, *et al.* 1987, Dyer and Paulson 1976, Ford and Randolph 1992, Packendorff 1995, Shenhar 1995). However, there continues to be very little focus on projects per se. In organization theory, the study of project management is a relatively young area of research recognized to suffer from a lack of theoretical basis and concepts (Ford and Randolph 1992, Packendorff 1995, Shenhar 1995, Stinchcombe and Heimer 1985). Thus, the study of projects and project management represents an important and under-researched organizational construct which potentially has significant impact on an organization's bottom line.

Existing research is based on two contrasting beliefs about the role of project management in organizations. The first stream views project management practices as a means to create order and impose control on organizational life through a determinant and closed process, following specific prescriptions and rules. The second stream views project management practices as emergent and open processes for making sense out of organizational action. The aim of this chapter is to delineate each of these streams of research and the theoretical constructs they encompass (summarized in Table 1), and to discuss their implications for a more inclusive, comprehensive and practical theory for project management.

Table 1 serves as a guide and summary for the rest of the chapter. In the text, each stream of research concludes with a summary of its contributions and shortcomings. In the section describing the sense-making perspective, several research questions are posed, which if investigated, would enrich our understanding of project management and project management theory. An overall summary and discussion of implications for future research concludes the chapter.

Table 1. Overview of Project Management Theories

I. PROJECT MANAGEMENT AS A MATTER OF CONTROL

    Major Assumption(s):
- Primary objective is to manage time, budget and quality
- Planning, structure, and formal procedures key to success

    Major Theories

      One Right Way

      Major Assumptions:
- A project has a clear and unambiguously defined task
  (Burke 1992, Frame 1987, Kerzner 1994, Lock 1992)
- Project management is an ideal form of organizing project tasks

      Key Areas of research and constructs examined:
- Project planning and planning tools
- Project control

- Identifying boundaries of projects
  (Ford & Randolf 1992, Knight 1976)
- Conflict resulting from matrix organizational form
  (Archibald 1992; Thamhain & Wilemon 1975; Wilemon & Baker 1983;
  Barker, Tjosvold & Andrews 1988, Butler 1973, Dinsmore 1983
  Hill 1975, 1977, 1983; Stinchcombe 1985b)
- Monitoring progress of project
  - Methods for comparing plans and budgets to outcomes
    (Ritz 1990)
  - Project Evaluation
- Critical success factors for project implementation
  (Cooper & Kleinschmidt 1987, Lechler 1997, Pinto & Slevin 1989)
- Reasons why projects fail
  (Hall 1980, Janis 1972, Kharbanda & Stallworthy 1983, Morris & Hough 1987, Persson 1979,
  Sapolsky 1972, Wilensky 1967, Kerzner 1994)

      Contingency Theory

      Major Assumptions
- All projects are not alike.
  (Pinto and Slevin 1989)

      Key Areas of research and constructs examined:
- Types of projects
  (Shenhar 1993, 1995; Hartman 1995; Packendorff 1995)
- Match between type of project and project management practice
  (Hartman 1995)
- Match between type of project and project success factors
  (Wideman and Shenhar 1996)
- Different levels of understanding project management
  (Morris 1994)

II. EXAMINING PROJECT MANAGEMENT AS A MATTER OF MAKING SENSE

> ➤ **Alternative roles for project management**
- Legitimation (Sapolsky 1977, Lundin 1994)
- Action generation (Starbuck 1984; Packendor 1995)
- As a form of organizing (Lundin 1994, Packendorff 1995)

> ➤ **Sense-making**
> Sense-making can be applied in two ways:
> 1) to explain how people interpret things, and
> 2) to imply a process that individuals and group use to make sense of new situations

Key Areas of research and constructs examined:

> ➤ **General understanding of theoretical foundations**

- Combination of ethnomethodology and cognitive psychology
  (Schutz 1969, Weick 1977, 1995, Berger & Luckman 1967, Gephart 1979, Garfinkel 1967)

- Cognitive psychology

  - – Implications of using a given interpretive scheme or knowledge structure
    (Walsh 1995, Axelrod 1976, Argyris & Schon 1978, Brunsson 1982, Meyer 1982, Fahey & Narayanban 1989, Huff 1982, March & Simon 1958, Ranson, Hinings & Greenwood 1980, Thorngate 1980, Mischel 1981, Gioia 1986, Weick 1977)

  - – Cognitive dissonance theory
    (Weick 1995, Festinger 1957)

> ➤ **Levels of sense-making –**
> (Wiley 1988)

- Individual level sense-making
  (Wiley 1988, Walsh 1988)

- Inter-subjective sense-making
  (Wiley 1988, Bittner 1967)

- Generic subjectivity
  (Barley 1986, Ranson, Hinings & Greenwood 1980, Gephart 1993; Walsh 1995)

- Extra-subjective
  (Weick 1995, Berger & Luckmann 1967, DiMaggio & Powell 1984)

> ➤ **Sense-making as a process**
> (Weick 1995)

EXAMINING PROJECT MANAGEMENT AS A MATTER OF CONTROL

Academic research into project management began with the precedence network diagramming techniques developed for the Polaris submarine project in the early 1960's. This project management literature reflects normative techniques and methods for project planning and control developed primarily by consultants and engineers. It tends to focus on the prescriptive, providing advice and principles for how to plan, organize and control project work; or the descriptive, entailing war stories about what happens on projects.

The underlying assumption of this literature is that the primary function of project management is to get something done on time, on budget and to a specified level of quality or functionality. Emphasizing the importance of formalization and rationality, the message is that successful project management requires high performance in project planning, proper choice of organizational structure, and formalized operating and management procedures (Archibald 1976, Cleland and King 1972, Frame 1987, Kerzner 1979, Lock 1977, Stuckenbruck 1982). Success is believed to be a result of efficiency in the project process accomplished through rationalistic project management procedures.

The great majority of the literature deals with techniques and procedures rather than management practice. Project management from this perspective can clearly be perceived as positivistic, technocentric and rationalistic. Project management entails planning work in small measurable tasks and tracking effort against outcomes. By dividing work into small tasks and monitoring activity through the subdivision of time and the temporal elaboration of activities, project management is a blend of disciplinary practices aimed at making project work predictable, calculable and manageable (Foucault 1977, Townley 1995). It is associated with a belief in linear progress, absolute truths, the rational planning of ideal social orders, and the commodification of knowledge and production (Harvey 1990). The application of project management to uncertain tasks is a way of imposing a scientific, rational control that increases the predictability of the outcomes. In this way, it is a prototypical example of the rationalization and technocratization of management -- a theory of control.

There are two ways to view project management within this framework of control. One way is to frame project management (the traditional model) as a one size fits all solution to all problems arising from temporary undertakings. A second framing of project management (the contingency perspective) incorporates the realization that not all projects are alike and recognizes that because of this project management principles must adapt to these contingent circumstances. This approach no longer looks for one best way to manage all projects, focusing instead on identifying the contingencies that matter and what to do about them.

The Traditional Model of Project Management -- One Right Way

Much of the research on projects and project management is based on the traditional project management model. This model describes the process of planning, organizing, directing and controlling professional staff for the relatively short-term objective of meeting externally established goals and objectives (Kerzner 1994). The fundamental assumption that a project has a clearly and unambiguously defined task (Burke 1992, Frame 1987, Kerzner 1994, Lock 1992) allows project management to build on the premise that the efforts of the project manager (and team) can be directed to the efficient use of resources and techniques. Thus, planning and control are two key components of project management research. Planning includes the preparation of plans and the operation of the tracking system. The organizing systems track appropriate activities against the plan and report deviations to management. Project control provides for control and projection of the critical elements of the project and its process (change control mechanisms) (Humphrey 1990). A second important, although often implicit, assumption is that project management is an ideal form of organizing for project tasks and increases the probability of project success. Hence, project evaluation forms a third key area of research.

Most of the early work on project management centered on the development of *planning models* in Operations Research areas in the 1960's. Later researchers sought to develop concepts such as life cycle planning, risk analysis and project valuation. The most commonly used planning techniques are: the work break down structure, the Gantt Chart, the critical path method, the program evaluation and review technique, and the graphical evaluation and review technique. While most of these tools originated before 1960, work on enhancing them remains an on-going effort of operations research typically pursued under the heading *of project planning.* Research on models and techniques of project planning is now a highly developed discipline where further discoveries are expected to be expensive relative to the effort necessary to uncover them (Packendorff 1995). However, many still view the project management field as composed almost solely of planning and control techniques. The advent of cheap and reasonably user friendly and sophisticated project management software for personal computers in the 1980's made it possible for project managers to apply the techniques to a wider scale of projects. Increased interest in planning (as evidenced in trends towards TQM and Re-engineering) coupled with efforts to develop project management expert systems (Schelle 1990) contributes to a renewed focus on project management as a technical discipline. Thus, work continues in this area primarily into ways to implement the planning models using computer software (Thamhain 1987).

There are two important streams of research literature dealing explicitly with *project control.* These include work concerned with identifying the boundaries of the project with respect to the parent organization, and those concerned with monitoring the project's progress against the plan. The boundaries issue usually arises out of the research on the matrix organizational form (cf. reviews in Ford and Randolph 1992, Knight 1976). Much of this work focuses on the conflict that arises as a result of the use of the matrix structure. The common understanding is that conflict is dysfunctional (Archibald 1992, Thamhain and Wilemon 1975, Wilemon and Baker 1983). Some, however, suggest that small doses of conflict stimulate creativity and innovation (Barker, Tjosvold and Andrews 1988, Butler 1973, Dinsmore 1984, Hill 1975, 1977, 1983, Stinchcombe 1985b). The second topic, the monitoring and follow-up on plans and budgets, gives rise to research on methods of comparing plans and budgets to outcomes. Creating functioning routines for cost control enjoy great importance in this literature. Most of these routines demand a highly structured organizational form and the use of high frequency information capture and examinations (Ritz 1990).

Very few theories of *project evaluation* exist. Evaluation is typically operationalized as degree of goal fulfillment. Studies using this measure aim to determine factors that influence good and bad performance on projects. They often seek to identify critical success factors for project implementation (Cooper and Kleinschmidt 1987, Lechler 1997, Pinto and Slevin 1989). Included in such universal lists of critical success factors are project mission, project planning and control, top management support, customer involvement, etc. The role of the project manager is seen as ensuring that these essential conditions are present and applying the traditional project management practices appropriately to manage the project risks arising out of the weakness of any of these conditions.

Studies addressing the underlying reasons for the success of the project are noticeably absent. It seems that successful projects are not in need of evaluation. The underlying assumption is that the success was due to the use of effective project management techniques. Project evaluation occurs much more frequently when projects fail. The key to preventing failure is assumed to reside in the application of the literature. Project failure is generally ascribed to one of two causes: 1) non-rational decision making, and/or 2) the ineffective implementation of project management planning and controls (Hall 1980, Janis 1972, Kharbanda and Stallworthy 1983, Morris and Hough 1987, Persson 1979, Sapolsky 1972, Wilensky 1967). Many practitioners and researchers adhere to the belief that more stringent application of project management approaches or development of better methods will result in more successful projects (Kerzner 1994). In general, these studies tend to provide case descriptions but superficial and atheoretical analysis.

From the above it is easy to see that there is a flourishing research agenda in he planning and control areas of project management based on an identifiable and extendible theoretical base. This may lead one to think that there is no need for further theoretical development in the project management arena and that only refinement and compilation of existing knowledge remains. However, projects often fail (cf. Kharbanda and Stallworthy 1983, Morris and Hough 1987). In addition, there is evidence that only the most basic project management models are used in practice (Liberatore and Titus 1983, Link and Zmud 1986) and that they are often not used as the existing project management literature leads one to believe (Nathan 1991, Sapolsky 1972). Finally, this research tends to be dominated by mechanistic understandings of organizations and projects. In most cases it follows closed model reasoning, based on the idea that a general theory of project management should exist and every project should be managed in this way.

At the same time, there exists a growing body of contradictory empirical research showing that:

- plans are not stable (Archibald 1992, Thamhain 1987),
- planning procedures often serve to legitimate the project rather than guide it(Sapolsky 1972),

- new and sophisticated planning tools are rarely used by practitioners (Higgins and Watts 1986, Liberatore and Titus 1983), and
- precise plans are not always the most useful management tools (Engwall 1992, Sahlin-Andersson 1992).

Clearly, evidence exists to support the claim that "the discipline as normally described is often incapable of fulfilling its objectives" (Morris 1994). Contingency approaches to the study of project management arose in the early 1990's as a direct response to recognition of these weaknesses in the model's explanatory power.

The Contingency Perspective of Project Management -- It Depends

The contingency model of project management is in its infancy. While still focussing on control of projects, it originates out of the empirical recognition that not all projects are alike and that we must resist the tendency to characterize all projects as fundamentally similar (Pinto and Slevin 1989). This results in an effort to identify critical contingencies and project characteristics in order to better apply appropriate project management tools and techniques.

The primary thrust of research based on the contingency approach has been the generation of ideal types (typologies) of projects. The largest sample study develops a taxonomy of types of projects. This taxonomy is based on a large and detailed project database of 127 projects and two data collection methods (Shenhar 1993, 1995). It suggests that the most important variable in classifying projects is their initial level of technological uncertainty. He describes the four types of projects as those using established technology, mostly established technology, advanced technology and highly advanced technology. Shenhar suggests that these varying projects are typically found in different industries. Another classification scheme categorizes projects by the level of complexity and by the uncertainty of the outcome (Hartman 1995). Complexity is measured in terms of the number of organizations or groups involved in the project. The range or volatility of the expected outcomes measures uncertainty of outcomes. Four major classifications are suggested, representing the four quadrants created by high and low measures on each of these two dimensions (complexity and uncertainty of outcomes). Finally, Packendorff (1995) suggests that not all of what are named projects fit a traditional project definition. He explicitly views projects as temporary organizations and categorizes them on the basis of their individual and structural characteristics. He suggests that projects need to be classified according to their level of formalized structure (explicit vs. emerging) and the degree to which the individual describes him- or herself as dependent on the project or the permanent organization in completing their work. This typology produces four ideal type projects: the "pure" task force, the functional matrix organization, the action group, and the internal renewal project.

The first and most important implication of recognizing the differences among projects is that this recognition provides further reason to question the usefulness of the efforts to derive a universal project management theory. This implication is explored next.

The researchers deriving these contingent typologies observed that not only does a difference in the nature of these projects exist, but that this difference also requires differences in how traditional project management practices are applied. Consequently, there began a move towards contingent application of the traditional project management model. For instance, Hartman (1995) asserts that projects with high levels of complexity and uncertainty were poorly served by traditional project management theory. He derived a new model of project management and tested its use on several projects using an action research methodology. On this small sample of projects, the new model appears to be quite successful, and further testing is planned to examine its validity (Hartman 1996). Wideman and Shenhar (1996) suggest that project success factors should match the type of project. They identify four primary categories of project success:

Internal Project Objectives –
    (1) efficiency during project;

Benefit to Customer –
    (2) effectiveness in the short term;
    (3) effectiveness in the medium term; and,
    (4) effectiveness in the long term.

Initial empirical results show some correlation between these term-based success criteria and project types. These researchers provide recommendations for how to apply project management practices given these differences however, they tend to be restricted to existing planning and control techniques.

Finally, Morris (1994) suggests that there are three different levels of understanding of project management. At its most basic, project management is a deceptively simple discipline based on integrating everything that needs to be done as the project evolves in order to ensure that its objectives are met. From this perspective, project management uses management practices (planning, organizing, controlling etc.) similar to other forms of management; the only difference being that it is time constrained and moves through a predetermined life cycle. A second level of understanding incorporates the first level and complicates it with additional tasks which have greater complexity (project definition, contracting, planning, measurement and team leadership issues). At its third and most complex level, project management includes the more strategic issues of project definition, policy, strategy, technology, legal, financial, environmental, community and others. At this level the project is no longer focusing solely on the task to be completed but also recognizing the environment in which the task must be completed. Morris (1994) suggests that most people's understanding of project management may go no deeper that the second level. This idea is based on the experiential knowledge of the author but lacks a basis in empirical evidence. The implications of these differing levels of understanding to the project management process have not been explored.

The contingency approach makes four contributions to the study of project management. First, projects vary on a range of significant criteria. Second, project management practices should vary with project type. Third, project success criteria should vary with project type. Finally, different project participants may have different levels of understanding of project management.

The contingency approach arose due to attempts to address the lack of empirical studies on the nature of projects and project management. It addresses issues of how to improve project management *within* traditional project management boundaries. That is, it attempts to identify the small number of significant contingencies and the related changes required to traditional project management. However, it continues to pursue a few key contingencies, which if identified in advance can be used to select and apply the appropriate predefined model of project management. Thus, the contingency model continues the mechanistic view of projects inherent in the traditional model of project management. The contingency view of project management also does not address the contradictory empirical evidence of project management practices relationship to project success.

The preceding two sections explored the status of the more traditional approaches to the study of project management. The next section introduces a new theoretical approach to the study of project management and poses research questions to enrich our understanding of these important practices.

EXAMINING PROJECT MANAGEMENT AS A MATTER OF MAKING SENSE

Much organizational theory now recognizes organizational experience as a social construction of reality, institutionalized and reproduced by the human actor (Berger and Luckmann 1967). Under this approach, projects, like their surroundings, are assumed to be institutions created out of the expectations, inter-subjective understandings and reproductive actions undertaken by the humans involved in them. Adjusting the methods and theories of project management research to these assumptions will require studying the individual conceptions of project reality rather than searching for universal truths and mechanisms of the unambiguous phenomenon of "projects". Such research explores understandings of project management's role in organizations other than those connected to rational efficiency goals.

Alternative Roles for Project Management

The alternative roles suggested for project management include legitimization; action generation; and organizing versus organization. As early as 1972, Sapolsky suggested that the *primary role of project management might be legitimization*; therefore formal project management tools simply provide a facade that symbolizes control, rationalism, power and efficiency (Sapolsky 1972). Work by Lundin and Söderholm (1995) and others using institutional theory to understand differences in the application of project management practices furthers this line of research.

Others have suggested that *project management's role in generating action* in organizations (Starbuck 1983) needs further investigation. The primary purpose of projects is to accomplish action. Studying projects as action systems means spending less time on what was meant to happen and more on what actually happens. It is the enactment of individuals rather than the behavior of individuals that is of interest; action can not be studied without also investigating the expectations forming the action base and the learning occurring as a result of the action taking place (Packendorff 1995).

Finally, some suggest (Lundin and Söderholm 1995, Packendorff 1995) that we should explore *project management as a form of organizing* rather than a form of organization. Rather than organization's focus on structure, 'organizing' views the actions of individuals and the processes they can form as the basic elements of inquiry. Weick (1979) defined 'organizing' as "...*a consensually validated grammar for reducing equivocality by means of sensible interlocked behaviors*". To organize is to assemble ongoing interdependent actions into sensible sequences that generate sensible outcomes" (Weick 1979: 3, Italics from original). This is very similar to how the word "project" is often defined:

> "Project: ...a temporary process composed of constantly changing collection of technicalities/operations involving the close coordination of heterogeneous resources to produce one or a few units of a unique product/service .... The essential characteristic of the process by which a project is performed is the progressive elaboration of requirements/specification." (Webster 1994: p. 22-8)

Each of these three perspectives on the role of project management serves to question the rational mechanism underlying management action. They represent a fundamental re-thinking of project management in organizations, and how to evaluate project success. Packendorff (1994) suggests that it may be time for project management to incorporate a broader view of project management in organizations but he warns that "Abandoning the notion of the project manager as a Homo economicus would be to question the very foundation of present knowledge on project planning and control" (1994: p. 212). To date these perspectives are considered radical, and have not received much acceptance in either the mainstream academic or practitioners' realm. However, they do indicate that project management theory is on the verge of major changes in its underlying assumptions.

These three perspectives have two things in common. The first commonality is a view of projects as emerging phenomenon; and of project management as means of clarifying what needs to be done and when; or for justifying what was done rather than just a means of controlling a project. For instance, Packendorff (1995) explicitly suggests that understanding the cognitive functioning around project management has a high potential to contribute to our understandings of project management. Engwall (1994) also suggests that "Project management theory might be instrumental as talk for some practitioners when they try to interpret and explain their organizational lives" (Engwall 1994). This comment signals a need to view project management as an open and emergent process of sense-making rather than a determinant and closed process of following prescriptions and rules.

The second commonality is that each of these new perspectives of project management strives to increase the complexity of our understandings of projects and project management. It changes our perspective of projects from rational to natural to open systems. In doing so, more ambiguity in structures, processes and environments is introduced. As the level of ambiguity increases, there is a greater need for sense-making (Weick 1995). The next section outlines a sense-making theoretical framework (Garfinkel 1967, Gephart 1978, 1993, Walsh 1995, Weick 1979, 1995) to synthesize these commonalities and provide a focus for further project management research.

The Sense-making Perspective

The term sense-making is commonly used in two ways. First, there is the theory of sense-making that is about the ways people generate what they interpret (Weick 1995). The second use of the term refers to sense-making as a process. From this perspective, sense-making includes the efforts of individuals and social groups as they seek, process and construct information to negotiate through new situations. This use of the term highlights the actions, activity, and creating – i.e., the process of sense-making -- that lays down the events that are interpreted and then reinterpreted. Both approaches to sense-making can make important contributions to our understanding of project management.

Sense-making theory explains how people construct meaning in their everyday lives and is derived from Schutz's (1967) phenomenology. It combines research from the areas of ethnomethodology and cognitive psychology. *Ethnomethodology* emphasizes accounting for what one does in the presence of others to prove social competence and the rationality of actions. To ethnomethodologists, sense-making means reasoning in ways that differ from those practices associated with rational decision-making (Weick 1995). Social psychologists view sense-making as making sense of actions that did not follow from beliefs and self-concepts (Weick 1995). This approach assumes that social reality is essentially socially constructed on an on-going basis (Berger and Luckmann 1967). It is the sociological investigation of every day life and social practices that form the basis for individuals to socially construct a sense of shared meanings (Gephart 1993). Thus, sense-making is the verbal, inter-subjective process of interpreting actions and events (Weick 1979, Gephart 1978).

Sense-making practices are based on assumptions that participants:

a) share a common perspective on the world (reciprocity of perspectives);
b) employ recognizable words and terms (normal forms);
c) will interpret comments if they are vague and that the comments can be clarified later in the conversation (the etceteras principle); and,
d) will attempt to understand any unclear aspect of conversation by using background knowledge (descriptive vocabularies as indexical expressions) (Gephart 1993).

These practices form the basis for constructing interpretive schemes that assist members in making sense of the world. When sense-making practices break down, situations become confusing or meaningless (Gephart 1978).

Cognitive psychology makes two main contributions to sense-making theory. The first is to delineate the implications of using a given interpretive scheme or knowledge structure (Walsh 1995). *[Note that knowledge structures are studied under a wide variety of names including: Cognitive Maps (Axelrod 1976); Theory of Action (Argyris and Schon 1978); Organizational Ideologies (Brunsson 1982, Meyer 1982); Causal Maps (Fahey and Narayanan 1989); Strategic Frame (Huff 1982); Frames (March and Simon 1958); Interpretive Schemes (Ranson, Hinings and Greenwood 1980).]* This body of research suggests that knowledge structures are templates consisting of organized information about an information domain. These templates simplify and speed problem solving by providing a basis for evaluating information. The basic premise of this research is that "individuals create knowledge structures to help them process information and make decisions" (Walsh 1995: p. 286). Knowledge structures are "a mental template consisting of organized knowledge about an information environment that enables interpretation and action in that environment." (Walsh 1995:286). These knowledge structures serve the purpose of transforming complex information environments into tractable ones. Knowledge structures encompass both content and structure, and are both enabling and limiting at the same time. The key advantages associated with the use of knowledge structures are that they improve the effectiveness and efficiency of information processing (Thorngate 1980) and so increase cognitive efficiency (Mischel 1981). On the other hand, in simplifying the information domain to allow processing some of the complexity is inevitably lost (Gioia 1986, Weick 1979).

The second major contribution of cognitive psychology arises out of cognitive dissonance theory (Weick 1995). Cognitive dissonance theory incorporates the idea that outcomes develop prior to definitions of the situation (Festinger 1957). In order to reduce the dissonance an individual feels surrounding the choice of one alternative over another, the individual enhances the positive attributes of the chosen solution and increases the negative features of the non-chosen alternative. In this way, the individual retrospectively changes the meaning of the decision by altering the nature of the alternatives. Thus, the outcome of the decision is made sensible by constructing a plausible story to account for it. From a dissonance perspective, sense-making often equates to self-justification. The individual chooses what to justify through retrospective sense-making. The discrepancies between what should and what does happen as a result of action on the part of the individual creates an occasion for sense-making.

Levels of Sense-making

Wiley (1988) identifies four levels of sense-making: individual, inter-subjective, generic subjective and extra subjective. Conceptualizing sense-making as being composed of different characteristics at different levels of analysis allows us to integrate somewhat the theoretical insights described in the previous section. The following describes each level of sense-making, identifies the key theoretical influences associated with each level, and presents some ideas of how these sense-making concepts will prove useful in the study of project management.

The first level of sense-making is referred to as *Individual level sense-making*. This level concentrates on discovering the ways individuals build or use existing knowledge structures to make sense of information and situations. Both structures of knowledge and content are relevant at this level of sense-making. It involves the creation and use of knowledge structures to make sense. Thus, social cognition and information processing theories have a strong influence here.

At the individual level, project managers' models of project management can be viewed as a knowledge structure that "orders an information environment in a way that enables subsequent interpretation and action" (Walsh 1995:281). Understanding how project managers' individually make sense of project management requires surfacing their knowledge structures and causal beliefs around the concept. Examples of research questions which would focus on this level of sense-making include:

> What do individually constructed knowledge structures pertaining to project management contain and how are they structured?

> What impact do these structures have on reflections of practices and post-project evaluations?

The second level of sense-making is called *Inter-subjective sense-making*. It involves the processes by which individuals construct social reality interactively, the primary focus of ethnomethodology. Inter-subjective sense-making is distinct from individual sense-making because it emerges from the interchange and synthesis of two or more communicating individuals creating a level of social reality (Wiley 1988). Inter-subjectivity facilitates 1) the perception of complex events, and 2) innovations to manage the complexity. Cognitive dissonance theory also come into play in exploring how individuals make sense of discrepancies between their individual sense-making of project management and the inter-subjective understandings that arise.

Exploring project management at the inter-subjective level requires that we determine its meaning in real scenes of action (Bittner 1967). Identifying the "taken for granted" background stock of knowledge necessary to make project management sensible will start to surface the important factors of project management not traditionally dealt with in the literature. Research questions grounded in the inter-subjective level of sense-making include:

> How do project participants use sense-making practices to create a sense of shared understanding of project management?

> How do project participants justify differences between project management models and project management practice?

The third level of sense-making is *generic subjectivity*. This level takes the form of 'scripts' (Barley 1986), 'interpretive schemes' (Ranson, Hinings and Greenwood 1980) or 'sense-making resources' (Gephart 1993) which allow people to substitute for one another and share an understanding of a situation. Generic subjectivity operates at the level of structure. The reification of previously negotiated inter-subjective understandings of roles and rules allow individuals to take action without having to re-negotiate their understanding of the situation on an on-going basis. This allows individuals to act without continually making sense of familiar objects and circumstances. Generic subjectivity facilitates control through the mindless application of routines independent of individual or intersubjectivity. Generic sense-making is built upon ideology, third order controls, paradigms, theories of action, tradition, stories (Weick 1995).

These theoretical constructs generate interest in determining if project managers' share a common knowledge structure recognized as "project management". Identification of this generic sense-making structure would go a long way to address the question of generic practices and terminology that frequently arises in the project management field (Morris 1994, Packendorff 1995, Wideman and Shenhar 1996). Walsh (1995) also suggests that an important question yet to be answered by organizational cognition is "how accurate a knowledge structure must be in order to be useful to the person employing it?....i.e. administrative scientists need to discover the nature of useful simplicity." (p. 303) He suggests that this must be done through post-decision assessments. By looking at post-decision project outcomes (judgments of success and failure) and assessing the generic and individual models of project management in place, one can explore: a) whether more complicated or simpler models are more often associated with perceived success or failure; and b) whether the sharing of project management models influences perceived success or failure of projects. Research questions of interest at this level of sense-making include:

> What role do local shared understandings of project management
> have in how individuals make sense of project management?
>
> How accurate are generic knowledge structures? What impact do
> they have on project management and its outcomes?

The fourth level of sense-making is the extra-subjective level. The *Extra-subjective* level of sense-making involves an abstract institutional field derived from previous interaction. These are almost cultural beliefs that exist without need for reconstitution on a regular basis. Weick (1995) describes this as 'a level of symbolic reality such as we might associate with capitalism or mathematics' (p. 72). This level of sense-making derives from institutional theory (Berger and Luckmann 1967, DiMaggio and Powell 1984). Finding common project management knowledge structures across project types and organizations would indicate the operation of institutional influences on project management practices. Given the unitary and generic assumptions of traditional project management model, the extra-subjective level's influence on sense-making around project management practices and definitions of success are bound to be important. Research questions of interest here include:

> What influence do institutional factors (PMI, PMBOK) have on individual's constructions of project management and project success criteria?

Project Management a Sense-making Process

Viewed as a process, sense-making includes the efforts of individuals and social groups as they seek, process and construct information to negotiate through problem situations. This use of the term highlights the actions, activity, and creating -- the process of sense-making -- that lays down the traces that are interpreted and then reinterpreted (Weick 1995). The key research question of interest here is:

> How do project participants use project management constructs to make sense of practices used on projects and project outcomes?

Another process involved is "organizational sense-making" (Weick 1995). Organizational sense-making occurs at the intersection of inter-subjective and generic subjectivity where interactions that try to manage uncertainty require a mixture of the inter subjective and generic subjective. Periods of stability reflect periods where generic subjectivity is the primary sense-making activity. Weick suggests that sense-making through generic subjectivity is a mainstay of organizational analysis. In times of stability, generic subjectivity takes many forms including rules and scripts. Inter-subjectivity is largely irrelevant as long as the script fits the situation. Turbulence or change requires more inter-subjective activity and the use of modified scripts. If the situation changes such that the script no longer fits and generic subjectivity is no longer sufficient to make sense of the circumstances, inter subjectivity is invoked to fill the gaps. Individuals interact to synthesize new meaning. This inter-subjective activity does not completely replace generic subjectivity. In fact, generic scripts of how to modify understandings may be invoked.

Organizational sense-making begins with either the action or the outcome and results in alteration of beliefs to create a sensible explanation for the action or the outcome (Weick 1995: p. 168). *Belief-driven sense-making* is based in beliefs arising from ideology or paradigms and occurs either through arguing or expecting. Arguing enables sense-making by putting forth opposing ideas and negotiating some common understanding. Expecting engenders sense-making through a sort of self-fulfilling prophecy. What is expected, and worked towards, happens. *Action driven sense-making* starts with an action for which an individual is responsible (commitment), or which has happened and that requires explanation (manipulation). Committing again facilitates accomplishing expectations because people strive to a) achieve what they have committed to, and b) make sense of the world in terms of these commitments. In this case, sense-making focuses on the question of why the action occurred. Finally, organizational sense-making can occur through a process of manipulating expectations to arrive at an expected goal. Here, sense-making focuses on defining what did occur. The research questions generated by these issues include:

> How do project management constructs provide opportunities for arguing or setting expectations that make sense of project reality or outcomes?

> How do project management constructs allow project participants to explain *what* did, in fact, happen; or to explain *why* a particular occurrence happened?

> Do different models of project management rely on different sense-making drivers? That is, do true believers use project management beliefs to justify or set expectations for future actions, while more politically driven managers use project management to explain actions already taken?

Unmet expectations or communication failures usually explain project failure. The sense-making approach provides tools to assist in examining the operation of project management in organizations, and to understand why expectations are unmet or communications fail. Expectations and communication rely on the existence of a common underlying understanding of key concepts. This inter-subjective or cultural world is constructed or produced through sense-making (Leiter 1980). If something disrupts the process and practice of sense-making, meaning begins to disintegrate (Garfinkel 1967) and both communication and expectations fail to be shared. In the traditional project management model, issues of failure of sense-making have largely been ignored by assuming a generic and unitary model of project management that applies in all situations. Consequently, project success criteria can universally be assumed to be based on schedule, budget and specification measures. However, if we throw out the generic, unitary view and turn to a socially constructed (Berger and Luckmann 1967) view of the world, it becomes necessary to understand project management through the experience of project participants, and to recognize the possibility of multiple realities.

CONCLUSIONS AND FUTURE RESEARCH

The fundamental difference between the control and the sense-making orientation for the study of projects and project management resides in their underlying assumptions. The control model views projects as a form of organization while the sense-making approach views projects as a means of organizing.

Using 'organization' as a foundational concept, the control perspective views a project as a relatively closed system, guided by objectives, managed through work division and specialization, and distinguishable from its environment. This concept of "organization" relates to rationalism and to tools. The basic idea inherent in the "organization" concept is to design, optimize, and be prepared for all eventualities before they occur. It is this concept that forms the foundation for most work on planning and control and project management in general. The implications for management and research based on this view is that there is a "best" way (or a few best ways) to manage projects; the sooner we discover and apply them the sooner we will have more project success.

'Organizing', on the other hand, refers to the deliberate social interaction occurring between humans working together to accomplish a certain task. Rather than organization's focus on structure, 'organizing' views the actions of individuals and the processes they can form as the basic elements of inquiry. Thus, a sense-making focus on project management directs us to look at the processes of action and interaction that enable individuals to make sense of organizational activities and to act. Managers are advised to be aware of the sense-making processes at work and how they interact to effect the emergent projects. Researchers are directed to explore ways to facilitate the inter-subjective sense-making to reduce communication failure and confusion.

Each perspective has a different set of implications which can be seen to be in direct conflict. Yet, each contributes in some unique way to our understanding of project management. The traditional model provides the tools and direction to begin a project. The contingency model reminds us to learn from the past and adapt the traditional model to fit the contextual details of the existing project. The sense-making models incorporate the socially negotiated order of human action and stress the complex and emergent nature of project activity.

Much research is currently underway in the control perspective of project management. What is needed now is research that adopts a sense-making perspective exploring the theory of project management as a process for making sense of organizational activity, and the levels of sense-making as they apply to project management. For an individual, sense-making is the process of creating and applying knowledge structures, negotiating their inter-subjective meaning and applying generic and extra-subjective sense-making tools where appropriate. All four levels of sense-making interact in the individual sense-making process to build a model of project management and project success criteria. Understanding how project team members are influenced by these different levels of sense-making in building models of project management has implications for improving practise.

Projects continue to fail, and the control-orientation towards project management fails to adequately explain why they do. If, as discussed earlier, projects are becoming a fundamental structural component in organizations; then it is imperative to understand how to effectively manage them. Research based on a sense-making perspective will help create and enrich this understanding. This chapter provides the theoretical basis and introduces the research questions generated by a sense-making approach to the study of project management.

Moreover, if chaos is the law of nature and order is the dream of man as professed by Henry Adams, then it is time to recognize that man's dream of order as reflected in the pursuit of 'best' project management practices be over shadowed by accepting nature's law of chaos. Applying a sense-making approach may allow us to understand projects more fully and make better use of the many project management tools and practices we have already defined.

CHAPTER 4

COUPLING, INTERDEPENDENCE AND CONTROL IN GLOBAL PROJECTS

Paul C. van Fenema, Erasmus University, Rotterdam School of Management, The Netherlands

Kuldeep Kumar, Erasmus University, Rotterdam School of Management, The Netherlands

ABSTRACT

Organizing projects across globally distributed sites is the most recent step in an ongoing process of internationalizing temporary work. These remote projects are becoming technically feasible and advantageous in a business community that becomes globalized and interconnected. Global projects differ from their local ancestors in multiple senses: contributors lack face-to-face interactions and have different cultural backgrounds, advanced information technology and infrastructures mediate remote cooperation, and time zone differences reduce real-time communications to only a few hours per day.

Organizations experience unfamiliarity in coordinating and controlling work that is accomplished at multiple sites. In response, a body of knowledge is emerging that seeks to understand the implications of global dispersion for project management. This chapter contributes from a coordination theory perspective. It elaborates 4 configurations of global projects based on the uncertainty of project interfaces, and the way work is assigned to project locations. The chapter analyzes each configuration in terms of interdependencies and coupling properties, and proposes strategies for improving coordination and control across sites.

TRANSITION TOWARDS GLOBAL PROJECTS

Over the past decade, many projects have undergone a major change. Increasingly, projects require close cooperation from professionals dispersed across the globe (Evaristo and van Fenema 1999). This is an extension of projects that are geographically distributed in, for example, the US or Europe. In the US, distributed projects are common in the aerospace industry, and experience in managing these projects has developed since the POLARIS project. In Europe, integration on a governmental and business level has promoted geographically distributed projects like the ESPRIT research programs, Airbus Industries, and projects from the European Space Agency (ESA).

Global projects extend the nature of distributedness as two or more sites across the globe are involved. For example, one site in the Americas, one in Europe and one in the Far East. Spearhead projects in the automotive industry include the Ford Mondeo project in which European and American units of the Ford organization cooperated in the development of a car benefiting from and suiting internationally merging tastes and needs (Andres 1992). Global projects are also becoming common in the financial sector, management consultancy, oil industry (Solomon 1995), hi-tech electronics & semiconductor industries, as well as software development projects. Examples of the latter include offshore outsourcing projects in which companies from Europe or the US develop Information Systems together with professionals from India (Rajkumar and Dawley 1997).

Due to the recent nature of global projects, professional experience and academic research is currently in its early stages. Some early contributions include examples from the automotive industry (Manheim 1993), R&D (Chiesa 1995) and offshore software outsourcing (Smith, Mitra, and Narasimhan 1996; van Fenema 1997). These initial experiences and research projects indicate some issues and problems in managing interdependencies and coordination needs in multi-site environments. Also, controlling performances of people across sites appears a challenge in projects where common project control strategies cannot easily be applied. However, systematic research based on a solid theoretical basis is only starting to emerge.

The purpose of this chapter is to develop a theoretical basis for assessing the impact of global distributedness on work interdependencies and processes of coordination and control.

Building on Project Management and Organization theory, we propose a matrix with two dimensions. First, the extent to which work packages or modules are assigned to a single or multiple location, and second the uncertainty of interfaces between modules.

The matrix yields four configurations of global projects. For each of these, work interdependencies and requirements for project coordination and control strategies are investigated. The proposed configurations bear relevance for practitioners and researchers in project management. Professionals who are expected to meet the challenges of global projects will find the configurations useful to assess the nature of their global project. Researchers can use the concepts as a point of departure for future research on the management of global projects.

WORK PARTITIONING, INTERDEPENDENCIES AND COUPLING

"Interdependence does not by itself cause difficulty if the pattern of interdependence is stable and fixed. For in this case, each subprogram can be designed to take into account all of the other subprograms with which it interacts.

Difficulties arise only if program execution rests on contingencies that cannot be predicted perfectly in advance. In this case, coordinating activity is required to secure agreement on estimates that will be used as the basis for action, or to provide information to each subprogram unit about the relevant activities of the others. Hence, we arrive at the proposition that the more repetitive and predictable the situation, the greater the tolerance for interdependence. Conversely, the greater the elements of variability and contingency, the greater is the burden of coordinating activities (...)".

March and Simon 1958, page 159

Turner (1993, p. 8) defines a project as "an endeavor in which human, material and financial resources are organized in a novel way, to undertake a unique scope of work, of given specification, within constraints of cost and time, so as to achieve beneficial change defined by quantitative and qualitative objectives". Because of their limited duration and pre-defined goals, project management concepts and techniques are aimed at enabling and ensuring performance in accordance with organizational expectations. In literature, two principles have been proposed that underpin the management of projects: differentiation and integration (Meadows 1996, Scott, Mitchell, and Peery 1981).

Differentiation
The accomplishment of project goals within resource constraints requires specifying and planning sequential and parallel steps and activities. Hence, work packages or modules are specified and assigned to teams or individuals. In project management, common differentiation concepts include the Work Breakdown Structure (WBS), Project Life-Cycle (PLC), and Organization Breakdown Structures (OBS). Differentiation and assignment of subtasks creates interdependencies between people whose tasks are linked in some way. Thompson (1967) introduced three types of interdependencies: pooled, sequential, and reciprocal. In pooled interdependence, people need the same tool or resource to accomplish work. Tasks are sequentially linked when accomplishment of one task requires completion of another one. If work flows back and forth between people, they are reciprocally connected. Van de Ven (1976) extended reciprocity with team interdependence, that is, individuals interacting simultaneously. A final type of interdependence is integrative interdependence (van Fenema and Kumar 2000), where deliverables are integrated to a single output (Crowston 1997).

Coupling Work Activities and Ensuring Performance
Differentiated work needs to be integrated, that is, managed in order to deliver the intended product or services. Project management literature has emphasized two aspects of integration: *Coordination* which includes planning work and promoting coupling among project contributors; and *Control,* that is, the process aimed at ensuring compliance of the project activities with the overall project design (Lester 1982).

Coordination. Organization literature distinguishes four types of coordination strategies. First, procedural coordination which includes mechanisms for managing work by specifications, like standardized work-procedures, outcome and process standards, project-plans, and schedules designed to coordinate work. Second, structural coordination, that is, the organizational structures of roles that enable work differentiation and interactions between people. Examples are the managerial hierarchy, steering committees, and linking pins between project units (Galbraith 1973). Third, Child (1984) pointed at the role of social integration which includes people dynamics and team building in projects. Projects requires frequent interaction, or "mutual adjustment" (Thompson 1967) to keep people in touch with each other and focused on project goals. Finally, projects are increasingly supported by sophisticated technical coordination mechanisms, such as planning and control software, packaged project management tools, work-flow systems, computer-supported collaborative work (CSCW) tools, and electronic media.

The four coordination mechanisms are connected, complementary, and substitutable (Mintzberg 1979). For example, plans and standards (procedural coordination mechanisms) are developed and institutionalized through structural mechanisms such as steering committees. They are communicated through a combination of structural and information technology arrangements. On the other hand, problems in developing standards, as in case of uncertain or complex work may be ameliorated by either the use of close managerial supervision (structural coordination) or social coordination mechanisms like mutual adjustment and sharing of knowledge among professionals (Krauss and Fussell 1990).

Control. Projects need mechanisms to ensure that performances of individual and teams comply with project planning and stakeholder expectations. Control processes includes an object of control and a subject (the controller) (van Fenema and Kumar 2000). The control object may include (1) inputs required for the project, that is, resources like time, people, money, and technology; (2) the transformation process, that is, the tasks and activities required to accomplish project purposes; and (3) the outcomes of project activities in intermediate or aggregated stages.

The controller has traditionally been seen as the project managers, being responsible for selecting people, specifying work expectations, setting work standards, monitoring actual work, and sanctioning or rewarding people accordingly. In large projects, possibly in an environment where reliability, safety and quality are important, managerial supervision is often supplemented by reliance on formal rules and work procedures. The controller role can also be partially accomplished or facilitated by advanced information systems. Current project management software allows project participants to represent past, current and expected work activities. In addition, software can help project participants visualize interdependencies between activities and actors, and reveal resource constraints. Control may also be executed by professional associations which certify people upon completion of professional (project management) training. Finally, as in many global projects, parts of the work are subcontracted or outsourced, clients will likely control vendor performance at regular intervals. Like the four coordination strategies, the modes of control provide project managers and stakeholders with a portfolio of strategies that are complementary and substitutable.

DETERMINANTS OF GLOBAL PROJECT ORGANIZATION

Global projects are analyzed along two dimensions. First, the division of project work in modules (work packages), and the assignment of these modules to sites involved in the project. Second, we look at the structurability of project work, in particular concerning interfaces between project modules. These two contingencies are considered important determinants of project coordination (Van de Ven, Delbecq, and Koenig Jr 1976). We then propose a matrix that combines the two dimensions and proposes four configurations of global projects.

Work Division, Interdependencies and Geographical Assignment

Global projects extend the challenge for project managers to partition work in smaller segments and assign these to teams or individuals. In co-located projects, work breakdown is an important consideration (Globerson 1994) since it creates interdependencies and information needs between actors, activities and resources (Malone, Crowston, Lee, and Pentland 1999). A diverse set of task interdependencies has been recognized in literature, like pooled (people working on the same job), sequential (people passing work on), reciprocal/team (people exchanging work asynchronously or synchronously), and integrative (people bringing their work together).

In turn, these interdependencies drive coupling and control needs in a project. Low levels of task interdependence (like pooled, or sequential), are associated with routine modes of coordination (Thompson 1967). More complex dependencies require more active, inter-human forms of communications (Van de Ven, Delbecq and Koenig Jr 1976). The complexity that WBS and interdependencies generate has led to the notion of semi-structured, modular work division. Here, the work is partitioned in loosely coupled modules with stable interfaces (Sanchez and Mahoney 1996). This allows actors to work in relative isolation on their respective portion *within* the constraints of the interface definition, but *without* the constant need to interact with actors involved in other project modules (von Hippel 1994).

In remote projects, the assignment of these modules is an additional dimension of the WBS that has implications for the coupling and management processes of the project. Understanding these consequences is important in global projects, since face-to-face interactions and problem solving are resource intensive in terms of money and time. In order to extend our insight in this problem, we distinguish two options for geographically assigning work packages. First, each site is completely responsible for a single module. Second, multiple sites work on the same module because, for instance, specialized know-how or equipment reside only at a single location (von Hippel 1998).

Structurability of Global Project Work

The second dimension, structurability, refers to the nature of project work as experienced by project participants. This includes various constructs from organization theory, like work variety, complexity (Hage, Aiken, and Marrett 1971), difficulty or uncertainty (Van de Ven, Delbecq and Koenig Jr 1976). *Complexity* refers to the fact that individuals lack the mental capacity to oversee large or complex projects in all its dimensions and interdependencies (Simon 1957). Complexity is related to the size of the project, the novelty of the project, and the level of experience of project participants. *Uncertainty* is caused by a lack of information on future contingencies and interdependencies (Tushman and Nadler 1978). For example, specifications of project deliveries is uncertain because stakeholders keep changing requirements, or the company depends on subcontractors for the design and manufacturing of key components.

If projects or subactivities are not fully specifiable and structurable, coordination by procedural mechanisms like plans and schedules is no longer feasible. Instead, literature suggests that structural and social coordination mechanisms are more appropriate that enable close coupling and mutual adjustment among project actors. Structural mechanisms include linking pins or teams that work across departmental boundaries (Galbraith 1973).

Similarly, structurability drives the modes of control. In case of unspecified work, project participants may have problems understanding performance expectations and ensuring compliance with project expectations. In addition, absence of clear standards deprives managers from a yardstick for comparing performance and rewarding people. Literature proposes alternative control strategies, like autonomously working teams (Jolivet and Navarre 1996; Wellins, Wilson, and Katz 1990).

For the purpose of this chapter, we assume that people working on the *same* module inherently will need to cooperate closely. What may vary, however, is the structure and stability of the interfaces *between* work packages. As indicated, well-defined interfaces allow people to focus on their particular module, while maintaining loose interactions with actors working on other parts (Sanchez and Mahoney 1996). However, project size and dynamics may imply that per-defined interface structures cannot be maintained because they do not cater for requisite changes and interdependencies between modules. The impact of global distributedness on this process will be explored in the next sections.

MATRIX OF GLOBAL PROJECTS: FOUR CONFIGURATIONS

When the dimensions are combined, four configurations of global projects emerge (table 1). Since the two dimensions (work partitioning and structurability) cover key aspects of any project, the configurations provide an interesting basis for investigating interdependencies, coupling and control in global, multi-site environments.

Using configurations for theory building is well accepted in organization theory (Meyer, Tsui, and Hinings 1993). Examples include Burns and Stalker's (1961) and Mintzberg's (1979) typologies of organizational forms. Among the unlimited variety of organizational forms in real-life configurations provide condensed templates. Based on variables that define key properties of organizations, these templates combine different settings of such variables. In this chapter the first dimension captures the extent to which geographical work assignment coincides with division of the project in modules (see rows in table 1). The second dimension varies the extent to which interfaces between the modules are structured (see columns in table 1).

Table 1. Four Configurations of Globally Distributed Projects

		Uncertainty of Interfaces between Modules	
		Low	*High*
Synchronicity of Geographical Work Allocation & WBS	*High*	**Configuration 1** Synchronous Allocation of Structured Work	**Configuration 3** Synchronous Allocation of Uncertain Work
	Low	**Configuration 2** Asynchronous Allocation of Structured Work	**Configuration 4** Asynchronous Allocation of Uncertain Work

The purpose of these configurations is to provide a conceptual framework for analyzing global projects, and for investigating the differences of coordination and control strategies. Configuration 1 and 2 comprise activities which have stable interfaces, allowing project actors to work in isolation on their respective modules. By contrast, interfaces in configuration 3 and 4 are not specifiable and require heedful coupling to manage cross-modular dependencies. The following sections discuss the four configurations. We assess the impact of the two dimensions on interdependencies and strategies for connecting and controlling work accomplishment. The discussion is clarified by four figures depicting each configuration.

CONFIGURATION 1. SYNCHRONOUS ALLOCATION OF STRUCTURED WORK

Figure 1 depicts the first configuration. We show 3 locations that are involved in the project. Per site, one or more professionals may contribute to the project. The figure also shows 3 modules (A, B, and C), in this case each is assigned to a single location. In this first configuration, project participants can break down the overall project goals in discrete activities or work packages. Modules are each assigned to a specific location that is fully responsible for its completion. This implies that every site houses the full set of resources and competencies needed for delivering the module. We assume here that interfaces between modules are stable and pre-defined, for example, because representatives have spelled out the WBS after project kick-off. This may include the main functional and technical specifications of the project and modules, as well as delivery dates and quality standards.

Site representatives are responsible for implementing these specifications at their site. One implication of this strategy is that mutual adjustments and coupling between locations become superfluous. Although interdependencies between the modules persist (deliverables need to be integrated at some point of time), they are "asleep" while people work on the packages. This allows each site to proceed in parallel, operating quasi-independently (March and Simon 1958). Examples from configuration 1 abound in car manufacturing, avionics, electronics, construction and the computer industry (Baldwin and Clark 1997).

Local work on modules contrasts with the structure and stability on an interface level. Professionals elaborate design specifications, and subsequently start executing these designs. Co-location fosters rich and frequent interactions as people collectively shape their module (Dougherty 1996). Since this process is incompletely defined in advance, it is controlled by carefully selecting team members, and empowering professionals to manage themselves as individuals and a team (Manz, Mossholder, and Luthans 1987). On an international, supra-module level, minimal coupling suffices to achieve concerted action (Thompson 1967), provided that each location sticks to the initial design of the project. Occasionally organizations will check key performance metrics to ensure compliance.

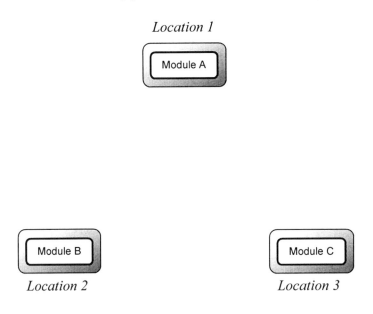

Figure 1: Synchronous allocation of structured work

Upon completion, each location delivers its performance as part of the aggregated project performance. Modules are integrated at a single location (in case the project is intended to deliver a single physical artifact like an airplane), or remotely (for example software modules). Control in this final stage is aimed at ensuring compliance of work packages with *a priori* defined standards. If such controls yield favorable outcomes, coordination is automatically achieved. Coordination between modules thus mainly relies on the initial and final stage of the project.

The specifiable and discrete nature of the WBS favors a governance strategy of contracting-out or outsourcing: expectations are easily transmitted and codified in contracts (Williamson 1986). Control is facilitated by the existence of these codifications. However, the distributed character of the project requires a way to observe progress of performance on a local level. Reliance on commitment, reputation and competence is supplemented with contractual incorporation of frequent reporting requirements to enforce contractual agreements (Kumar and Willcocks 1996).

CONFIGURATION 2. ASYNCHRONOUS ALLOCATION OF STRUCTURED WORK

In the second configuration, each module is assigned to multiple locations. The bold lines between modules depict interdependencies between professionals working on the same module (figure 2). The divided involvement in work packages may result from an organization's specialization mode. For example, each site contributes only to a particular dimension of modules, like engineering, product design, manufacturing, sales. Such a functional concentration promotes interactions among professionals with a similar background (Chiesa 1995). Yet from a project and work process perspective, it generates cross-site dependencies. Each site contributes in sequence or parallel as their competencies are required in the overall accomplishment process.

Because interfaces are structured, interdependencies between modules remain passive and unobserved. People can work on their module without taking heed of contributors to other modules (Weick and Roberts 1993). Although connections between modules are not necessary, they *could* easily take place as people are co-located. For example, staff working on module A and B at site 1 could interact without much effort.

By contrast, professionals involved in the same module, for example C, must work remotely. Assuming that the modules themselves are not yet fully elaborated and structured (unlike the interfaces), interdependencies between contributors to the same module arise. Hence, close coupling and exchanges between sites evolve as professionals shape their module.

Remoteness changes the way people cooperate. Professionals working on the same module experience the impact of distributedness in multple ways. First, electronic media are used to mediate communicative actions between sites. Scholars have observed that electronic media differ in the number of cues transmitted, and their suitability to support more complex exchanges between actors (Daft and Lengel 1986). So-called "lean" media like email allow users to send textual messages, whereas "richer" media (i.e., more cues) like phone or videoconferencing mediate someone's voice and image. People cooperating on difficult, intertwined tasks will prefer richer media to clarify the work and mediate expectations. Second, people lack a shared repository of documents related to the module they are working on. Instead, each site must receive updated replications of documents enacted by contributors at the counterpart site. This encourages the use of digital documentation and automated exchange of files and databases, for example overnight. Third, time zone differences limit real-time communications to small windows. Communication patterns thus become more asynchronous, mediated by email and voice mail. In urgent cases, people may even have to temporarily adjust their normal working hours to enable remote, real-time exchanges.

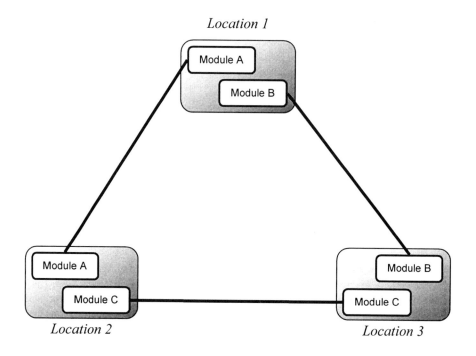

Figure 2. Asynchronous allocation of structured work

Remoteness also limits some control modes used in co-located situations. Like directly observing team members, or informally checking the status of a task. In dispersed settings, these direct interactions are substituted for more formalized reporting, output controls, and reliance on professional reputation of counterparts. Contributors heavily depend on information technology (hardware, software, communication technology) for transmitting and receiving messages, for liaising, and documenting. For the remote part of their work, they interact with a mediated, represented and selectively replicated environment.

CONFIGURATION 3. SYNCHRONOUS ALLOCATION OF UNCERTAIN WORK

"Nondisclosive intimacy is a sufficient ground for relating as long as the task stays constant and the environment remains stable."

Weick 1993, page 647

Configuration 3 is an extension of the first configuration. In each case, modules are exclusive assigned to each site. However, the type of project here is different since the interfaces cannot be specified in advance. As depicted by the dotted lines in figure3, this implies that both within and between modules work activities are uncertain, unspecified and interdependent. Although the aggregated work is roughly shaped in separate modules, its novelty prevents defining clear demarcations between these. For example, at the initial stage of a New Product Development project, experience tells contributors what the product will look like by approximation. Yet apart from some general dimensions, like functionality and overall shape, they cannot yet outline *en detail* the design, manufacturing processes, or materials to be used. The need to integrate modules at some stage in the project suggests that interdependencies between professionals involved persists. This extended need for (remote) coupling differentiates the way this configuration is coordinated and controlled from configuration 1.

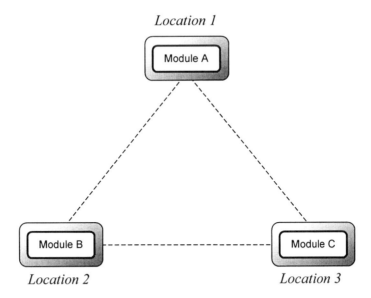

Figure 3. Synchronous allocation of uncertain work

The complexity that arises here is that sites do not work in a stand-alone mode. The shaping of their local work package remains linked to what people are doing at other sites. Changes proposed by a local site may affect other sites as well, adding complexity to local design efforts (von Hippel 1990). Strategies for dealing with such connectivity may include one of the following trajectories. First, sites may freeze their local efforts and empower a group of local representatives to elaborate stable interfaces. When interdependencies are thus resolved, the project will resemble configuration 1. Second, in case this path is not feasible or desirable, organizations may adapt the way sites cooperate to accommodate for increased coupling and information processing needs (Galbraith 1973). To this end, several coupling and control mechanisms are at their disposal.

In configuration 1, structured interfaces reduce linkages to occasional interactions among site representatives. But here, coupling needs become more dense, in the sense of being *broader*: more facets and perspectives need to be taken into account. And *deeper*: exchanges cannot remain on a superficial update and reporting level, but must get closer to the core of module design and activity planning.

It is unlikely that site representatives embody all the knowledge required for handling these increased coupling needs (Grant 1996). Hence, professionals are put in direct contact with their counterparts from other sites. The formation of such a more elaborate network across sites implies building working relationships and mutual knowledge (Krauss and Fussell 1990). This enables actors to use multiple communication channels and enhance the effectiveness of media usage (Gabarro 1990). It also induces people to anticipate and enact the impacts of their work on tasks accomplished at other sites (Weick 1993).

As local work becomes more embedded in a networked project setup, on-site forms of control are complemented with cross-site mechanisms of tracking and tracing work progress. This is triggered by the persistence of cross-dependencies, meaning that work designs and progress are frequently transmitted between sites. Advanced technologies play a pivotal role here in replicating databases and workflow representations back and forth.

Finally, these properties suggest that when each location stands for a different company, their transactions are incompletely specified. Besides, the work remains tightly connected and requires remote interactions among professionals. Organizations therefore carefully select counterparts to ensure their reliability and may even opt for building longer term relationships (Kumar and van Dissel 1996).

CONFIGURATION 4. ASYNCHRONOUS ALLOCATION OF UNCERTAIN WORK

> *"Collective mind is conceptualized as a pattern of heedful interrelations of actions in a social system. Actors in the system construct their actions (contributions), understanding that the system consists of connected actions by themselves and others (representation), and interrelate their actions within the system (subordination)."*

Weick and Roberts 1993, page 357

The basic setup of the fourth configuration is similar to the second one. People liaise across sites to collectively shape the module for which they are jointly responsible (depicted by the bold lines between modules). Unlike the second configuration, however, the overall design of the project is only roughly conceived, and by far not crystallized out. Interfaces remain fluid and adaptable, although the major chunks (A, B, and C) have been defined and each assigned to 2 locations. The fact that modules must be integrated at some point of time, combined with the lack of structured interfaces imply that people involved in different packages are interconnected (see dotted lines in figure 4).

Contributors to each module experience that their work depends on the evolution of work on other packages. To illustrate the complexity of these linkages in configuration 4, suppose that someone wants to change the design of Module A at location 1. First, you need to liaise (remotely) with colleagues working on the same module at site 2. Next, you need to elaborate how changes in module A impact the other modules. Unlike configuration 3 however, representatives of module B and C are dispersed across two sites, totaling four separate groups that need to be involved.

The communications and time needed to incorporate changes across the various modules may easily explode. Not only because so many groups are involved, which increases the potential number of exchanges (i.e., the dotted and bold lines in figure 4). Most interactions are remote and may suffer from time zone differences. As working hours only partially overlap, people rely on asynchronous media like email or voice mail. Communicating back and forth takes longer as counterparts may not respond quickly and need additional feedback loops for clarifications. Hence, the capacity of such a dispersed and connected network to handle unstructured work may prove incapable of adjusting in a rapid and flexible manner (March and Simon 1958, Volberda 1997).

Several directions may promote a more balanced interaction process among participants. We propose three, supposing that resource immobility makes centralized co-location not feasible. First, organizations reduce the number of connections by regrouping actors in accordance with configuration 3. This implies co-locating people working on the same module. Second, the current division of work is maintained, but only after the structure of interfaces has been enhanced. This enables moving to configuration 2. The specification of interfaces removes coupling needs between project groups, allowing them to concentrate on shaping their particular module which still requires remote exchanges.

Finally, configuration 4 could be maintained with some changes in *communication routing* and *remote work support*. Currently, people exchange information rather broadly which results in an organic, fluidly connected network. This could be slightly restrained even though interfaces remain incompletely specified. Structuring patterns of interactions means they become more channeled and formalized instead of random and as extensive as depicted in figure 4. For example, external contacts for each local group working on a particular module are handled by a single representative, thus reducing the number of connections substantially. The same principle applies to entire modules. Routing external communications through a single gateway may, however, reduce information processing capacity since local team members loose direct contacts with counterparts. Since liaisons absorb the ramified exchange network, they complement inclusion in their own group with strong external relationships. Still, this makes the communication structure fragile as groups depend exclusively on intermediaries' competencies and reliability for external information processing.

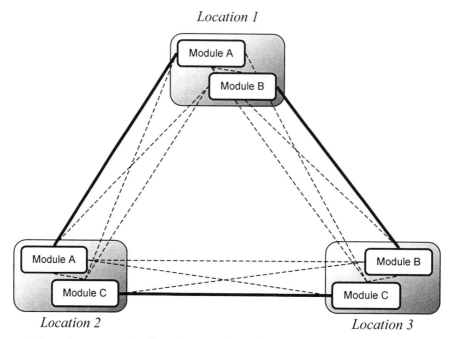

Figure 4. Asynchronous allocation of uncertain work

Remote, intertwined cooperation implies that actors rely on updates of work progress at other sites (Weick and Roberts 1993). The process of reciprocal updating among sites is time-related as project contributors engage in a recurrent flow of conceiving work, executing activities, and documenting their accomplishments (Clark 1990). Hence, distributed sites fine-tune *ex ante* work planning, they update each other on work progress as activities evolve, and they exchange *ex post* documentation of accomplished work. This process enables actors to spot interdependencies and enact coupling moments. The fluidity of module interfaces enhances the frequency and completeness of cross-site work replication. Actors need (within the limitations of their role definition) instant access to schedules, work progress reports, and activity logs to embed their contributions in the overall system (Hutchins 1991).

CONCLUSION

Globalization adds new dimensions to the configuration and functioning of temporary systems. The allocation of work across multiple sites generates different types of interdependencies and coupling needs. Consistency of work processes and outcomes must be guaranteed in a situation where people contribute with diverse cultural and professional backgrounds. Parts of the work are often outsourced to benefit from a vendor's unique competencies or cost advantages. And project sites operate in different time zones, reducing real-time interactions between sites to only a couple of hours per day. This chapter adopts a coordination theory perspective to enhance our understanding of this new phenomenon. It elaborates 4 configurations based on the structure of interfaces between work packages, and the way the modules are assigned to one or more locations. Four figures clarify the configurations.

In the *first* configuration, project modules are each assigned as a whole to project locations. Structured interfaces minimize interdependencies between sites, and reduce coupling to occasional updates. The *second* configuration combines the same interface stability with asynchronous assignment of modules. This means that multiple sites are responsible for each module, and professionals liaise remotely with counterparts. They concentrate on their own work package without taking heed of people involved in other modules since interfaces have been specified in advance.

This assumption is released in the *third* configuration. Activities for each module remain connected and can no longer be worked upon in isolation. Professionals combine tight local coupling for their own module with remote exchanges to manage interfaces with other packages. The *fourth* configuration combines unstructured interfaces with asynchronous assignment of work packages. Remote interactions among project participants may easily explode: people contact counterparts at other sites working on the same module, and also liase to manage interfaces. As an alternative, communications are more formally routed and channeled through representatives. In addition, advanced technologies support distributed contributors by replicating work planning and progress reports between sites.

Each configuration represents a unique combination of key variables characterizing temporary systems. These defining properties have implications for work interdependencies and coupling modes. Anticipation of connectivity among sites allows organizations to refine their processes of shaping and managing global projects. They can balance performance criteria and resource constraints to improve the feasibility and performance of distributed, remote work accomplishment.

Finally, the proposed configurations provide a condensed template of real-life phenomena as a starting point for academic understanding and research. In practice, projects may represent multiple configurations at the same time or in a sequential pattern. Besides, complementary perspectives are required to enrich the description and analysis of distributed temporary systems. Researchers may want to take up the challenge to investigate these intricacies and extend our knowledge of global projects.

CHAPTER 5

TEMPORARY ORGANIZING - CHARACTERISTICS AND CONTROL FORMS

Jonas Söderlund, IMIE, Linköping University, Sweden

ABSTRACT

Temporary organizing might be viewed along two different dimensions. One is the structure dimension, which has been the focus for much research on project management and temporary organization, the other one is the participation dimension, which has been the focus for parts of the literature on career theory. This chapter attempts to integrate these streams of research in order to shed light on different temporary forms of organizing and to outline control forms for organizing. In doing so, I rely on writings not only on project management and temporary organizations, but also on literature that deals with increased interfirm mobility and use of temporary employees. More specifically this chapter (1) identifies the main characteristics of temporary organizing, and (2) identifies and analyzes the control forms connected with different temporary forms of organizing. A main conclusion is that network and professional control represent important mechanisms of temporary organizing.

THE COMING OF TEMPORARY ORGANIZING

In recent years a fairly well established strand of research has emerged concerning the phenomena of projects and temporary organizations (Lundin 1998, Lundin and Söderholm 1998). Such organizations seem to permeate much of our lives, although as individuals we might not realize it or understand its consequences (Lundin 1995:315). Many researchers, managers and consultants have presented similar arguments (Bridges 1994, Huey 1994, Peters 1992, Richman 1994). The underlying rationale for project-based organizations and the increased use of it has been demonstrated in Whittington *et al.* (1999). They claim, based on a survey of 450 large and medium sized European companies, that project-based organizing has increased by 175% between 1992 and 1996 and that the trend seems to be continuing. Furthermore, Hobday (1999) and Weick (1996) suggested that the studies of projects and temporary organizations provide more fruitful avenues in order to increase the knowledge of the processes and structures of organizing in the new economy.

Several concepts and metaphors have been suggested to depict the firm in a so-called "temporary lens," i.e. highlighting the temporary or time-limited processes and structures inside and outside the firm. In this specific research stream several concepts, mainly highlighting the same thing, can been identified, including "project-based organization" (Faulkner and Anderson 1987), "project-based organizing" (Pettigrew *et al.* 1999), "project-based enterprise" (DeFillippi and Arthur 1998), and "project-oriented companies" (Gareis 1991). In this literature there is a more or less implicit recognition that temporary systems differ from their permanent counterparts (Palisi 1970). However, one observes few attempts to explicate the areas of divergence and similarity (Packendorff 1995).

I will argue that the distinction between *permanent* and *temporary* is an important one for project researchers. This has also been emphasized by recent writings of Ekstedt et al (1999), Lundin and Söderholm (1995) and Packendorff (1995). The idea of *permanence* in organization theory probably has its roots in the era of industrialism. As argued by Lundin and Söderholm (1995), mainstream organization theory is based on assumptions that organizations are permanent. This could also be seen in many of the assumptions regarding the principle of going-concern in accounting theory and systems theory's general idea that every organization strives for survival in the long run. As put by Lundin and Söderholm (1995:439):

> "Permanent organizations are more naturally defined by goals (rather than task), survival (rather than time), working organization (rather than team) and production processes and continual development (rather than transition)."

Temporary organizations, such as projects, on the other hand have a predetermined lifetime. This has led, for instance, Lundin and Söderholm (1995) to formulate a theory of the temporary organization based on the four building blocks, task, time, team and transition/transformation (Lundin 1998, Lundin and Söderholm 1995). However, their theory mainly focuses on the structure and processes at the organizational level, not about the other side of the coin, i.e. the individual's relation to colleagues and the rest of the organization. In my opinion this is just as important in order to elaborate a theory of temporary organizing.

Miles (1964) and Bennis (1968) were among the first writers to delve on the concept of temporary systems. Miles (1964) offered a broad typology of different types of temporary systems, including such diverse settings as conferences, projects and prisons. Bennis (1968) proposed a departure from the machine model of organization and suggested organizing through adaptive structures (or temporary systems) to cope with rapidly changing technologies, unique customer requirements, and the need for multi-disciplinary teams to solve complex problems. Bennis further argued that the temporary systems of diverse specialists would gradually replace bureaucracy as we know it (1968:74). In the writings by Bennis one observes the starting point for the research focus on temporary organizations. The type of organization suggested by Bennis has a strong resemblance with the organic model of organizing (Burns and Stalker 1961). However, one observes an additional dimension, i.e. since such systems are formed for a limited purpose, they tend to include members who have never worked together before and who do not expect to work together again (see also Goodman and Goodman 1976, Meyerson, Weick and Kramer, 1996).

One who discusses both the dimensions of structure and participation is Heydebrand (1989) in his treatise on the "post-bureaucratic organization." He characterizes this type of organization as having the following distinctive features. Its purpose is mission-oriented and flexible rather than jurisdictional and fixed. Itts authority structure is based on project teams and task forces, open communication, diffusion of authority, and substantive rationality rather than on a hierarchy involving formal-legal rationality. Moreover, its rules are seen as subordinated to the purpose, and its decision-making style is participatory and problem-centered, with heavy reliance on delegation. In terms of the individual-organization relationships, Heydebrand states that its careers are characterized by multiple and temporary affiliations, with a high reliance on subcontracting and experts who have an autonomous professional base.

Obviously there are many forms of temporary systems and organizations. Despite the plethora of temporary systems outlined by Miles (1964), the traditional literature on projects and temporary organizations has mainly focused on the structural dimension of temporary organizations. This means that temporary organizations are considered to be responses to task requirements within a particular firm with participants who are mainly seen as having a permanent relationship to each other and the firm. Furthermore, much effort has been put into analyzing why projects exist and what a project is, which has led researchers to explore the characteristics of different tasks in terms of, for instance, complexity and uncertainty. A temporary organization is thus depicted as a response to time-limited tasks of high complexity and high uncertainty. In this chapter, however, I will discuss other cases of temporary organizing to complement the prevailing structural images. In doing so, I relate to some recent writings on the increased use of project structures and the increased inter-firm mobility and temporary participation/employment observed within particular firms and industries (e.g. Jones 1996, Saxenian 1996).

PURPOSE AND OUTLINE

The growing number and importance of projects and temporary organizations makes one question the role of the firm as a permanent social reference for individuals' work life. The question here is also what new patterns will emerge for the individual-organization relationship (Lundin and Midler 1998:3). This, along with the puzzling concept of temporary organization, is the main theme of the present chapter.

In the chapter I will (1) identify the main characteristics of temporary organizing, (2) identify and analyze the control forms connected with different temporary forms of organizing, and discuss some problems of temporary organizing for firms and individuals. The chapter is structured in the following way. The next section discusses different examples of inquiries into temporary forms of organizing. The section outlines different explanations to increased project intensity and increased inter-firm mobility as observed in many industries. The following section identifies the characteristics of temporary organizing and a typology is suggested identifying the control forms associated with temporary employment, project organizing and temporary organizing. Recent literature and studies are reviewed to substantiate the analysis. The chapter ends with a concluding discussion that underlines some proposals for future research.

EXAMPLES OF TEMPORARY FORMS OF ORGANIZING

There are different explanations for the increased use of temporary forms of organizing. One explanation is oriented towards strategy, another has a focus on task characteristics, and a third one is related to participation issues. The different streams are emerging as separate, but related, inquiries about the modern form of organizing and, in my mind, into the explanations of temporary forms of organizing in a general sense.

In the part of strategic management that focuses on temporary forms of organization, strategy is not conceived of as a matter of building long-term competitive advantage, but instead as seizing the opportunities at hand and gathering strength to exploit a "window of opportunity." (Tyre and Orlikowski 1994). Obviously, in this conception, strategy has effects on the design of organization. The strategy is typically pursued and carried through by the use of a focused (temporary) project organization. Broadly speaking, pursuing such a strategy is a matter of initiating, executing and completing a single project (cf. Brown and Eisenhardt 1998, DeFillippi and Arthur 1998). Hence, the main argument by some of the strategic management scholars seems to be that projects and temporary organizations are vehicles for pursuing a strategy. Thus they seem to view temporary organizing as a "strategic choice" to gain competitive advantage.

Whereas the example taken from strategy theory emphasizes the importance of the choice of strategy for understanding organization design, the example taken from organization theory points to task and task environment as key traits. Hence, the reasoning builds in part on the structural contingency theory of organization. For instance, projects could be viewed as similar to "unit production," as depicted by Woodward (1965). The underlying explanations for organizing by projects have, of course, been commented upon by several authors in the area of project management and temporary organization. The basic question here is: why do projects exist? One work frequently referred to is the one by Goodman and Goodman (1976), which views projects as responses to, among other things, problems concerning the complexity and uncertainty of the task, the complexity among the interdependent activities, the task's uniqueness, the lack of standardized procedures and the temporary nature of the task (see e.g. Lundin and Söderholm 1995, Pinto and Prescott 1990, Shenhar and Dvir 1996).

An additional example of literature that has discussed different temporary forms of organizing is career literature (Arthur, Hall and Lawrence 1989, Arthur and Rousseau 1996). Among other things, they stress the significance of time for all participants in organizations, i.e. membership is often assumed to be temporary, be it participation in a permanent structure or participation in a temporary project. In the same vein, Weick (1996:45) claims that a "boundaryless" career signifies small projects rather than large divisions, "temporariness" rather than permanence and self-design rather than bureaucratic control. Part of the career theory thus questions the permanence view of careers and organizing and points to careers as movements among projects. This is yet another example of a temporary form of organizing, however, quite different from the previous two examples given above. In career theory, as depicted here, temporary forms of organizing means, among other things, temporary participation in permanent structures, such as stable firms, or temporary structures, such as time-limited projects.

THE CHARACTERISTICS OF TEMPORARY ORGANIZING

In the above sections I have summarized three closely related and relevant streams of research that all point to the need of taking a closer look at projects and temporary organizing. In order to zoom in on the nature of temporary organizing, I will attempt to identify some distinctive features of such a setting. The underlying rationale is that temporary forms of organizing might include either temporary structures or temporary participation. "Pure" temporary organizing, on the other hand, is considered here as a situation where both temporary structure and temporary participation are present. In the remaining parts of the chapter I will refer to "temporary organizing" as a situation where:

1. project participants with diverse skills are assembled by a contractor to enact expertise in order to carry out a project (cf. Goodman 1981), and
2. project participants have a limited history of working together and limited prospects of working together again in the future (cf. Meyerson, Weick and Kramer 1996).

The characteristics lead to several interesting inquiries from a theoretical perspective. For example, game theory often assumes that there are no "finite games" (cf. Kreps 1990). Furthermore, mainstream organization theory often assumes that partnerships that are characterized by repeated trials introduce considerations of reputation, trust, retaliation, and learning that are not present in single-trial situations. The basic argument here is that repeated games have both a history and a future; hence participants can promise retaliation or reward in the future, depending on how well behavior conforms to current standards. This combination of greater information and opportunities for retribution makes, according to March (1994:133), partnerships involving repeated interactions distinctively different from single-play partnerships. However, these differences have not been studied or discussed in any straightforward manner. The game theory analogy is one way of discussing the differences between temporary and permanent organizing.

TEMPORARY VS PERMANENT ORGANIZING: A TYPOLOGY

In order to further mark out the meaning and characteristics of temporary organizing, I propose a typology identifying four types of organizing. The typology will also be the introduction to a discussion about the control forms apparent in the different settings where temporariness, contrary to permanence, is a key feature. The typology is based on the two arguments put forward earlier in the chapter, i.e. a distinction between temporary and permanent structures (the "structural dimension") and between temporary and permanent participation/employment (the "participation dimension"), has to be made. The important facet is here that people assume (know) that either the structure they are working in and the relationships are of a temporary nature, or know (assume) that their participation in the structure is temporary. This recognition is likely to affect both the ways in which their participation is perceived and the appropriate management and organizational apparatus relative to permanent systems. Members of permanent organizations that turn out to be temporary (due to bankruptcy or whatever) have little, if any, recognition of the temporary nature of their organization, at least not until fairly late in the sequence of events (Bryman et al, 1987). In other words, it is the recognition and anticipation of temporariness that constitute the key trait of different temporary forms of organizing (cf. Miles, 1964). In Figure 1 four situations of organizing are depicted.

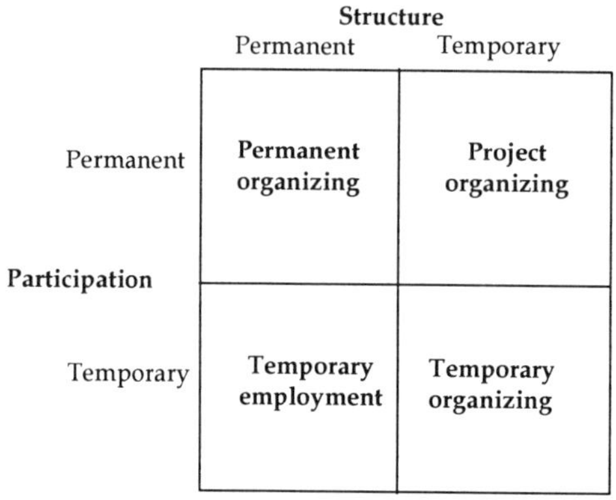

	Structure	
	Permanent	Temporary
Permanent	**Permanent organizing**	**Project organizing**
Temporary	**Temporary employment**	**Temporary organizing**

Figure 1. A typology of permanent/temporary organizing

Permanent organizing
As a point of departure to clarify the different forms of organizing and, more specifically, each situation's relationship between individuals and organization, I will outline "permanent organizing." The principles of organizing could be either cultural and/or regulatory in formal ways, such as rules, standard operating procedures, etc. As membership and participation builds on a permanent relationship with the organization, such as the case of lifetime employment, the relationship between an organization and its members would then be guided by long-term perspectives from both parties. Commitment can in such situations be said to be to the organization and/or the individual's profession. I mainly consider bureaucratic or clan-control to be "most likely" in an analysis of control forms relative to a focal firm, emerging either through division of labor, formalization of roles, etc. or culturally oriented dimensions, such as long-term commitment. To depict the member of this type of organization I have chosen the metaphor "official."

The two trends discussed in previous sections, i.e. increased project intensity and inter-firm mobility, lead to what might be considered a "failure" of permanent organizing. For example, formal rules and standard operating procedures as control mechanisms prove to be obsolete due to, among other things, increased competition, changing technology and customer requirements (Bennis 1968). Furthermore, Ouchi (1980), for instance, stresses long-term employment and stable career patterns as a main precondition for clans. The postindustrial temporary organization, as discussed above, however, might take on the opposite characteristics. Typical examples would be rapidly changing relationships, open social circles and increased mobility of personnel (Heydebrand 1989).

Temporary employment

During the past decade, organizations' use of external workers, such as temporary workers, leased workers, and independent contractors has increased tremendously. There is a plethora of references for this. Several studies indicate both a rapid increase in the number and knowledge profile of temporary workers (e.g. Applebaum 1987, Belous 1989, Davis-Blake and Uzzi 1993). In the study by Applebaum (1987) the majority of externalized workers no longer performed unskilled clerical tasks, many were professionals, such as engineers, nurses, accountants and management consultants. Moreover, the temporary-service industry has expanded tremendously in recent years (Scott 1998). For instance, the largest firm in terms of number of employees in the United States employing nearly one million workers is Manpower Temporary Services (Scott 1998:23). The trend towards temporary employees has also been identified in other countries (see e.g. SAF 1997).

Obviously the relationship between individuals and organization is puzzling when temporary employees are analyzed. Several of the mechanisms guiding and controlling behavior in more traditional organizations will be vague or even completely nonexistent, such as socialization, culture, expectations of future returns, etc. One way of guiding and controlling behavior is through forms of contracting, most notably in formal ways. Naturally, different forms of personal ordering, trust, and more socially oriented mechanisms do exist, one example of such a mechanism is professionalism.

Garsten (1999) analyzes the temporary employees as being "betwixt and between" organizational structures. In her conception, employers push for more flexible work conditions and flexible employment contracts. Companies thus seek to minimize the number of regular full-time employees (Greer, Youngblood and Gray 1999). Although some might argue that temporary assignments are the first step towards a permanent position, I argue in line with Garsten, that there is evidence of "permanent temps" (Garsten 1999:607). Temps, however, might be seen as "strangers" in the workplace, just temporarily passing through, and thus running the risk of being "socially undermined." One might argue that temps are not clan members as they lack the togetherness that often springs out of long-term emotional investments (Garsten 1999:607). The reason being that temps, due to their high mobility, do not tend to invest much of their emotions in particular colleagues or places of work. They are also, because of their inherent mobility and transience, detached from local and collegial ties (Garsten 1999:616). Frequently temps have also been interpreted as lacking the drive of a strong professional ethos. However, Garsten observes, there have been changes also in this respect, for instance, by altering titles to "consultants" and an increased importance of reputation.

I consider two fundamental forms of control to be apparent in this form of organizing, namely bureaucratic and professional control, where the trend due to increased knowledge intensity seems to be toward different forms of professional control. One might view the individual as "bee-like" following a "free agent route"

(Jones and DeFillipi 1997), moving from opportunity to opportunity always entering yet another permanent structure. In such situations the individual seems to be very much like a "loner," i.e. a person that does not belong to any organization permanently and who does not attach her long-term fortunes to the fates of a single organization, i.e. in the words of Garsten "betwixt and between" organizational structures. However, the loner is "socially competent" and able to swiftly build relationships with new people, but also being able to let go of these relationships. As it seems the loner does not invest much emotion in the relationships.

Project organizing
Project organizing, as understood in this chapter, involves individuals with a more or less permanent relationship with each other and the firm. Projects are frequently described as unique events, as "organizational experiments," and as learning processes. In such a context it seems to be, not only, difficult or impossible, but sometimes also inappropriate to rely on ordinary bureaucratic forms of control. Instead, organizations turn to or rely on more clan-like forms of control (Ouchi, 1980). Thus, one may expect, even though individuals move from project to project, they have a permanent relationship (non-finite) to the overall organization. Two famous examples of such organization types are the Adhocracy (Mintzberg 1983) and the Prospector (Miles and Snow 1978). These types of organizations largely operate by the use of project structures where "mutual adjustment" is viewed as the prime coordination mechanism (Thompson 1967, Mintzberg 1979). However, mutual adjustment does not give any insight into the individual-organization relationship and about the governance structures (or the modes of governance) that I am interested in here. Although mutual adjustment could be seen as one source from which clans are being developed and maintained (cf. Meyerson, Weick and Kramer 1996), the social orientation, the willingness to act on behalf of the organization, etc. is not necessarily associated with this coordination mechanism. My analysis here points to the importance of the clan form of control when discussing project organization in general.

In a sense, the project participants can metaphorically be depicted as members of a "nomadic tribe" (cf. Slater 1968) who move to new contexts or new projects, constantly seeking new challenges within the firm and often together with each other. The latter is probably also of importance for transferring knowledge between projects, as the knowledge developed within projects to a large extent is tacit and thus difficult or impossible to transfer to other project teams (Lindkvist, Söderlund and Tell 1998). One might assume that within these tribes a strong "local culture" and a strong sense of belonging are developed and promoted. Thus, the conception of the individual greatly differs from the bureaucratic type of the "official," which builds on a static, permanent form of individual-organization relationship. In the case of project organizing a person moves from project to project, but mostly together with people who are known and with whom the person has been working together before, or at least probably will be working with again in the near future. In such situations an individual-organization relationship appears to be quite long-term, either historically or future-oriented.

There are, however, some important shortcomings of the conception provided by scholars focusing on project organizing. The basic one being that it builds to a large extent on the assumption about permanent membership. For instance, the use of temporary workers, temporary hired consultants, etc. is not discussed in any further detail. The focus is, e.g. in the studies of Adhocracies and Prospectors, on the corporate level and the role of outside aspects is under-emphasized. The problems of establishing clans in situations where temporary participation is a key feature lead to a different conception. This leads us to zoom in on the situation of simultaneous temporary structures and temporary participation.

Temporary organizing

Several studies have been published that explicitly stress the need for focusing on projects instead of individual firms (see Hobday 1999, Weick 1996). Furthermore, one observes several examples of temporary organizing, i.e. organizational settings with a temporary structure and with temporary participation. Typical examples here would be the organization of the Olympic Games (cf. Løwendahl 1995, McDonald 1988), the organization of the EU Cultural Capital (Stockholm Cultural Capital 1999). However, more recent experience similar to temporary organizing would be the organization of some projects in Silicon Valley, the making of a film in Hollywood (DeFillippi and Arthur 1998) or even when Toyota hires engineers on a project-by-project basis (Berggren and Nomura 1997). In situations of temporary organizing, there is no real form of permanent structure, and participants are involved on a temporary basis with no long-term membership in the organization. Individuals are most typically seeking new adventures, and are hired on professional grounds and reputation (Meyerson, Weick and Kramer 1996). Therefore, the most dominant form of control would probably be "professional control" and/or loyalty to other institutions and "networks "that reside outside the focal firm or organization, such as industrial or professional networks.

Empirical support is found in Saxenian (1996) who studied IT specialists in Silicon Valley, and in Morley and Silver (1981), and DeFillippi and Arthur (1998) who studied film making in Hollywood. A common denominator in these studies is the emphasis on networks instead of firms, projects instead of departments, and mobility instead of fixed positions. Both these industries are to a large extent project-based and associated with high uncertainty and complexity. The similarities with project organizing, as analyzed previously, are thus obvious. The main difference, however, is that the relationships to the contractor and to the colleagues, as in these situations no permanent relationships exist. Instead, people gather and are being gathered for a fixed period of time in order to carry out a certain project, be it developing a new software package, setting up a single play or doing a live TV show. It is a matter of "once-in-a-lifetime events" with people who have no history of working together and limited prospects of working together again. However, which is of importance here, they are members of the same (or overlapping) networks. The boundaries of these networks are, frequently, highly unclear, changing constantly and intertwined in different ways. Some networks are tightly coupled others are not, which also effects the possibilities of the network to balance long-term equity among participants. Furthermore, a constantly changing network with new members entering and old members leaving, is also a complicating factor for the possibilities of network control.

Saxenian (1996) argues that the region and its relationships, rather than the firm, is the key definer of the opportunities for individuals and collective advancements in Silicon Valley. However, the relationships are not like any labor market, instead they are strongly socially embedded (Granovetter, 1995). Successful careers in this region are largely explained by participation in local networks of social relations, i.e. the professional and social networks outside the control of a single firm. These networks are important for building ones' reputation and searching for new opportunities. As one of the engineers in Saxenian's study put it:

> "In this business there's really a network. You just don't hire people out of the blue. In general, it's people you know, or you know someone who knows them" (Saxenian 1996:27).

Furthermore, "job-hopping" is common in this region. Engineers have shifted so frequently in the past, and still do, that mobility has not merely been socially accepted, but rather has become the norm (Saxenian, 1996). Hence, a defining feature of the processes of technology development in Silicon Valley is not that the engineers have developed loyalties to individual firms, but to the network, to their crafts and to the quest for technological advancement. For example, one of the CEOs in a Silicon Valley firm claimed:

> "Here in Silicon Valley there's far greater loyalty to one's craft than to one's company. A company is just a vehicle which allows you to work. If you're a circuit designer it's most important for you to do excellent work. If you can't in one firm, you'll move on to another." (Saxenian 1996:28)

The image of the individual in this type of organizing is similar that of an "adventurer" who moves from one temporary structure to yet another one, always looking for new challenges, and new learning opportunities. Other examples of temporary organizing are found in March's (1995) treatise on the "disposable organization," in Mintzberg's (1983) analysis of the "temporary adhocracies" and in Toffler's (1970:133) examination of organizations as "throw-away tissues." The common feature is here an organization that integrates specialists to carry out a project, and after completing that project the organization dissolves.

CONTROL FORMS: A CLOSER LOOK

In Figure 2 I have integrated the typology of forms of organizing with most likely expected control forms. I have argued that permanent organizing basically would be guided by bureaucratic principles such as rules, routines, etc, or at least have the possibilities of under certain circumstances bringing about bureaucratic control. Although in some cases this might prove to be difficult and the organization would rely on either clan-like or professional control. In the typology professional control is always present. On the other hand, in the case of temporary employment, I believe that professional and bureaucratic forms of control will emerge as the ones impacting behavior. Due to a lack of long-term commitment and emotional investment, I conclude that clan-like control will be difficult to establish. This is certainly a narrow definition of the clan form of control. However, my argument is basically that clans build on a long-term relationship with a particular firm. Clans are not equivalent to "self-control" or "professional control" in a general sense. Clans, as conceived of by Ouchi (1980), develop to a large extent on participants' assumption that the clan is able to balance in the long run, by means of rewarding and retaliating, the clan members' performance. Furthermore, in this conception, a clan denotes common views and social relationships within a firm, involving trust and confidence in the long-term equity of reward distribution (Alvesson and Lindkvist 1993).

The third type outlined in the typology, i.e. project organizing, calls for different control forms as compared to bureaucratic principles due to adjustments to local circumstances. I have shown earlier that typical examples would be the Prospector and the Adhocracy, with their relatively strong local cultures, the clan-like controls and importance of professional control (cf. Alvesson and Lindkvist 1993). However, I am not arguing that clans are easily developed in these settings.

	Structure	
	Permanent	Temporary
Permanent	Bureaucratic and/or clan control	Professional and/or clan control
Temporary	Bureaucratic and/or professional control	Professional and/or network control

Participation (vertical label on left, spanning Permanent / Temporary rows)

Figure 2. A typology of control forms

In situations similar to temporary organizing, I believe neither bureaucratic nor clan-like control will function very well, nor have the real possibilities to come about. The reasons being high task variety, high complexity and high uncertainty along with the lack of history and future for the participants, at least towards a focal firm. This leaves us with professional control as one important mechanism. Professional control basically builds on the standardization of skills, the standards of ones profession and the willingness to work in line with ones professional ethos. It is thus a control form that is internalized by the individual, and partly developed and maintained in the process of a project. However, the roots of professionalism reside outside the project, for example in terms of education, membership of a particular professional community where certain skills, attitudes, etc. are being explored and diffused. On the other hand we have what might be labeled "network control mechanisms," e.g. fear of bad reputation, loyalty to overall structures, such as ones industrial network, different forms of "reputation-based" (Söderlund and Andersson 1998) or "network" control. The point is that network control is different from professional control as it to a large extent is based on mechanisms that are not internalized by the individual. Instead, network control resides outside the control of a single individual. Meyerson, Weick and Kramer (1996) have analyzed this in a fruitful manner. Their main argument is that people are afraid of bad performance, or at least that rumor is being spread about bad performance. Figure 2 summarizes the arguments put forward.

PROBLEMS OF TEMPORARY ORGANIZING: A DISCUSSION

There are certainly a plethora of advantages of temporary forms of organizing. My belief is, however, that the need for a review of its advantages is not as important as an analysis of its disadvantages and dangers. The reader can pick up any of the handbooks on project management, management books or articles that summarize some of the good results from organizing by projects (e.g. Gareis 1990, Pinto 1999), and temporary organizing (e.g. Saxenian 1996).

Temporariness points to some interesting features of organizing settings and processes. Above I have focused on some of the consequences in terms of control forms pointing to an increased importance of professional and network control. Transience as discussed here is not necessarily about "change" in a general sense, but on assumptions about structures and participation as being time-limited. There are several dangers connected to "temporariness," which have attracted the interest of Handy (1996) who discusses temporary forms of organization. A danger, Handy argues, is the lack of long-term thinking and a lack of belonging if individuals are only the members of exciting project teams that may not be there tomorrow. If one does not handle this problem, Handy fears, society might degenerate into a culture of "temporariness, of selfishness and opportunism" (p. 185), which will be good for some but bad for most parts of society. As pointed out in the previous analysis other control forms seem to be replacing the control forms typically associated with control inside a particular firm. However, from a perspective of a firm, there are a few other problems that should be analyzed, namely that of the role of the firm in the knowledge process. The point of departure is here Goodman (1981) who illuminates the risk of project organizing as eroding individuals' knowledge and skills. The basic argument, by Goodman, is that project participants are primarily recruited for what they know, not on their possibilities to learn. This coupled with the often stressful environment that characterizes many projects led him to hypothesize projects as a way of "deskilling" project participants. More recently, there has also been a public debate on several important issues connected with project and temporary organizing. One such topic is the problem where project participants are caught in the "honey trap," i.e. the case when people work on projects, they tend work so intensely that they lose the social grounds and thus their position in the overall network. Hence, they experience problems in getting new challenging projects (Broomé and Persson 1999).

In studies of firms, the importance of organizational learning is often discussed as a means to sustain competitive advantage and develop organizational capabilities. As stated by Pisano (1994), it is hard to imagine from where a firm's unique skills and competencies would come from if, it was not from learning. Obviously, these capabilities emerge from continuous learning accumulated over time. A firm is not merely a transaction cost reducing entity but also a solution that is superior to market alternatives at sharing and transferring knowledge of individuals and groups within an organization (Kogut and Zander 1992). The problem of making individual learning organizational, and thus retrievable for other members of the organization, seems to be extremely important here (cf. Hedberg 1981). From an organizational point of view, issues such as organizational memories, preserved behavior patterns, and standard operating procedures are key as mechanisms for transferring knowledge and storing organizational knowledge. I argue that these ways of transferring and storing organizational knowledge are not sufficient to fully understand the logics of different temporary forms of organizing. For instance, a temporary system seems to search for autonomy and a free-standing position of history at an organizational level. A project is also per se cut off from the rest of the organization and its environment in order to stimulate action and learning within the limited cognitive capacity given to man. The danger of "learning myopia" might thus be a problem in a project context (cf. Lindkvist, Söderlund and Tell 1998). This has also been the argument of Lundin and Söderholm (1998:50) who argue that projects "are allowed to die without leaving any serious traces."

One way of looking at the modern firm is that of a conveyer of knowledge to different temporary projects. However, the mobilization process has proven to be associated with several problems, and several researchers observe that projects tend to start a life of their own and become organizationally isolated (Boklund 1996, Sahlin 1996, Levin 1996). Furthermore, Wheelwright and Clark (1992) claim that project participants frequently take little or nothing as given and that they expand the bounds of their project definition. Another example is Hedlund and Ridderstråle (1995) who argued that handover, e.g. from project to the rest of the organization, takes just as long as the project itself, and when handover is completed the risk that the "window of opportunity" is already closed is obvious. A famous example here is DEC who was not able to integrate its projects in Silicon Valley with the rest of the firm. Because of this DEC had to shut down its West Coast activities (Saxenian 1996).

I have pointed to several problems with temporary organizing so far. The main issues have been related to control forms and problems from a knowledge perspective. A caricature here would be a firm with no control and no knowledge. Here a firm functions merely as an "address list" (Hedlund and Ridderstråle 1995) that might be caught in the "knowledge trap" of adding little or no value. The point made here differs from the one Goodman (1981) put forward in his famous book "Temporary systems." His argument was mainly that participants are hired on the basis of their existent knowledge and skills. Hence, there are, he argued, obvious risks that the individual's skills would be obsolete in only a few years time. My argument being made in the present chapter has gone in another direction, pointing to the obvious risks of eroding the knowledge base and role of the firm in industries with a high reliance on temporary organizing.

CONCLUSIONS AND FUTURE RESEARCH

The main theme of this chapter was set by the use of different streams of research outside the field of projects and temporary organizations. This was the starting point for a closer look at temporary organizing and its specific characteristics. From that followed a typology identifying different types of control forms. The basic argument was here that "project organizing" cannot rely on bureaucratic control mechanisms, "temporary employment" cannot rely on clan control, whereas "temporary organizing" cannot rely on either bureaucratic or clan-like control mechanisms. Instead, professional and network controls were considered to be the most important ones in such contexts. This was also evidenced in the empirical illustration of Silicon Valley. The discussion about control forms and the point of a decreased role for control forms that reside inside a single firm was followed by a more general discussion about temporary organizing and its possible problems. The main argument was the obvious risk of temporary organizing being a device for "deskilling" the firm where the firm was depicted by the metaphor of an "address list." The chapter thus points to an increased awareness of control forms that to a large extent reside outside the control of a single firm. Moreover, the importance of networks was highlighted, both in terms of control and from the participants' point of view in pursuing a career.

Project management research, in general, is in need of both integration within and stimulation from outside perspectives. The present chapter took ideas from strategy theory, organization theory and career theory. However, there are a lot of other perspectives that might be used in future research. Although, I believe it is of importance to keep a balance between inside and outside perspective. In terms of empirical studies, there is a great need for in-depth studies of the structures and processes of what in this chapter has been labeled temporary organizing. Future studies should also focus on different levels of analysis of temporary organizing, for instance both at individuals and at organizations. It is, of course, also of great interest to keep an ongoing vital and critical debate about the drawbacks of temporary organizing, such as the "knowledge trap" and "honey trap" problems.

Acknowledgements: I would like to thank Professor Lars Lindkvist, Professor Bo Hellgren, Econ. Lic. Fredrik Tell and my colleagues at Linköping University for helpful and critical comments on this chapter. The comments and suggestions by the editors of this volume have highly improved the quality of the chapter for which I am very grateful. I would also like to thank Dr. Ralph Levene at Cranfield School of Management for his insightful comments and supportive approach. The research has received financial support from IMIE, The Foundation for Strategic Research, and The Jan Wallander and Tom Hedelius Foundation for Social Science Research.

BUSINESS ISSUES AND PROJECTS

CHAPTER 6

MANAGING PROJECT PORTFOLIOS

Barbro Anell, Umeå School of Business and Economics, Department of Business Administration, Umeå, Sweden

ABSTRACT

In this chapter we endeavour to discuss some of the problems associated with leading project-based companies. Several researchers maintain that the world of work is becoming more "projectified", hence the art of managing in such a context ought to be seen as an important business issue. However, the problems of managing project portfolios have been scantily treated in the literature, so far. This chapter identifies some current issues such as protecting and developing the organisation's distinctive core competence and adapting to fluctuations in demand as well as to demand shifts. Management ought to regard the firm's set of projects as a portfolio. Systematically evaluating and monitoring the portfolio as a whole, that is, attracting and selecting projects that fit into the portfolio and effectively discarding inappropriate projects are of utmost importance. The choice of customers, the definition of projects, the allocation of organisation members' time and energy, as well as other resources to projects, must constantly be paid attention to. In short, the critical managerial skill needed is to balance the various aspects of the project portfolio against each other and over time.

BACKGROUND

The single project has been the main area of interest in project management studies (Packendorff 1993). The bulk of both the descriptive and the prescriptive literature on project management concerns single project problems. However, many researchers as well as practitioners maintain that an increasing projectification of society might be expected (see for instance Lundin and Söderholm 1998). The demands for more flexible companies that are voiced by business and its various interest groups, such as the Swedish Employers' Confederation in Sweden, and the debate concerning the possibilities of increasing the flexibility of the work-force will perhaps also add impact to the trend towards a transformation of working life into more project-based activities (Galbraith 1993). This will in turn mean that most top managers will have to learn to handle more complex project structures and processes than running large, single projects beside the main set of routine activities, as their operations increasingly grow project-based. They will not find much help to do this in the existing management literature. Project management handbooks mainly contain more or less sophisticated prescriptions on how to successfully run the single project (see for instance Turner 1993).

Furthermore, the focus of the normative literature is on planning and control as solutions to project management problems. Standardisation of models for executing projects and routinisation of project activities might, of course, be one way of reducing the complexities and uncertainties that project work entails. We are not certain that this approach will function very well, as complexity and uncertainty are embedded in project work, at least in multi-project contexts. Besides, introducing standardisation and routinisation will mean that that the benefits from flexibility and creativity in project work will diminish.

A shift towards projectification of activities will also mean a power shift in the organisation as project leaders take over more managerial responsibilities, which must be taken into account when management style is being considered. A clan-like style of management might be better adapted to the context of organising by projects and leading a project-based organisation, than the traditional command and control style (Ouchi 1979). But the central question of how a more or less project-based company should be run remains. Which are the critical considerations for management, where do the pitfalls lie? Some aspects of managing project-based companies will be discussed in this chapter. The central theme concerns creating and maintaining a balanced project portfolio.

In most definitions of the concept "project", it is stressed that a project has a goal (or goals), that it consists of a set of complicated and/or interdependent activities, that it is subjected to time and resource constraints, that it is more or less kept separate from the routine activities and that it has a more or less non-recurrent character. (Packendorff 1993, Eskerod 1997). It has also been stressed in the literature that several projects in various stages of completion might be going on at the same time in the firm, sharing a common resource pool, where, of course, the human resources are central. Members of the firm might work in several projects at the same time. A project leader, it is also said, has the responsibility for delivering the desired end result, for ensuring that the customer is satisfied, and for keeping time and budget limits. The logical conclusion of using this definition of a project is that all other activities or activity patterns are considered as routine, or to use another, perhaps more apt term, as repeated, standardised cycles. If this definition is accepted, the number of wholly project based organisations must be very low. Project based firms might, however, be categorised along a continuum, where one end-point is represented by firms which run only "one of a kind" projects and the other by firms which run projects that vary in scale and scope, but are guided by routines, norms, rules and recipes, which is increasingly the case - perhaps for reasons of governance and control.

Most project-based firms probably fall between these extremes. As a rule a project-based organisation has a backbone of routines that lends some stability to its activities. Typically routines for writing contracts, for writing reports, for paying salaries and for controlling the economic situation exist. And routinisation has a tendency to grow, as it is time and energy saving. Members stay on for extended periods of time to carry out a number of projects. More or less original recipes for how a project should be carried out develop, as patterns of co-working in teams take form. This might sometimes lead to a development of sub-cultures in the firm which might lower its efficiency, as the pool of human resources will not only be differentiated according to competence, but also according to "school". Examples of how companies are split between different schools, fighting for hegemony or even leaving to found another company, are not difficult to find in our experience.

However, an academic discourse on multi-project organisations has started with the seminal work of P. Eskerod (Eskerod 1997). Management of multiple simultaneous projects was, however, discussed earlier in an article by Payne, who identified five dimensions of the multi-project setting, viz. (Payne 1993):

- capacity
- complexity,
- conflict
- commitment
- context

Payne stated that, according to his experiences, as firms try to keep down costly over-capacity, by cutting down on personnel and taking on new projects, the ensuing result often is capacity shortage instead. This is a frequent problem and a popular scapegoat in multi-project settings and Payne recommends a more systematic selection of projects as a cure. However, he does not discuss the concept of a project portfolio.

Complexity relates to the multiple interfaces within and between projects, between projects and the organisation as a whole and between the involved parties inside and outside the organisation, and concerns questions of co-ordination and control. Reducing the degree of complexity by integrating only the part of projects that are common and not whole projects is a way for management to lessen this problem. This, Payne maintained, might lead to the development of subcultures within the organisation, which in turn might exacerbate eventual conflicts within the organisation.

Conflicts may arise over people issues, systems issues and organisational issues, according to Payne, who recommended the promotion of a professionally stimulating environment, a thing easier said than done, as a means to alleviate the problems. Such a climate might also be beneficial in other aspects. A professionally stimulating environment might increase the organisation members' commitment to their work and to the company in question.

In Payne's article, commitment was related to the resource providers' engagement in the different projects, where perceived importance of a particular project played an important role and where project size, not its contribution to the organisations goals or its profitability, in turn influenced perceptions. Context was related to the setting of projects, for instance the culture existing in the organisation and in the environments of different projects, but context might also be related to various issues, such as people or systems questions. Variations in context were also introduced by the structural choices management made, concerning both the whole firm, as well as the positioning of the projects within it.

Payne concluded by observing that in the literature on multi-project management, however scarce, it was assumed that projects were treated as if they were homogeneous, a premise he himself doubted. The variation among projects in a multi-project setting is often too large to allow such groupings. This also speaks for grouping projects into categories within a portfolio. The obvious conclusion for management of mixed multi-projects is that a flexible and varied management style must be adopted, otherwise management will have difficulties in responding adequately to the different demands. Another solution is, of course, to try to diminish the diversity by choosing projects that fit into an organised portfolio. This approach might have some drawbacks as it lessens the company's efficiency in terms of size of market and its flexibility, increases risk in demand shift situations and gives rise to conflicts within the organisation, as project leaders will fight for "their" projects. But, it is argued here, it will help ensuring company's survival by giving management information about the current situation and warning signals about future problems.

In multi-project settings, many projects are accepted ad hoc and just "happen" to run simultaneously, they do not form a larger overall programme. And even if management conceives that the company has a programme or a portfolio, a systematic analysis of the current set of projects might indicate that such is not the case, as is illustrated in the article by Wheelwright and Clark (1992). The article refers to product development projects. The company Wheelwright and Clark has studied handled more projects than management was aware of, in fact two to three times more development work had been undertaken than could possibly be completed within its three year planning horizon. Delays in some projects spilled over on to other projects, spreading problems of broken time and budget limits through the organisation. It was also found that the employees were not concentrating their time and efforts to the projects that were most critical for business, instead projects were chosen on the basis of the challenges they offered or because customers or other departments in the company in question required them. Furthermore, the project leaders often spent a significant part of their time in non-project related work.

In this chapter managing project portfolios is seen as different from multi-project management. The term multi-project management implies handling a number of more or less different projects, that just "happen" to be started by the firm at the same time, while the term portfolio is meant to indicate a planned composition of projects, balancing various aspects of a number of projects over time to ensure long-range survival of the firm in question. The lack of studies of managing project portfolios and practical guidelines for doing so is obvious. Financial theories of portfolio management might be one source of inspiration. The central question in this case is how to analyse the risk/return characteristics of the portfolio's possible contents and finding the efficient set or sets of contents. (See for instance Elton and Gruber 1995, Farrell 1996, Haugen 1997, Sharpe et al 1995). The portfolio concept has been fruitfully applied in other contexts such as when talking about product portfolios, customer or supplier portfolios in marketing Friis Olsen and Ellram 1997). "Holes", "heaps" and other signs of imbalance and inefficiency in the portfolio, whatever its contents, can be detected by this type of analysis. One important difference between financial portfolios and project portfolios must, however, be pointed out, viz. that entrance and exit problems differ in a project setting from those in a financial setting. For instance, a project that meets the criteria for inclusion in the portfolio might not easily be acquired or if it does not meet the criteria, it cannot easily be discarded, as no market for projects exists.

Might models and practical guidelines be developed by studying existing, project-based firms? The firms having a project-based organisation are by tradition those that thrive on catering to individual customer service needs, such as architectural firms, legal firms, advertising companies and all kinds of consultants. In this chapter the discussion will be based on experiences from working with or in a number of traditional, project-based firms, among them consulting firms, advertising agencies and independent, non-company and non-governmental research organisations. These experiences will be used to exemplify a number of problems that this kind of organization faces as well as the solutions tried and found to work, in order to try to throw some light on the tricky questions of project portfolio management.

PROBLEMS OF PROJECT PORTFOLIO HANDLING

Building a balanced portfolio over time concerns several problems for management, such as defining the desirable characteristics of the portfolio, where the dimensions profitability and strategic importance – that is enhancing distinctive competence or enlarging the possible market for the firms activities – are central, generating and accepting projects to fill "holes" in the portfolio, and discarding projects that are accumulated in "heaps" of identical projects or do not otherwise live up to standards, in a changing and uncertain environment.

The Desirable Portfolio

When should a potential assignment be accepted in the portfolio and when should it be turned down? Two criteria must be combined: Profitability and strategic importance. Unprofitable assignments are not interesting in themselves, but sometimes even such projects must be accepted as having strategic significance, as for instance when they are thought to have good demonstration effects for potential customers or when the firm wants to enter new fields. Such projects might be labelled "competence enhancing" ventures or projects for the exploration of possible markets, that is market enhancing projects (March 1991). Unprofitable assignments are not interesting in themselves, but sometimes even such projects must be accepted as having strategic significance, as for instance when they are thought to have good demonstration effects for potential customers or when the firm wants to enter new fields and wants to acquire competence in those fields. Such projects might be labelled "competence enhancing" ventures or projects for exploring possible markets (March 1991). A simple analysis of potential assignments could be a good help in screening potential and existing projects. Even if it is very easy to carry out, it is seldom undertaken. And evaluating the project portfolio by this method is a good - sometimes both frightening and illuminating - exercise. (This analysis is also recommended for personal use when deciding about one's own work). All assignments should be placed in the matrix below:

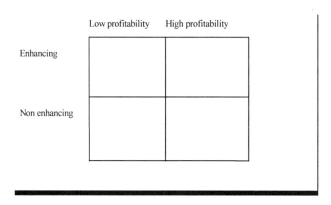

Figure 1. The analysis matrix

Aspiration levels concerning the portfolio's balance must be adjusted with an eye on the inflow of project proposals and outflow of terminated projects versus existing capacity. Assignments that are placed in the upper right-hand corner are, of course, clear yes-cases, (if capacity allows it), and assignments in the lower left-hand corner clear no-cases. Unprofitable projects that have no strategic significance should be quickly terminated or discarded in other ways, as they are just encumbrances. The choice between assignments in the remaining squares ought to be dependant on the composition of the portfolio as a whole. If the portfolio consists of a number of profitable but non enhancing projects, the firm can afford to take on a not very profitable project that strengthens its competence or position in new markets, but if the portfolio consists of mainly low profit projects, some profitable ones should be accepted, even if they mean nothing for competence development or market development.

The matrix, as depicted, represents the firm's view of projects. (A similar matrix might be drawn from the client's perspective). Projects that are enhancing competence or market development might be quite profitable for the firm and should be a significant portion of the portfolio. On the other hand, a major danger is being attracted by the low profitability, competence or market enhancing projects. These should be selected primarily when they are of strategic significance, that is when they are aligned to the vision about the company's future.

If the new projects are generated by outside clients, as is very often the case, the firm has limited influence on its influx of project proposals. How to build a good customer base is, however, discussed in a following section of the chapter. A stream of in-house projects might be better controlled, but those have a tendency to grow in size and number. For instance, Moss Kanter's book gives good advice to potential intrapreneurs about how to build support, acquire resources and launch projects (Moss Kanter 1983). The advice might as well be followed by members of a project-based company who wish to further their interests and circumvent top management.

Balancing a project portfolio requires a fine sense of when to say yes to proposed assignments and the courage to say no to some. Systematic evaluation of the portfolio's balance creates the feed-back necessary for learning.

Splicing Projects

One very important aspect of balancing the project portfolio is ensuring that the projects mesh into each other smoothly, creating neither overload nor gaps in resource use. Contracts with customers must be negotiated so that the start and end times of their projects as well as project length and resource demands fit into the existing portfolio of projects without too much re-organisation and re-negotiation with other clients. Some negotiations with project-leaders must also take place, in order to introduce new assignments in their individual project portfolios. It is, of course, vital that every project in the portfolio meets its resource- and time-budgets, as overdrafts in one project often create serious problems for on-going projects and for the possibilities of accepting new assignments (Wheelwright and Clark 1992). Therefore discipline ought to be strict. In our experience with project-based firms, a basic element in the culture of successful firms is regarding delivery dates as sacrosanct and the members are expected to work night and day if they suspect they will not be able to meet them with a normal input of time. We have found that the members who do not live up to these expectations will be sorted out, either in a more or less hidden process, where they are not chosen as co-workers by project leaders or in a more formal way, when top management recommends them to look for other jobs that would suit them better.

The project-leaders must also be disciplined enough not to accept assignments without checking how these fit into the overall portfolio. It is a constant temptation for project leaders to take on new projects. Being able to bring home new profitable contracts is meritous and the salary system is usually constructed as a constant remainder of the fact. A policy where the CEO of the firm has to accept all new assignments may exist, but other members might sometimes be over-eager in acquiring new contracts and will disregard it. The danger of constant overload on resources is always present when times are good. In this case the influx of new projects needs to be monitored.

Balancing a project portfolio demands skill in splicing projects, which in turns demands negotiation skills and a high degree of discipline among the project-leaders. Monitoring the influx of new projects is an important task for management.

Generating Projects

Having a stock of high status and satisfied customers is of great importance for this type of firm for several reasons. The self-evident reason is that such customers generate new projects. Satisfied customers have a tendency to come back, as their problems are not permanently solved, or the solutions create new problems or circumstances change, creating new problems. As assignment is added to assignment, the firm and the customer build knowledge about each other, trust is established, and the foundations for a stable relationship are laid. The loyal customers are not necessarily the ones that provide the most profitable single assignment, but they generate a steady income, even if the profitability of each single project is low.

Another reason is that marketing the firm's services through the usual channels, advertisements or mail, is often not very efficient. Word-of-mouth is more important for gaining new customers. Satisfied customers spread the word. And the higher the status of the customer, the higher the worth of the customer's recommendation. High standing, satisfied customers are used as reference objects in order to attract new customers. This is considered one of the most important ways of demonstrating the competence of the firm and the quality of its services to potential new customers.

In managing project portfolios, the careful building of a base of satisfied, loyal customers of high standing is of central importance.

Defining Projects

Some project-based firms have a well defined sphere of activities, others have not. Management consultants, for instance, have a tendency to aspire to be all-embracing and are often tempted to take on projects where the context or the problem or both are not very well known by the consultants beforehand. This is, of course, a way of learning by doing, both for senior and junior members of the firm. But there is also a tendency to redefine assignments to suit existing competence and existing recipes, a practice that does not always provide the best solution for an individual customer. Procrustes' way of handling clients must be avoided.

However, the customer does not always have a clear picture of what he or she wants or what the problem "really" is. Or, as in some advertising firms, what the customer wants is not up to the standards of excellence that the firm has set itself. The diagnostic phase then becomes critical, as it implies an interpretation of the situation that gives hints or clues of what actions to take in order to solve the client's problem. The procedure often follows a pattern that bears close resemblance to medical practice. First a diagnostic reading of the situation being investigated takes place, then follows a critical evaluation, and finally prescriptions are given, that is remedies are proposed and interventions made. (Morgan 1997). It is important that this "sense-making" of what the problem consists of and what ought to be done about it takes place in a consensus shaping dialogue with the client. (Weick 1995). Without this agreement, a discussion between consultant and client about what has been delivered and when the project is finished might ensue, as we have seen in some instances. But in most cases, the check-up of the patient's well-being after the cure is rarely undertaken, hence an opportunity for learning is being missed.

The interpretation of the situation will act as a blinder to other interpretations and their train of treatments or solutions. A narrowing of alternative interpretations and actions takes place. For instance, if a certain problem is diagnosed as one of low productivity instead of as one of low morale, the measures taken will vary and so will the results. In company A, an advertising company, much effort was spent on persuading unsophisticated customers to accept A's more refined and sophisticated ideas of how to carry out a campaign. No experiments were made to ascertain the effects of the different designs on the consumers.

Learning by doing is essential to project-based firms. Learning opportunities should be exploited. Awareness of the threat of becoming home-blind is needed.

Discarding Projects

A project is defined as a set of goal-directed activities, constrained by a time budget and a resource budget. But even with these built-in stops, projects sometimes have to be killed. If the project has an external customer the problem of finishing off projects is not so severe as when the project is intended for in-house use. In the case of the external customer the project dies a natural death when the intended result is achieved. If the goal is not reached by the time the resources are used up, the problem becomes one of making a graceful exit, that satisfies the customer's demands as far as possible with a minimum of extra resources and without disturbing or cannibalising other on-going projects.

In-house projects have a tendency to make themselves permanent. Even failed projects show a surprising capacity for survival. The immunisation strategies are many, but they might be summarised into three categories, viz. ensuring a lack of precise goals, ensuring a lack of relevant feed-back and ensuring a lack of alternatives. (Beckman 1979). Special skills and techniques are needed to kill projects that have survived themselves, as the hindrances are many and varied. The defenders of status quo are easily rallied. Yet getting rid of resource-consuming projects is necessary in order to create room for new ones. The problems and obstacles of the disinvestment process have been the object of several studies by Anell and Persson. (Anell, Lindell and Persson 1982, Anell and Persson 1982, 1983, 1984, 1985, Anell 1985).

To manage a portfolio of projects well, the skill to make a graceful exit and the courage to kill projects that shows tendencies to grow into surviving failures are necessary.

Demand Fluctuations

Handling variations in demand is a recurrent problem for the project-based firm. When demand is high, a certain amount of overload can be handled through the flexibility of the firm's members. They, as a rule, are loyal to the firm and prepared to put in considerable amounts of extra work, when it is deemed necessary. But they cannot sustain constant overload. Solutions have to be found, either by scaling down the project's demands or by allocating more resources to it. Both ways are difficult. Raising prices in order to narrow the stream of incoming projects without cutting profit is a strategy that might work. Sometimes, however, this has no effect on demand.

Another type of overload is when a single assignment is considered attractive, but too large-scaled to be handled by any amount of stretching by the firm's members. When the amount or size of current assignments becomes too big, having a network of trusted partners and sub-contractors is a well-tried solution. Building networks of reliable partners and sub-contractors offer the same kinds of investment problems as building a customer base. Creating trust and knowledge about each other takes time and effort, as well as the ensuing necessary co-ordination and integration.

Overload might also occur for more sinister reasons, that is when already existing projects take more time and or resources than allotted and encroach on other projects. Capacity problems and conflicts about resource allocations seem to be the most common trouble in project-based firms. Eskerod's dissertation focuses on the allocation of scarce human resources to projects, a process which is carried out through negotiations. (Eskerod 1997). Eskerod's contribution opens a rich area for research. Especially interesting were the possibilities of seeing projects as competing for resources in times of overload and resources as competing for projects in times of underload. Payne, for instance, pointed out the risk of projects being dragged on to ensure an extension of job security. (Payne 1995).

If the project-based firm is small and its assets mainly consist of the human capital of the members, its networks of customers, partners and sub-contractors, the problem of demand fluctuations is aggravated by the difficulty of building reserve capital, as the restrictions in Swedish tax laws make efforts in this direction rather expensive. The tax laws recognise only substance. Hence, investments in human capital and in networks do not show in the accounts and cannot be depreciated. Other solutions to the problem of reserve building might, however, be dangerous as the firm has to enter markets it knows little about. An example can be made of the successful data-consulting company, E, which tried to find a way out of this problem by entering the real estate market in order to increase its fixed assets. But lacking competence in this special field, it did so at the wrong time. When prices in the real-estate market fell sharply, it lost a considerable amount of money and had to be reconstructed. How to acquire resources for competence development is still an unresolved problem in the human capital intensive firm.

When demand is low, other problems surface. There are always things to do that have been neglected during times of high demand, such as writing reports and catching up on relevant literature, but these activities bring no profit. Necessary competence-maintenance and -building might be undertaken, but the problem of keeping the necessary inflow of money is a constant worry. Laying off members is to be avoided at almost any cost, as the firm stands and falls with their tacit knowledge, loyalty and enthusiasm. Eroded human capital can not be restored in the same way as eroded material assets can be rebuilt. Members of the company might instead seek work as temporary helpers in other firms' projects. The net-work of partners and sub-contractors is useful in this context also, as news and jobs are shunted through it. Another way of easing the burden is through flexible salary systems. In meagre times, the members' salaries are cut. The eventual bonuses disappear, of course, but also the basic salaries might, by mutual agreement, be cut down for a period of time. But just as overload can not be endured for long periods of time, trimming and slimming activities can not be enforced for ever.

Managing the product portfolio when demand is fluctuating needs flexibility in many aspects. The demand for flexibility is most taxing for the members of the firm.

The ground for that flexibility must be laid beforehand.

Demand Shifts

Building a base of loyal customers takes time and effort. A good customer base is a strong competitive advantage that cannot easily be copied by other firms. On the other hand, it can turn out to be a kind of prison, as was the case in company I. Company I was a small consultant firm whose very good customer base consisted of Swedish communes. When the communal budgets diminished, company I's order book also shrank, and the company tried to enter the private enterprise market, but found this almost impossible. The potential customers saw themselves and their problems as too different from Swedish communes and their troubles and did not find Company I's competence relevant for the problems at hand.

This example has of course more general implications, as it illustrates the problems of any specialist. Convincing potential clients of the scale and scope of the specialist's competence might be difficult. A worse problem is, however, when the niche of the specialist diminishes or disappears, as his or her competence then decreases in value. It is difficult to build new competence and to communicate the fact that it has really been done.

Shifts in demand for competence are more serious threats to project-based firms than to most manufacturing firms. The latter might import knowledge and competence, in the form of knowledge embodied in new employees, in artefacts such as machines and in implementing new routines. Of course the project-based firm might import new competence by hiring new members, but hiring is not an attractive option in times of adversity. And socialising the new employees to the firm's special culture and recipe for working might take some time. There will be a period when the new member does not cover his or her costs, and yet another period before he or she shows a profit. Shifts in demand can also be destructive for investments in different kinds of networks.

Managing a project portfolio implies the need to take a proactive stance in competence development and networking, in order not to become entrapped in the firm's particular niche.

Maintaining Core Competence

The largest part of the core of distinctive competence of a knowledge-intensive, project-based firm consists of the tacit knowledge of its members. Another part consists of their ability to complement each other, to work smoothly with each other, to develop knowledge together and to share knowledge with each other. When a good member leaves, he or she leaves a gap in the core competence. As this is distinctive and mainly tacit, it is not easy to replace him or her, as no labour market exists for this type of competence.

The maintenance of core competence means that layoffs during periods of low demand, as mentioned earlier, must be avoided at almost any cost. Defections for other reasons must also be prevented. Often the more creative members of the organisation want to create their own company culture and try out their own recipes, but such jump-offs should be counteracted for as long as possible. Successful members of a project-based firm are often tempted to start their own firm, when they perceive how much they bill their customers and how low their salary is in comparison. Bonus systems for profitable members are created to counteract this feeling of being exploited. To keep members in the firm, a system for becoming partners or share-holders is often created. This might be difficult for new partners in successful firms, but the bonus system opens a way of financing the buy-ins. The salary system is one that not only remunerates members for their contributions to the firm, it is one that must restrain urges that might lead key members to leave. It is now common knowledge that salary is not a motivator, but it can be a dissatisfier to key personnel. (Herzberg, Mausner, Snyderman 1959). Motivation for the key personnel tends to come through the work, so personnel must be assigned to projects that sustain their sense of contribution.

Problems of growth are severe for the project-based firm, as no market for relevant competence exists. Most firms of this type prefer to recruit young members and to train them for extended periods of time in thinking and acting in accordance with the local culture. The clan management style flourishes. Common activities in the members' free time are frequent, and rituals and symbols abound, all with the intent of creating the sense of belonging to a family or clan.

To manage the people who comprise the core competencies of a firm, security and adequate remuneration must be provided, but motivation comes from the product portfolio itself.

CONCLUSIONS AND FUTURE RESEARCH

Projects are so deceptively successful in getting things done that sometimes it is easy to forget that they need management, and often management of a kind that differs from traditional management or management as prescribed in normative text-books on planning and control of project.. They do, of course, both with regard to operations and strategy. This chapter dealt with the strategic management of projects – particularly the portfolio that project firms must have. The need for balancing the portfolio regarding the two central dimensions, profit and enhancement of competence or market is underlined. However, this is only a first step into the interesting research area of managing several projects at the same time, and how to manage project-based operations in various types of organizations.

CHAPTER 7

PROJECTS AND PROPOSALS IN BUSINESS SERVICES

Tim Wilson, Clarion University, Clarion, Pennsylvania, U.S.A.

Marcia Seidle, Clarion University, Clarion, Pennsylvania, U.S.A.

ABSTRACT

"Business services" are those services provided for business customers. History has indicated that this service sector has been the largest and most rapidly growing of all service sectors in the U.S. Of course projects, proposals and planning for projects are important in these services. In-depth interviews with managers thus have been completed in the eight segments that comprise approximately 80 percent of the revenues that are attributed to this sector. Results suggested that two elements were important in arriving at an understanding for a project in these services – the "nature" of the interaction and the "content" that these interactions tended to take. This two-element model is thought to be generally applicable across business services and may be a special case of the application of communication theory as developed for national cultures. Significant differences in detail appear to exist, however, in the eight segments and some of these differences are described. Qualitative association may be made with observations on profitability made in business service segments.

BUSINESS SERVICES AND OUTSOURCING

History has indicated that the business service sector has been the largest and most rapidly growing of all service sectors in the U.S. Wilson and Smith (1996) reviewed the eleven industries generally comprising the Department of Commerce listing in this sector and noted the overall growth of business services in that sample was 11.7 percent per annum (p.a.). Further, every segment in that study outperformed GDP growth (6.7 percent p.a.) during the comparable period.

One factor cited as contributing to the growth of business services was downsizing, coupled with attendant outsourcing (Wilson and Smith 1996). This tendency is likely to continue. According to research from Dun and Bradstreet (Ozanne 1997), "Outsourcing, once used mainly for downsizing and cost reductions at major corporations, has become a strategic tool that has a powerful impact on corporate growth and financial stability." The Dun and Bradstreet study suggested outsourcing would grow 23% over a 12 months period to become a USD180 billion business world-wide. Companies were reported to utilise outsourcing for several reasons. The main purpose was access to specialised expertise in selected management support functions. Additionally, workers associated with outsourcing have been cited as "hidden assets" (Clark 1997). It was reported that when DuPont reduced its labour force over the last seven years, approximately 30% of the former employees returned as vendors or contractors. One executive was quoted that he "keeps 100 temps working at all times because he likes the flexibility and the chance to try out potential permanent hires." Dobler and Burt (1996: 409) have noted that service procurement may amount to as much as 25 percent of an organisations' expenditures. Further, when "qualified personnel are involved, savings of approximately 25 percent are enjoyed with equal or improved quality."

The widespread popularity of this outsourcing apparently assures business services growth over the immediate future. Further, projects, proposals and planning for projects are important in business services -- at least professional ones. Peters (1992) spent four chapters on these topics in a recent text. Thus, the importance of these topics appears assured in a practical sense for the same period. Nevertheless, there does not appear to be a general model for the marketing of business services. Clearly, this model would focus on pre-task activities. The purpose of this chapter is to identify concepts and issues associated with the successful initial marketing of business services. Necessarily, this description will focus on initial activities of suppliers across a range of business services. Because of the importance of the project concept in business services, this model warrants discussion in this section of the text relating to projects in business.

BUSINESS SERVICES IN THE LITERATURE

Projects in Business Services
Projects appear generally associated with business service provision. Agreement on project selection and conduct thus is a necessary preliminary step in interfirm discussions. Harvey and Rupert (1988) identified the "test" project as being an essential element of final selection of an advertising agency. This project was to be paid for by the potential buyer so that the agencies would receive some compensation for their work on "speculative" assignments and consequently the client would "own" the output after the presentation. Day and Barksdale (1992) also cited "satisfaction with previous *projects*" and "has worked on similar *projects* in the past" (emphasis added) as an indication of quality by clients in supplier selection.

Two things are worth noting with regard to these observations. First, the concept of the project as both an organisational unit and as a work unit in business services is undoubtedly universally applicable. That is, when the supplier agrees with the client to supply a certain service it invariably is a service that involves a task with a certain uniqueness, a predetermined date of delivery, one or more performance goals, and a number of complex and/or interdependent activities. These attributes are the elements that define a project (Packendorff 1995).

The second note is that although projects are undoubtedly associated with the supply of business services, the nature of the projects themselves is likely to vary in a manner dependent upon the industry sector and task at hand. One manner is project uniqueness. It would seem implausible that service projects developed by advertising firms would be similar in detail and complexity to projects developed by building and dwelling service firms, or even accountants. The former would tend to be more unique, whereas the latter would tend to be repetitive, or even mass produced. Of course even these "mass produced" projects would necessarily be client specific viz. a viz. the suggestion of Jackson and Cooper (1988) that "industrial services can be characterised by their customisation to their customer needs."

Packendorff (1993), in this regard, indicated that "uniqueness" of projects can be considered a variable. That is, both the delivery process and actual output must be considered in ascertaining uniqueness. Using this approach, three types of projects were identified -- mass produced, repetitive, and truly unique projects (1993: 17-19). In structuring a theory of temporary organisations, Lundin and Söderholm (1995) further added to the concept of repetitive and uniqueness the ideas that goals, experience, competence, evaluation and learning tend to differ in the two extremes of projects.

Although Peters (1992) devoted four chapters to projects, he primarily focused on "creative" projects in professional firms. These descriptions tended to place most emphasis on group interactions. He evidently envisioned a normative approach in which group members were involved from initial, brainstorming sessions throughout the process necessary to satisfy clients. This process, of course, involved clients as well as provider firms. Little insight was given on how these projects were obtained. Instead, it was noted that, "If a job is won, a project team is cobbled together" (1990: 163).

Purchasing of Business Services
Purchasing of business services has a long-standing history. In this regard, the purchase of services tends in general to be somewhat different than the purchase of industrial goods. For one thing, the U.S. Universal Commercial Code exempts coverage of services (Dobler and Burt 1996: 700). For another, there is the tendency for the specific service to be tailored to specific customers (DeBrentani 1989). Consequently, suggested purchasing practice tends to be discussed in terms of "contracting" rather than "purchasing."

The process in general procurement involves a statement of work, which has been labelled "most critical in the successful procurement of services." This statement is supposed to protect the buyer's interest while encouraging the supplier's creativity. This statement is incorporated into a request for proposal, whose purpose is to elicit a performance plan, quality monitoring system, personnel plan and performance and payment bonds. Selection of "right" sources has been associated with selecting established, reputable firms who satisfy needs at reasonable prices. Text treatments tend to result in a rather stylised approach for the purchasing of services, which in turn is complemented by negotiations concerning details (see, for instance, Dobler and Burt 1996: 408-422).

Business Services Marketing
The "textbook" approach to marketing of business services recognises the variation that may occur in this process. For instance, "Buying motives and practices may differ greatly depending on the type of service involved. The contract for janitorial services, for example, may be straightforward and simple, ... On the other hand, a contract for engineering services may be quite complex and require considerable negotiation. ..." (Haas 1995).

Marketing oriented descriptions of the selection process in service sectors has been a popular topic of academic study, but these studies have tended to be quite industry specific. Dawes, Dowling and Peterson (1992), for example, studied a range of management consulting services provided to organisations under consultancy agreements in Australia. It was concluded that existing clients represented the most probable (and most profitable) sources of new business. In a somewhat similar manner, Woodside, Wilson and Milner (1992) used in-depth interviews to develop a relationship model for Certified Public Accounting (CPA) service marketing. Wheiler (1987) had previously indicated the importance of referrals in not only CPA services, but also in bank and law services as well. A study by Harvey and Rupert (1988) suggested changing agencies was the specific consideration an industrial firm might need to make in regard to advertising services. Day and Barksdale (1992) attempted to gain insight into the process by which business clients selected and evaluated architectural and engineering service firms. Not surprisingly, factors contributing to overall satisfaction or dissatisfaction were very similar to quality evaluation criteria. It appears that less attention has been paid to the purchase criteria used in selecting suppliers of MRO (Maintenance, Repair and Operation) services. Jackson et al (1988, 1995) noted merely that MRO services might be purchased by a different set of buyers than production services.

The European literature has tended to emphasise the relationship nature of services marketing. This approach recognised the active nature of both marketing and purchasing firms (IMP 1982). Yorke (1990) studied both financial and legal firms and concluded that "traditional marketing strategies may not be entirely relevant to the needs of the market. A more convincing solution ... must recognise the desire of many clients that their supplier firms should work with rather than for them." It was noted that few banks have been able to implement an effective relationship banking strategy (Turnbull and Gibbs 1987) -- corporate customers tend to be transaction oriented. The successful licensing of technology, on the other hand, required a continuing commitment to the process of relationship building (Welsh 1985).

Business Services Characteristics
It has been suggested that business services tend to fall into three groups (Wilson and Smith 1996). One grouping was the *Professional Business Services* grouping. This group represented high revenue/employee and high pay/employee and included Computer and Data Processing Services, Legal Services, Advertising, Engineering and Architectural Services, Management Consulting and Public Relations, R&D Laboratories, and Accounting, Auditing and Bookkeeping. Skilled individuals of

these firms could be staff members of client firms. It might be thought that these firms succeeded by "renting" their rather highly pair personnel to client firms. Insofar as customers, or clients, of these Group I firms were also businesses by definition, these customers would be expected to develop capabilities to sustain their own routine activities. Thus, it followed that the revenue produced by each Group I employee, or employee group, must be something especially valuable. In general, this "special" offering would be expected to be a unique capability supplied by the service provider, tailored to meet the needs of the customer, or client.

In a second group representing low revenue/employee and low pay/employee (Group II) were Personnel Supply Services, Detective Agencies and Protective Services, and Service to Dwellings and Other Buildings. This grouping was thought of as the segments providing the *MRO Services* described by Jackson et al. (1995) and Jackson and Cooper (1988). It would be expected that these firms would be supplying relatively standard offerings to their clients. It would follow that jobs done by firms in this group would have to be relatively standard because low paid (relatively unskilled), or part-time (relatively uncommitted) personnel are used in the production of these services. Client firms could conceivably produce these services for themselves, but elected not to because a specialist may produce them cheaper, or because the client may not want to bother with them.

Equipment Rental and Leasing Services was an obvious outliner in the study and thus was taken to be a third, separate industrial group (Group III). Firms in this segment tended to be characterised by very high revenues per employee produced by moderately paid employees. This grouping was the *Equipment Rental and Leasing* grouping. The relatively large difference that existed between revenue/employee and pay/employee was a consequence of "rent" on equipment supplied to clients.

Although there appeared to be a single relationship that covered revenue generated from provider's services, it was apparent that profitability varied considerably among the individual segments. Profit before taxes was used as a measure of "bottom line" profitability. Values ranged from 1.9 percent for Services to Dwellings and Buildings to 14.7 percent for Legal Services. Further, group association did not in itself determine profit level. Services to Dwellings and Buildings (1.9%) and Detective Agencies and Protection of Group II, from the "low" pay group, were the two lowest profit level segments. Personnel Supply Services of the same group, however, rated higher than five groups in Group I, the "high" pay group. Thus, it appeared necessary to go through the listing segment by segment to appreciate relative profitability levels.

FIELD INTERVIEWS AT SELECTED FIRMS

The investigational portion of this study consisted of exploratory interviews designed to identify the nature of pre-project discussions for a range of business service offerings. A convenience sample of firms was drawn with the assistance of the local Small Business Development Center to represent the major categories of business services, one firm per segment. Reliance upon a small business sample in this study appeared consistent with previous observations that the typical size of these businesses was about ten employees (Wilson and Smith 1996). Eight of the eleven major segments, including all three of the Wilson/Smith (1996) groupings, were covered. In-depth interviews were conducted with executives of these firms. These interviews were guided by a questionnaire designed to provide consistent coverage across interviews.

The instrument consisted primarily of open-ended questions and was comprised of three major parts plus two minor ones. The first part led the respondent to select a successful, first-time sale with which they were personally involved and which represented a typical portion of their business. The exploratory nature of the research was explained as well as the desire not to be intrusive into confidential aspects of their business. The situation that had been voluntarily selected by the respondent was then described by him or her in some detail. The second portion of the interview then asked specific questions about details leading up to the close of business -- who was involved, number of meetings, where these meetings were held, and subsequent meetings after the close of sale. The third portion of the interview got into even greater detail about the situation leading up to the close of sale -- whether a written proposal was required, the nature of presentation if necessary, where in the sequence of meetings the proposal was made, whether a contract was signed, and who signed it if one was. In a fourth portion, the general nature of pricing was also determined in this sequence. In each case, it was asked if this sale was typical of the respondent's business. Finally, general demographic information was obtained on the respondent and his/her firm. Field responses were subsequently summarized and coded.

The field questionnaire was tested by the leading author of this chapter. Subsequently, interviews with the MRO and equipment rental and leasing firms were conducted personally by the authors. Interviews in the professional segments were primarily conducted by graduate students in a service marketing course. These students were of course briefed on techniques and applications prior to their actual field work. Actual results and interpretations were also reviewed by the leading author. The authors express their appreciation for these student contributions.

PROJECTS AND PROPOSALS IN BUSINESS SERVICES

Initial Deliberations in Business Services
As suggested by Haas (1995), a wide range of behaviour was noted in the deliberations leading up to the close of first-time sales of business services. Nevertheless, the picture that evolved was one in which four steps were common to all situations:

1. An initial meeting was held in which needs were assessed and comfort was built between potential supplier and customer.
2. A proposal was developed.
3. A price or a price schedule was set.
4. A contract, written in seven of the eight cases, was agreed upon.

Of course there were differences across the segments and these differences are noted in Table 1. The initial meeting was held at different places - two at the supplier's, but six at the customers; the number of pre-sale meetings varied as did the formality of proposal and personnel involved in these meetings. Further, there were a number of segments in which post-sale meetings seemed to be accepted practice, particularly in the professional services. There was also a difference in the usage of the term "project" in the interviews. Respondents in the professional services tended to use this term to describe their activities, although attorneys tend to use the term "case" or "docket." The rental respondent did not describe the rental as a project, but talked about the renter using the equipment in his "project." MRO respondents tended to use the word "job" in their interviews, but that was a term all respondents used at some time in interviews to describe activities.

Relevant detailed observations from the interviews in the eight segments along with organisational descriptions also are shown in Table 1. Interviews suggested that simplest interactions came in the *equipment rental segment*. There, potential clients would check to assure equipment availability and then come to pick up the equipment. The contract was on the reverse side of the rental agreement, and prices were set by national averages. Prices tended not to be negotiable although the firm did provide credit for its local customers. On the other hand, the most complex behaviour appeared to occur in the advertising industry. There, activities appeared to be customer oriented, but provider intense. Four meetings were required to close the sale -- all at the customer's location and at the owner/ manager's convenience. Both the provider's capabilities and expected outcomes had to be sold. Subsequently, eight to twenty meetings were arranged over a period of time to assess outcomes -- relationships were important in providing ongoing business. To some extent, the pricing schedule reinforced ongoing business insofar as a schedule of discounts was used.

Naturally, a range of behaviour was noted between these two extremes. In general, the *professional business services* (Computer and Data Processing, Management, Consulting and PR, Engineering, Architectural) tended to be like the advertising example -- a number of meetings, primarily at the customer's location, and devoted to understanding needs while selling the capabilities of the provider. Legal Services provided an exception to this general behaviour. In the particular situation that was discussed, a mining situation, the client arranged a meeting with the attorney at the law firm's office, explained the situation, heard the attorney's suggestions, and then the attorney took charge of subsequent developments. Fees, etc. were agreed upon in advance and the client subsequently was billed for services. In certain respects the deliberations were more like the equipment rental situation than the other business services.

Table 1. - Summary Observations: Business Service Pre-Project Activities

SIC	SEGMENT/FIRM	NATURE OF INTERACTION	CONTENT OF INTERACTION	PRICING
Group	I – Professional Business Services			
737_	Computer & Data Processing - Custom Programming Firm	Three pre-sale meetings at supplier. "Lots of time after installation."	Needs assessment. Proposal at second meeting. Subsequent to how used, feedback and changes.	Two-tier: one existing system. Another for modifications. Rate for extras.
874_	Management, Consulting & PR – Complete Care Firm	1st contact at special trade show. Subse- quent calls and meet-ings to cement deal. Supplier initiated.	Contract written for 1st meeting (at customer). Walk through and examination of records to identify problems.	Flat fee plus % of gross revenue.
731_	Advertising - Cable Time Supplier	Four meetings to close sale. 8 to 20 subse-quent meetings.	Introduce capabilities to potential client. Subsequent to assess results and build relationship.	Set rates, discounts for multi-system.
81__	Legal Services - G&L Partnership	Initial contact followed by meeting at law firm. Ongoing as necessary.	Client presented situation. Attorney explained needs.	Fees, expenses, + billing hours.
871_	Engineering, Archi-tectural – AEDS Group	Initial meeting followed by proposal meetings. Subsequent meetings.	Firm and capability important. Understanding of problem. Fees and approach separate.	Initial proposal + negotiation.
Group II – Equipment Rental & Leasing				
735_	Equipment Rental & Leasing – State Rental	Customer call. Customer pick up.	Availability and terms.	Used national averages.
Group III - MRO Services				
734_	Dwelling and Building Service - M's Cleaning Service	Two meetings for pro-posal. One subsequent	Walk around to understand needs. Discuss written proposal. Adjust rates (only one with oral agreement).	Formula on sq. ft. basis. Adjustment for extras.
7381	Detective Agencies and Protection - GRS Security	Three pre-sale meetings. 2 or 3 after sale.	Needs and capabilities. Walk around for specifics. Work out extra requirements. Educa-tional and comfort building.	Formula - number required.

Firms in the *MRO sector* tended to be less formal in their approach to the marketplace. To be sure, a number of meetings were required to close a sale, but formal presentations apparently were not required. Instead, both respondents indicated a "walk around" played a role in discussing apparent needs and potential solutions. In this exercise, supply firm representatives literally walked around the potential customer's plant with representatives of the decision committee. Needs and possible approaches were discussed during this working tour. A subsequent proposal was required, and price was settled somewhat separate from this proposal.

It was not the purpose of this research to make an extensive study of pricing, but pricing was clearly important for both parties in these pre-project deliberations in business services. It was a topic on which both parties must agree; it also was, and is, a determining factor in establishing profitability of the firm. Respondents appeared to favour formula pricing. In seven of the eight interviews, a formula was definitely used to establish an initial asking price by the provider. Although bases varied across segments, this approach apparently served the dual needs of supplier and customer.

As an aside, it might be noted in the headings of Table 1 that SIC (Standard Classification Numbers) are included as a first column. This addition permits association with the broader industries that these specific firms represent. To the extent that these cases may be thought of as being typical of broader behaviour, the observations may be thought of as industry behaviour.

Substance of Pre-Project Discussions in Business Services
The picture that evolved across the segments that were studied was that certain generalities could be made about these pre-project, or pre-task, discussions and an attempt is made to reflect these generalities in Figure 1. First, there was the "nature" of the interaction. To some extent, this construct was reflected in the number of meetings that were required to close the sale. It also depended, however, upon the nature of the meetings. That is, were they relatively simple, i.e. one buyer and one seller, or did they become more complex -- adding people to both the selling team as well as the decision group as necessary through the sequence of meetings that occurred? Second, there was "content" within these interactions. For instance, in the MRO segments, participants "walked around" with their potential customers at the customers' place of business. During this time, substantive discussions were held -- informal, but focused, that led to the contract. At the other extreme, the advertising and engineering interactions required formal, and elaborate, presentations that "sold" the potential client on firm and project. Subsequently, further substantive discussions were held on terms.

These two constructs define a space that can be used to position the pre-project, or pre-task, discussions described in this study. Qualitative locations of all the interviews are shown in Figure 1 for this model. In general, they run from the lower left-hand quadrant to the upper right. That is, discussions that tend to be high-content also tend to require high-interaction. Likewise, low content tends to require low-interaction. Equipment rental set the apparent lower level, advertising the upper. In between, there were some perturbations. The attorney's case, for instance, required a single meeting to set up his task with his client, but the attorney's initial input into the process consisted of expertise, a fairly high content contribution – considerably different than the single meeting of the equipment rental firm. By comparison, the security firm required more interaction by way of meetings to settle agreement on its task than the building service firm.

In general, one might make note of the functional similarity between Figure 1 and observations made by Usunier (1993: 102-105) concerning communications in different cultures. There are obvious differences, of course, but in both cases segments were important, message content was relevant, and some aspect of interaction was identified. Further, results could be depicted as swinging in a monotonous fashion from lower left to upper right.

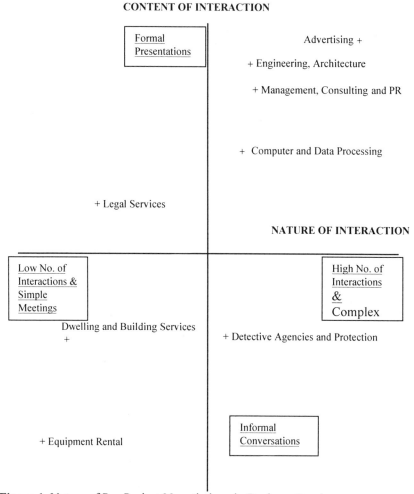

Figure 1. Nature of Pre-Project Negotiations in Business Services

REFLECTIONS ON FIELD INTERVIEWS

Business services are not produced until <u>after</u> they are sold, and they tend to be produced in a manner specific to purchaser's needs (Jackson and Cooper 1988). An important function of business service firms is thus to market their services. With respect to project literature, this effort would be regarded as pre-project activity. That is, it relates to the efforts on the part of both the buyer and seller to negotiate a satisfactory agreement for the timing, scope and outcome of a task. These pre-project activities are interesting for three reasons. First, these activities represent a significant portion of the promotional effort of service firms. Second, incremental product development is done during this stage of activity, and third, the project itself is planned by supplier and user representatives as a consequence of these activities.

Due to the importance of the business service sector (Wilson and Smith 1996) and the relatively high usage of outsourcing in which firms participate (Clark 1997, Nicklin 1997, Ozanne 1997, Dobler and Burt 1996), understanding of this process is thus fairly important. In this regard, preliminary results suggested there may not be a single process that describes efforts in the segments that comprise the majority portion of business service activity. Nevertheless, a generally applicable model could be identified that suggested that a four step process tended to be followed in each case. Further, the nature of interaction necessary to develop the business and the content of pre-project interactions were found to be important, and cases could be characterised on this basis. That is, both numbers of meetings, etc. and communication materials tended to vary among cases.

To the extent that these were "typical" cases, the study suggested there were distinct variations in behaviour among segments. The characteristics of this behaviour were more along the lines suggested by a general marketing approach (Haas 1995) than a purchasing approach (Dobler and Burt 1996). That is, it was generally the seller who appeared active. With the possible exception of the engineering/architectural firm, which happened to be involved in some state work, there were no indications of buyer-generated statements of work as appeared important in a purchasing approach (Dobler and Burt 1996). Likewise, there was no indication that a project team was to be "cobbled together" after the project was won as described by Peters (1992). Instead, it appeared as if respondents had a good idea of "who would do what" when the presentations were made. On an overall basis, the observations may be a portion of communication theory as identified by Usunier (1993) for national cultures.

Relationship building also was not mentioned by respondents and may not be as important as some literature appeared to suggest (Yorke 1990, Welsh 1985). Rather, "comfort" might be a better term for buyer-seller interactions -- especially in the lower content cases. Nevertheless, relationship building undoubtedly was part of the routine in higher content examples as evidenced by the number of meetings required. It also might be noted that the tendency to unbundle price in these situations also contributed to the number of meetings that were required.

Some clarity could be added to observations by considering these interactions as tasks that had to be successfully completed before work could start for potential clients/customers. In this regard, the classification of Lundin and Söderholm (1995) of repetitive and unique tasks appears appropriate. Equipment rental and the aspect of legal services reported here appear clearly repetitive. The approaches to obtaining first-time clients in advertising and engineering, etc., on the other hand, tend to be more unique. This observation might be anticipated because of the nature of tasks in these segments, which tend to be repetitive and unique respectively. Nevertheless, projects and pre-projects do not necessarily have the same characteristics. For instance, actual work in the building service and protection sectors tend to be quite repetitive, but aspects of pre-contract negotiations could be described as unique.

Interest in this aspect of the observations is related to profitability. Work that must be done before initiation of paid activity, either as a project or "job," represents overhead for the firm. Thus, the observation of a wide variation in profitability across sectors (Wilson and Smith 1996) is not completely surprising – again to the degree that these in-depth cases represent industry behaviour.

Pricing, of course, plays a role in any profitability determination and thus cannot be eliminated from consideration. Nevertheless, it is understandable why legal services led the profitability list for business services. With a single meeting, supplier located, this sector clearly would carry a low overhead. Combined with a pricing approach that included direct payment for time spent on services plus fees and expenses, relative profitability would be expected to be high. Likewise, the equipment sector would be expected to do well, as suggested by the simplicity of practice in that sector. As long as reasonable rents could be charged, overhead would be expected to be quite low. On the other hand, it is easy to see why some of the professional services had lower profitability. Obviously more money was spent in getting work as suggested by the number of meetings that was required to get and keep work. Evidently, from profit figures, these costs could not be fully recovered and thus had to be absorbed as overhead. Thus, simpler approaches may be associated with higher profitability in industries that tend to adopt simplified protocol. Lower profitability, on the other hand, may be associated with complex protocols. The observations of this study thus appear to be qualitatively consistent with previous, broader observations (Wilson and Smith 1996).

This study thus provides potentially practical assistance to individuals involved in setting up their projects with potential customers. Implicit in this approach is the assumption that some flexibility is available in the type of work and customer base that could be pursued. The legal service model would seem to present an optimal approach for other service providers. In the case reported here, the provider was able to supply a relatively repetitive service (for him) to a client who perceived it to be unique. Further, the supplier was able to obtain this work with minimal up-front expense.

On the other hand, this study has obvious limitations at this point. It involves a case study approach and might be considered as a work in progress; some major assumptions have been made in generalising results and really such generalisations should be treated as hypothetical at this time. Clearly, further studies of a descriptive nature are in order to assure generality. None the less, the purpose of this paper was to present a model for marketing practices, and it is felt that some conceptual contributions have been made in that regard from empirical observations. Further, with the tendencies for single companies in individual situations to adapt to industry cultures, the single case observations may not be as tenuous as might be suspected.

CONCLUSIONS AND FUTURE WORK

A model has been developed from field observations that suggests that pre-project, pre-contract interactions can be described by a two factor model related to the <u>nature</u> and <u>content</u> of interactions. These observations were in qualitative agreement with relative profitability levels found for business services earlier. Of course this study was exploratory and quite preliminary. Further work of a descriptive nature should be done in support of hypothetical observations developed in this study. In particular, it would be of theoretical importance to know how generalities of communication observations might be applied to pre-project practice. Included in this work should be both pre-project characterisations and pricing practices. Both appear important in rationalising profitability of business service practice.

It has also been observed that positioning of business service firms in the nature-content space could be consistent with an unique/repetitive characterisation of tasks. Routine provision carries with it expenses that can be anticipated and thus controlled. Unique situations, on the other hand, carry more risk. It would be interesting to determine the degree to which firms across sectors provide routine (for them) services that provide unique benefits to customers. Reflection on the factors in a portfolio and their contributions to profitability could provide an interesting addition to management practice.

CHAPTER 8

PROJECT SUCCESS AND CUSTOMER SATISFACTION: TOWARD A FORMALIZED LINKAGE MECHANISM*

Jeffrey K. Pinto, School of Business, Penn State Erie

Pekka Rouhiainen, Aker Rauma Offshore Oy, Houston, TX 77079

Jeffrey W. Trailer, School of Business, Penn State - Erie

ABSTRACT

The successful strategic management of projects is based on an organization's understanding that an effective project is only as good as its capacity to satisfy customer requirements. In an increasingly competitive international marketplace, successful firms are typically those that have worked to establish a cooperative relationship with their clients, based on their desire to provide better service. This sense of better service typically refers to the willingness of these companies to evaluate their project management practices in terms of external, client demands along with the more traditional and internally-focused efficiency measures such as schedule and budget adherence. Through this use of Value-Chain Analysis, organizations are able to compete more effectively through understanding how best they can bring value to their customer's business activity cycle. This chapter reports on the results of a series of efforts by Aker Rauma Offshore Oy to develop a customer-based project success measure to ensure positive long-term relationships with customers. Among their findings is the need to differentiate among various stakeholder constituencies within the same client organization and develop service strategies to address each sub-group's needs.

THE APPROACH

The pursuit of project excellence follows a path with no existing endpoint in sight. Project organizations routinely face almost insurmountable obstacles in attempting to develop and operate their projects, through working to satisfy large numbers of

---

* Portions of this chapter appeared as "Customer-based project success: Exploring a key to gaining competitive advantage in project organizations," *Project Management*, vol. 4 (1), 6-11, 1998. Used with permission.

stakeholders, adhere to strict profit guidelines, maintain difficult schedules while conquering a series of technical challenges. However, when these firms critically examine their operations, they often founder on efforts to develop accurate measures of project success. Traditional views of success no longer necessarily capture the demands and constraints placed on firms operating in stiff, global competition. Put more simply, it is ironic that many project-based firms continue to view "success" through flawed parameters.

This chapter examines the approach currently being taken by a Finnish firm with a clearer understanding of what successful project management means. In redefining concepts of project "success," this organization has chosen to go back to basics, believing that true success can only be understood when looked at through the eyes of the customer. In formulating this seemingly simple, but ultimately radical shift in operating philosophy, they offer a unique model that will likely become a bellweather for other project-based firms, abandoning out-dated views of project success in favor of a more clear-eyed vision (Pinto and Rouhiainen 1998).

THE COMPANY

Aker Rauma Offshore Oy (ARO), a wholly-owned subsidiary of Aker Maritime, is headquartered in Pori, Finland. One of the company's key products is the Spar Hull and Mooring System. Spar is one of today's most promising deep-water offshore oil and gas development concepts. Currently, the largest market for Spar is the Gulf of Mexico. The four main components of the facility are: 1) the cylindrical hull that gives bouyancy to the facility, 2) the mooring system to keep the facility in the desired location, 3) topsides that contain the processing and drilling operations, and 4) riser systems that are used to transfer the hydrocarbons from the ocean floor well heads to the surface facility and back from the facility to the sea floor pipeline. In typical Spar projects ARO is responsible for delivering to the oil company customer the hull and mooring system, including project management, engineering, procurement, and fabrication.

The projects themselves are technically challenging and expensive: the spar hull can contain over 30,000 tons of steel framing and plating, the hulls are budgeted to take upwards of 18 months to design and fabricate and can cost over $100 million USD. In sheer dimensions, these spar hulls can be intimidating. The most recently completed hull measured over 200 meters in length and was almost 40 meters in diameter. Before lifting the Topsides facilities on the top of the hull at the final site at the Gulf of Mexico, the spar hull is fabricated in Finland in two pieces, transported across the Atlantic with a heavy transportation vessel, joined into one piece at the Gulf of Mexico yard, towed to the final site, upended and moored. By the time the total Spar project is completed, including drilling the wells, installing the pipelines for hydrocarbon transfer from the wells to the Spar facility and to shore, the total project can cost upwards of $1 billion USD. As these facilities are ordered by and for the use of major oil companies, ARO's role consists as that of a subcontractor to the overall construction effort.

ARO has been growing at a 40% compounded rate for the past nine years, primarily since it embarked on a radical refocusing of project management operations to become more customer-driven in its strategic project management. At the same time, the organization has worked to develop a customer-based project success measurement device in order to better understand: 1) the specific needs of each customer, 2) how well those needs have been addressed, and 3) how the organization can improve the project management contracting process in order to maintain positive relationships aimed at future partnerships. This process has confirmed for ARO the importance of introducing, in addition to the traditional determinants of project success (Time, budget, and performance), a Client-driven model in which a commitment to quality and customer satisfaction drives all strategic project decisions. This report will demonstrate that when such an external focus is encouraged, it will create an internal corporate culture conducive to competing successfully in the global marketplace.

TRADITIONAL PROJECT SUCCESS MEASUREMENT

ARO, along with many similar companies, had traditionally bounded its project success measurement along the more well-known project metrics of time (adherence to schedule), money (adherence to budget), and performance to specification. While well understood and relatively easy to measure, these traditional measures also present some important difficulties, including (Pinto and Slevin 1988; Wateridge 1998; Shenhar et al. 1997):

1) the tendency to sacrifice external concerns for internal performance. In other words, when a company measures their performance in terms of only how they developed the project internally, the natural by-product is to discount or minimize legitimate customer concerns. For example, if a project manager gains maximum corporate credit for simply bringing in projects under budget, it generates a temptation to continually cut corners or make decisions leading to a poorer project in order to improve margins. The irony is that when using this model, it is possible to create a "successful" project that does not attempt to directly satisfy the customer. While the company will be pleased with the result, the customer could end up with a project that is sub-standard.

2) the potential to develop adversarial relationships with contractors. A common problem that underlies the "contractor-subcontractor" relationship is the desire of the various "subs" to squeeze every last drop of profit out of the contracted relationship. The irony is that this difficulty chiefly arises from prejudicial attitudes by both the contractor and the subs. When the up front assumption from the project contractor is that all subs are out to gain as great an advantage as possible, at the expense of the contractor, it causes contractors to go into a project relationship with a firm degree of distrust. From this point, any disagreements with subcontractors merely solidifies, in their minds, this preconceived attitude.

3) the habit of treating all project relationships as "short term," rather than focusing on long-term partnership building. A common result from the traditional success approach is to treat each project as a discrete operation. To a degree, there is nothing wrong with this mentality - certainly projects are one-shot activities. However, the more important long-term relationships between customers and contractors are then often ignored. Once a subcontractor has completed its phase of

the project, communication breaks down and both parties go their own ways. This "transaction" orientation approach to customer-client relationships promotes the fragmentation of a firm's business activities and relationships into short-term expediency. The results promote an environment of "quick marriage and early divorce" between the contractor and customer.

As a result of the drawbacks with traditional project success assessment, ARO has shifted its focus to including customer satisfaction as a fourth success constraint. The inclusion of customer satisfaction acknowledges a fundamental truth in project-based firms: "successful projects" are only truly successful if they are seen that way through the eyes of the customer. The obvious benefit from this thinking is that it naturally moves ARO toward a externally-focused mindset, rather than reinforcing excessive concern for internal control processes based on simply adhering to the triple constraint.

ARO'S GOALS

ARO's interest in developing their customer-based project success evaluation system is derived from three important issues:

1) There is a perception within the organization that ARO does not possess enough real information on customer satisfaction. Generally, this information is informal or anecdotal, often going through several levels before reaching the management team at ARO. They need to get better, more timely, comprehensive, and objective data on satisfaction.

2) ARO wants to better understand customer needs. Through a more complete understanding of customer-based project evaluation, they can get a clear sense of the core dimensions that customers hold dear (as discussed with Value Chain Analysis).

3) Developing a well-performing evaluation process will also have beneficial effects through establishing ARO more favorably in the minds of their customer base. In effect, this process will give ARO significantly more favorable "brand image" with clients.

The above points are based on ARO's perception that in a highly competitive industry, superior products go hand-in-hand with superior service. Their goal is long-term viability: something that can only be achieved through working to maintain positive relationships with present and past customers in order to develop future business opportunities. It was with this philosophy firmly in mind that ARO has set out on a unique approach to better understanding how project success and their success are inextricably linked to customer satisfaction.

VALUE CHAIN ANALYSIS

In exploring ARO's motivations for establishing customer-based project success metrics, it is useful to refer to Michael Porter's (1985) Value Chain Model. Value Chain Analysis suggests that companies can compete most effectively if they clearly understand how they help create value to their customer's business activity cycle. To be successful, value chain analysis requires an organization to not only understand its own strengths and weaknesses, but those of potential customers. In this manner, they are better able to address and appeal to the most critical aspect in the customer's business operations. For example, ARO routinely engages in value chain analysis in order to tailor their project bidding to areas in which they can significantly enhance their clients' operations, through developing the delivery process of the spar hull and mooring system in a manner and for a price that gives the oil company an advantage over using alternative methods or competing contractor firms.

There are four distinct steps in performing a value chain analysis:

Step 1) Construct the value chain of the client. It is imperative that the subcontractor organization clearly understand their role in the customer's value chain. Each firm is composed of a sequence, or chain of activities, beginning with inputs bought from suppliers and ending with delivery to the customer, and after-sales support (See Figure 1). Activities define the process by which a firm creates value through transforming raw materials into finished goods or services. It is important to note that it is possible to attain competitive advantage in any activity in the chain; it is not necessary that all activities be superior to the competition. Figure One shows a simplified value chain for an oil company customer of ARO. Note that ARO's contribution to this company's value chain lies primarily within its operations activities - ARO provides superior quality and lower total costs and risk by effectively managing the engineering, design and fabrication of the spar hull and mooring system used in offshore oil exploration and extraction.

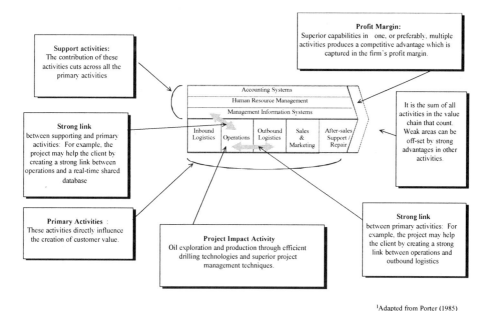

[1]Adapted from Porter (1985)

Figure 1. Value Chain Analysis[1]

Step 2) Identify activities and linkages that are superior compared to the competition. Activities in which the client has a cost advantage over the competition and activities that allow the client to produce a unique product or service are drivers of competitive advantage. It is important to discover whether the customer firm is driven primarily by low cost or product or service differentiation advantage. Understanding the customer's focus will enable the project organization to appreciate the project's impact and help guide choices which best fit the client's strategy. At the same time, project sub-contractors (e.g., ARO) need to engage in a straightforward assessment of their own strengths and weeknesses to ensure a close fit between what they do well and what the customer seeks. ARO has been highly successful in working with its customers to ensure that the operations and outbound logistics of oil field development are cost effective while maintaining a strong emphasis on quality.

Step 3) Identify activities and linkages that are inferior compared to the competition. These activities are a drag on the performance of the firm. For each inferior activity, a superior activity is necessary to offset the effect. Overall performance is enhanced when these activities are improved to, at the very least, meet the capability of the competition. Finally, it is important to note that a successful project need not create a competitive advantage. It can be equally effective through eliminating a disadvantage. As long as the client has a source of advantage in other activities, they will reap superior returns when the comparative disadvantage is corrected.

Step 4) Target activities and linkages with high potential for impact. Communicate to the client project options and alternatives, in order to "fit" the project to:

- improve activities to create a new competitive advantage(s)
- enhance existing competitive advantage(s)
- improve activities to eliminate competitive disadvantage(s)

Step 4 becomes the key starting point to developing a protocol for partnering with clients in order to enhance their business operations. The better able the project organization is at helping customers increase competitive advantage, the greater their own strategic position becomes vis-à-vis their competitors. In effect, ARO seeks to give other oil companies a compelling reason to select them as a sub-contractor.

One important key to ARO's success lies in their ability to offer the client organization competitive advantage through its own commitment to project excellence. This is accomplished in two ways: first, by viewing project success through the clients' eyes, rather than based simply on historical parameters of time, budget, and specification. Secondly, ARO actively seeks to redefine itself as a partner, rather than simple subcontractor. This partner relationship is reinforced by the attention they pay to the overall project, rather than simply their contracted sub-component. For example, in developing design and engineering aspects of the spar hull, ARO also looks to improve the overall project through close collaboration with other subcontractors (those developing riser systems, topside works, etc.) to give the customer enhanced value. This relentless pursuit of project excellence is based on a corporate philosophy which suggests that where the technology is to a great extent undifferentiated, what characterizes competitive advantage is often superior service through project development in active partnership with client firms.

THE CUSTOMERS AND THEIR NEEDS

From ARO's point of view, the "Customer" is seen as a set of stakeholders consisting of multiple levels. The levels nearest to ARO are the site team and the project team. Above these are the project management and upper management levels. Behind these direct interfaces there is the end user who eventually will make use of the project. Typically ARO is communicating during the project with the site team, project team, project management group, and to some extent, with members of upper management. After the project has been delivered the contacts to the customer are limited to discussions concerning possible new contracts.

In discussing customer satisfaction, we will divide the project life cycle into three phases: 1) sales, 2) execution, and 3) operation. The project's life cycle will typically last from 3 to 4 years. The complete life of the product (drilling and production platform) is 20 - 30 years. During the sales phase, ARO is normally competing with other firms in bidding the project. During this time customer expectations are built based on both the end product and the project execution process itself. Experience has shown that to win an order, in addition to having a competitive price, it is also important to reduce the customer's risk contingency by demonstrating the sophisticated project execution procedures employed. By the end of the sales phase, both these customer expectations have been built up to the point the contract is signed. During this phase there is an important step in the customer relations process: distinguishing between generating expectations and meeting expectations. One could reasonably argue that the goal of contract development is to create a set of positive expectations in the mind of customers - what the project can and cannot do, how we will do it, what performance criteria you can expect from us, and so forth.

There is a natural phenomenon present when establishing a project development relationship with a contractor. The phenomenon refers to the nature of customer expectations and attitudes across the project life cycle. Early in most projects, there is typically a positive relationship between all parties. The contract has been negotiated and signed and both the contractor and sub-contractors settle in to develop the product. During the execution phase, disagreements often begin to surface. Confusion over the initial contract terms come out, goals start to conflict, and members of both the contractor and sub-contractors start to maneuver for maximum advantage vis á vis the other project partners. As a result, initial expectations, set so high, begin to crumble. Bickering and arguing set in and the project's atmosphere become more adversarial. While some readers would argue that this is a natural side-effect of contractor - sub-contractor relationships, ARO believes that there is a better way: working to maintain positive relations throughout the development process through strong communications and a commitment to customer satisfaction.

Customer satisfaction in the contract stage hinges on ARO's ability to create positive and reasonable expectations in the minds of customers. During the balance of contract performance (execution and delivery), the company's primary goal naturally shifts to meeting these expectations. Consequently, a key to good customer relations is to create a clear set of deliverables during the contracting stage that can be met during the project's subsequent life cycle. While this point may seem obvious on the surface, it is important to note that within many organizations, particularly when internal communications between marketing and engineering are poor, it is common to inflate initial expectations too high based on questionable promises. The project team then is doomed to spend the balance of the project fending off requests and complaints from an increasingly disillusioned customer who correctly perceives that they were sold a lie during the contracting phase.

RESEARCH PROTOCOL

Creating a customer-based project success metric has involved several steps. ARO company members have been actively pursuing an agenda based on the following discrete phases:

1) Getting a list of key informants from the major customers. The list of key informants consists of those individuals knowledgeable enough and qualified to comment on the various activities of ARO and give their opinions as to the effectiveness of these activities. Some of these individuals may be high ranking members of the customer organizations and others are key project management personnel.

2) Asking these key informants about their decision process and criteria. ARO eschews simply holding post-project "lessons learned" feedback sessions in favor of a series of regular meetings with customers. While feedback conferences may yield good information for better project management in the future, their biggest flaw is that they allow no opportunities for process improvement to an ongoing project. ARO's preference for concurrent project control allows them to get answers to some fundamental questions, including: What are their key values and success criteria? What are their key concerns? How can ARO continue to satisfy their needs? What is ARO doing today that could be done better tomorrow? How does ARO operate to put itself at a strategic advantage with other competitors? These questions and their answers are key to understanding what specific decision criteria ARO's customers employ. Note that the intent of the questions asked at these meetings is not to simply adjudicate disagreements and "fire fight" current problems. Problem solving is important but the company also strongly feels that the best method for fixing problems is addressing and clearly understanding customer goals before misinterpretations lead to downstream problems.

3) Developing and refining the list of key issues. These issues are the key to ARO's continuing strategic advantage. They identify the areas that are important to customers, and ones they feel ARO performs either; a) well or, b) poorly relative to their competition. This list becomes the key starting point to developing an in-house Quality Assessment device that allows ARO to continually track future projects to

ensure that they are being developed in accordance with customer needs and expectations.

4) Deciding on measurement parameters. Once the list of key issues (critical success factors) has been developed, the next step is to determine the various parameters of actual data measurement. The key parameters revolve around the effective administration of the customer satisfaction measurement instrument. There are essentially three issues that required immediate attention:

a) Method - how should the data be measured? Should ARO employ a qualitative device based simply on interviews with customers? Should they use some "gap" measurement device to judge the difference between expected and actual results? It was subsequently determined that a combination of the two approaches was ideal. ARO is currently collecting data from customers that will allow a comprehensive questionnaire to be constructed for in-house quality control.

b) Timing - when should this information be collected? Clearly, it is necessary to do it at different points during the development process. There is little immediate benefit from getting the information about a finished project if it allows no opportunity for correction. On the other hand, it is also important to reflect on the appropriate points in the current project when this information is most useful. ARO's QA department can be most effective with this data if it is timely and "actionable" - meaning that the findings can lead to immediate corrective action. Part of the answer to the timing question lies in the length of the project undertaken. If, for example, a spar hull takes 18 months to design and fabricate, ARO will work with customers initially to address their chief concerns. Then, at various stages of project completion (e.g., engineering and design, procurement, fabrication), the organization assesses their own performance to date based on the identified key success factors. Likewise, these event points also allow the company to update customer expectations, answer questions, and strengthen communication links.

c) Feedback - how should the results be fed back to key personnel? As with the issue of timing mentioned above, it is vital that the data collected be done in a short period of time, that it be done concerning issues that are immediately relevant, and that it should be reported back in a timeframe that allows ARO to take corrective action, if necessary.

At present, the success measurement process is in operation. We are currently conducting the key interviews with site-team members from the contracting firm and assembling the important data that will be used to develop internal quality assessment protocols. The current timeframe calls for similar interviews to be conducted with other identified stakeholders constituencies within the client organization, including top management, engineering, QA, and operations. Once these interviews are completed, we will analyze the data in terms of similarities and differences that exist among the various constituency groups. To illustrate, for members of the client's site team, many satisfaction issues are related directly to the ease of transition into the local Finnish community for their families (e.g., schools, housing, and so forth). On the other hand, engineering groups are far more concerned with ARO's ability to response rapidly to exception reports and technical delays.

WHAT HAS ARO DISCOVERED?

Customer-based project success operates under a radically different philosophy from the traditional "triple constraint" approach to success assessment. While we have only been able to analyze preliminary findings based on interviews with one client firm, we have found some recurring themes. There are three important components of this philosophy:

1) The project organization must shift from a sub-contractor mentality to a partner mentality.

This shift will be difficult for both parties. It will require the main contractor to look upon these contracted firms as full partners in the project, having a vested interest in working with the lead firm in a collaborative effort to make the project succeed. Too often in the past, "sub-contractor" mentalities translated into sub-contractor attitudes, leading many firms to cut corners, withhold important information, resist full disclosure, and save costs in order to get the maximum advantage out of the contractor - sub-contractor relationship. Inevitably, this leads to an adversarial relationship rather than a partnering one. The lead contractor cannot fully trust the subs to operate for the good of the project rather than their own good. The subs automatically assume that they are not trusted, resent excessive oversight from the lead organization and the result is endless bickering, negotiating, and mistrust. Once the job is completed, the atmosphere may have become so fouled that neither party wants to work with the other again.

Creating a collaborative partnership redefines the nature of the relationship. Now, the former sub-contractors are treated as equal partners in the project's implementation. The goal for both sides is maintaining the basis for long-term relationships. When relationships are the goal, the mentality of both partners becomes helping rather than advantage seeking.

2) When customer satisfaction drives the process, everything else falls into place.

One of the biggest mistakes we continually make is to assume that schedule, cost, and performance will automatically create customer satisfaction. Our whole model is predicated on the idea that it is customer satisfaction that drives project development. Consider Figure 2.

The traditional model, which we have argued against, suggests that the better organizations manage the project internally, the greater the likelihood that it will be viewed positively by the customer. While this statement is highly arguable, an alternative model suggests that if our underlying goal is "external effectiveness;" that is, working to satisfy the customer, the other internal metrics will fall into place. Put another way, if our main driver is to satisfy the customer, we will do everything possible to adhere to mutually agreeable schedules and budgets, working to ensure that both the product and the project execution process meet specifications that will satisfy the customer.

One objection that is sometimes advanced states that too much concern for the customer will actually throw the project behind as we open the floodgates for endless rounds of change order requests and spec changes. Actually, while this might happen to a minor degree, it ignores the fact that the customer also wants the project completed in a timely fashion. If we are working with them in a collaborative partnership, are maintaining open channels of communication, and are seeking to develop trust, we will be able to overcome the difficulties related to change orders. Ultimately, the customer will begin to understand project tradeoffs from our perspective (our schedule and cost challenges) and work with us to mutually solve them. The key lies in redefining the nature of the relationship. We are not adversaries, we are long-term partners.

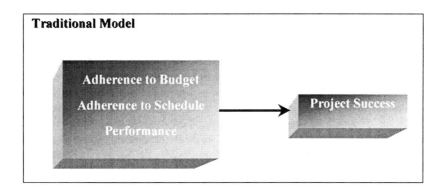

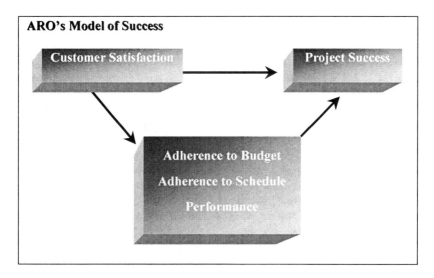

Figure 2. Traditional versus ARO's View of Project Success

The other benefit of such a partnering mentality is that it sows the seeds for long-term relationships. When customers understand our unique mentality of working to please them as our main motivation, they also begin to look on the relationship in a different way. Now, instead of constantly battling for percentages and minor advantages, both parties come to value the relationship itself, perceiving that in it lies the key to a longer-term, positive working climate.

3)   The key to in-process course corrections is possessing "real time" data from customers.

Too often, customer satisfaction consists mainly of post-project review sessions, such as "Lessons Learned" meetings. While the obvious benefit is that it gives us a chance to learn what we did wrong, the main drawback is that this approach gives the project organization no opportunities to correct these problems. To use an American idiom, it is the equivalent of closing the barn door after the horse has bolted. Yes, we can learn from these points for future projects but cannot do anything about them for the current one just completing.

ARO's goal of better understanding customer needs consists of generating real time data on project quality. Indeed, the customer-based project success model will be blended in with other quality control measures used at ARO to maintain their high standards throughout the development process. The benefit to ARO's customers is that it maintains a formal feedback and corrections channel as part of the ongoing project implementation. Customer needs, suggestions, and concerns are solicited on a continuous basis in order to make sure that good relations persist, the project is doing what both parties understand it should be doing, and formal and informal communications are maintained.

CONCLUSIONS AND FUTURE RESEARCH

In an increasingly competitive business environment, organizations are seeking new and innovative methods for gaining advantage. Project organizations, faced with strong international competition and shrinking profit margins, must look for project management approaches that offer them a method for positioning themselves as both unique and offering a superior product. Customer-based project success is a technique that has been earmarked by ARO as a key to maintaining close and positive links to clients, not only for projects currently under development, but as a "leg up" for creating future business. While still in its early stages, preliminary results and reactions to their initiative have been very positive, with clients discovering ARO's willingness to go the extra mile for customer satisfaction.

Future research needs to continue to identify relevant stakeholder groups within client organizations and investigate their expectations – how they mirror and how they differ from other stakeholder groups within the organization. Further, it is necessary to answer the ultimate question: Whose opinions truly matter? That is, there is a strong likelihood that, just as multiple stakeholder constituencies have been identified, differences in opinion among these groups will emerge. The question then becomes finding the best method for determining whose opinions matter most. Second, is there an issue of timing that needs to be considered in addressing stakeholder needs? Some groups, such as the site team, require early attention to ensure their satisfaction with the working relationship, transition to a foreign country, and so on. On the other hand, engineering groups may not enter the equation until much further downstream, when technical problems begin to surface. As part of the research protocol for addressing customer-based success, it is necessary to map out a preliminary plan for dealing with the various client groups.

Finally, it will be necessary to continue to expand the work being done into value-chain analysis to determine how the company's various customers parallel and differ with each other. Value Chain Analysis offers an important method for enhancing customer satisfaction through addressing their supply chains. Ultimately, however, true customer satisfaction is likelier to emerge from making the necessary adjustments to address the differences in priorities of each customer. A generic model may not be a useful model. On the other hand, a satisfaction protocol that understands and best addresses the individualized needs of each customer offers a great deal of promise.

CHAPTER 9

THE MANAGEMENT OF PROJECTS AS A GENERIC BUSINESS PROCESS

Graham M. Winch, Bartlett School of Graduate Studies, University College London

ABSTRACT

Perspectives derived from business process analysis and reengineering have become very influential in management research and practice over the last few years. The proposition of the chapter will be that the management of projects is a generic business process across a large number of industrial sectors ranging from cars to construction, and film to pharmaceuticals, and that defining the management of projects in information processing terms is central to its more widespread acceptance as a key management discipline.

Drawing upon BT's multi-level approach to business process analysis, the chapter will identify five principal project processes - defining the project mission; mobilising the resource base; riding the project life-cycle; leading the project coalition; and maintaining the resource base. These will be illustrated by reference to a variety of case studies of managing projects in a variety of industries. In conclusion, the chapter will advocate the place of the management of projects amongst the existing business disciplines, and indicate the ways in which it is at the core of the issues in the management of innovation.

BUSINESS PROCESS ANALYSIS AND THE MANAGEMENT OF PROJECTS

One of the principal reasons for the wide impact of the various formulations of business process analysis (BPA) is the way in which they reconceptualise the firm as consisting of customer-orientated processes, rather than functionally structured tasks. Coombs and Hull (1997) and Davenport (1993) trace some of the lineages of this view, identifying from the standpoint of economics resource-based rather than environment-based perspectives on the firm, and from the standpoint of management the development of performance improvement programmes such as *kaizen* and total quality management (TQM). While many of the opportunities for radical re-engineering of business processes are derived from information technologies, business process analysis can be considered to be the more fundamental - in the sense of both essential and prior - partner to business process re-engineering (BPR).

The aim of this chapter is to combine this approach with the management of projects, and to argue that the contemporary approach to the management of projects has much in common with that of business process analysis. Moreover, many of the problems of poor performance that business process analysis is trying to solve are exactly those that the management of projects is also trying to solve. This is clear from Davenport's (1993 p 5) formulation of a business process as "a specific ordering of work activities across time and place, with a beginning, and end, and clearly identified inputs and outputs: a structure for action". However, the strength of a management of projects approach as opposed to the approach of business process analysts is its ability to handle equally intra- and inter-firm relationships along the entire value system. This chapter will firstly define the management of projects, and then go on to identify five first order project processes before drawing some concluding thoughts on the role of the management of projects in the innovation process.

What both BPA and the management of projects have in common is their critique of the traditional organisation of production around functionally organised capital and human resources where information and materials are passed sequentially from one to the other and finally to the customer. Attempts to improve the customer focus of the functional approach have led to organisation by product rather than by function, but this tends to compromise the efficiency of resource use. Matrix organisation developed in order to have the best of both these worlds, but is seen as unstable and conflictual, and not widely used. However, a version of the matrix form - project organisation - is well established in a number of industries, and the evidence is that its use has been spreading rapidly in the last 10 years (Whittington *et al. forthcoming*). Its main distinction from matrix organisation is that it is temporary in character (Bryman *et al.* 1987, Lundin and Söderholm 1995). While the life of a matrix organisation is normally indeterminate, the life of a project organisation is clearly determinate, normally with a delivery date identified as part of its declared objectives. The aim of a project organisation is to mobilise the capital and human resources required to meet a client's specific demands from the resource bases that hold them. These resource bases are usually either functional departments within the client firm, or independent specialist firms. Thus resource bases participate in portfolios of projects, and projects mobilise networks of resource bases.

The time component of project organisation lends a particular characteristic - a determinate life cycle. All projects consist of flows of information which define, initiate, and control flows of materials (Winch 1994). There is an inherent level of uncertainty at their inception, because projects are only mounted when an innovation is required, otherwise the client would purchase the good or service "off the shelf". These flows of information and materials can, therefore, be seen in information processing terms as a process of reducing uncertainty through time through the project life cycle. At project inception very high levels of uncertainty are experienced, but it is at this stage that most of the major decisions that will determine the performance of the project are taken. At project hand-over all the information that is required for the project is available, but it is too late to act upon this information. Here lies the principal paradox of the management of projects.

The contention here is not that all projects are the same, but that there is a generic form that can be called project organisation. It is worth articulating difference before emphasising commonality. A first distinction is between *innovation projects* and *implementation projects*. Innovation projects create new value in the sense of an exploitable asset - be it Spielbergs's *Saving Private Ryan*, Microsoft Office 2000, the Jaguar XK8 or the Boeing 777. Implementation projects create change, they reorganise, but they do not create new value in this sense. BPR projects are implementation projects; the discussion in this chapter will be of the similarities between BPA and innovation projects. A second distinction is between *capital projects* that possess real clients as articulators of demand, and *new product development projects* where the client is virtual. On capital projects, the government procures a nuclear submarine or a road; a company invests in a new oil rig or an information system. Without the command from the client, work does not start. On new product development projects, it is the marketing department which acts as a proxy client articulating the needs of the target body of customers. In both cases, the project itself remains a one-off activity; the principal difference is that on capital projects, manufacturing is also organised on a project basis, while on new product development projects, the project finishes with "Job 1", and volume production is organised on a mass or lean basis. The discussion will cover both types equally. Thirdly, the distinction can be made between *major projects* where the level of resources deployed is a significant proportion of total resources available, and *routine projects*. The definition here is relative - a major project for a small firm may be a routine project for a large one - the issue is the criticality of the project for the client organisation. The discussion here will tend towards the major project end of the spectrum.

Porter's (1985) notions of the value system and value chain have important business process aspects (Davenport 1993 p 30). The project process as the creation of new value is distinct from the exploitation of that new value, This new value takes the form of assets that can then be exploited through distribution processes such as for films, manufacturing processes in the volume manufacturing sectors such as cars, and various forms of service operations such as transport systems and hospitals exploiting constructed assets to deliver movement and health care respectively. The assets created may also move beyond use-values and take the form of cultural/symbolic assets such as the Millennium Dome or public assets such as defence systems. While projects create new value in the form of assets owned by clients, they also create value for the members of the project coalition. This value takes the form of both profits for firms participating in the project - indeed that is their principal incentive to participate in the project – and the generation of human resources in the sense of the learning gained from participating in an inherently innovative activity.

What all these project organisations have in common is that they operate in networks. Construction is often seen as the classic network industry, but volume industries such as cars also work in networks for their capital projects. For instance, 85% of the investment value for the Twingo project was spent externally to Renault, compared to the 70% spent on the external supply chain for its exploitation in manufacturing. (Midler 1993 p 151). Thus it is appropriate to talk of the network of independent firms participating in the project organisation as the *project coalition* which comes together on a temporary basis to achieve a specific end. Secondly, what they all have in common is the matrix structure described above, where the project organisation draws on the separate resource bases - be they internal or external to the client firm - for a predefined period to deliver value for the client. Thirdly, project organisations are not economic actors in their own right - they are capitalised by their clients, whose resources they use to recompense the resource bases. Fourthly, all projects can be abandoned before they have run their intended course. Obviously, the risks of this are greatest in the earlier stages, when less capital has been invested, but in some cases, particularly in areas such as pharmaceuticals, abandonment can come very late as a new drug fails to perform as expected in trials (Giard and Midler 1993 p 51).

Project-type organisations have a venerable history; what defines the management of projects is the emergence of separate organisations specialising in the coordination of the resource bases to meet the client's demand. This was first implemented at Pratt and Whitney in the 1930s (Womack and Jones 1996), and is strongly associated with the early post-war US defence and space programmes (Morris 1994). It is, therefore, essentially an organisational innovation, but it became more widely associated with the management tools that were developed by the US military project management offices - especially Critical Path Analysis for the control of programme, Work Breakdown Structure for the control of budget, and Earned Value Analysis for the reconciliation of programme and budget. Cost benefit analysis was developed within the World Bank from 1968 on as a project appraisal tool. On this basis, the discipline of project management developed and diffused as "a collection of organizational, schedule, and cost-control tools - a largely middle-management intra-organizational skill" (Morris 1994 p 104) embodied in the various project management Bodies of Knowledge. For this reason, Morris prefers the term "management of projects" to capture the entire range of challenges of managing projects.

The management of projects is practised at three distinct levels within the project coalition (Winch 1994 chap 8). This first level is that of the *project manager* who manages the team within the resource base which is allocated to the project. At NASA, project managers in charge of each of the Shuttle sub-systems report to the *program manager* (Vaughan 1996). This term is typical in the aerospace industry, and also used in Ford (Walton 1997). Other terms for this function include the *acteur-projet* (Giard and Midler 1993), *shusa* at Toyota (Womack *et al.* 1990) and Vehicle Director in Rover. The program manager works at the level of the firm as a whole, ensuring effective project management across all the resources within the firm. The third level is the *prime contractor* which is responsible to the client for the delivery of the entire project ready for exploitation. Other terms for this role are systems integrator (Miller *et al.* 1995) and the construction manager in US and UK construction. The prime contractor may be a wholly owned subsidiary of the firm providing many of the key resource bases, as is normal in aerospace and power engineering or it may be an independent firm as is more commonly the case in construction. Not all project coalitions all three levels - new product development projects typically only have the first two, but prime contracting is becoming increasingly important in capital and defence project coalitions.

There is some debate about the number of business processes an organisation can have. The approach adopted here is that of BT (cited in Davenport 1993 chap 2), who identify five first order processes (Manage the Business; Manage People and Work; Serve the Customer; Run the Network and Support the Business). They then identify some 15 second order business process within these five. The following sections will draw upon the body of empirical studies on the management of projects to identify five first order project processes (Winch 1996b) - Defining the Project Mission; Mobilising the Resource Base; Riding the Project Life-Cycle; Leading the Project Coalition; and Maintaining the Resource Base.

DEFINING THE PROJECT MISSION

The identification of a clear mission for the project is widely considered to be essential for the effective management of projects. Yet this is difficult for two sets of very good reasons. Firstly, the cognitive horizon of strategic decision makers is usually shorter than the lead times of major projects, and quantitative planning tools cannot provide more than a rudimentary basis for decision. Elapsed project time in cars averages 4.5 years (Clark and Fujimoto 1991 table 4.1); in pharmaceuticals, it averages 12 years (Giard and Midler 1993 p 40), and 4 to 8 years in biotechnology (Powell *et al.* 1996). Thus the chances of the potential market for the product under development having changed dramatically by the time it is delivered are high. In some cases, such as the Trans-Alaska Pipeline, where the OPEC embargo broke the environmental opposition to the project (Morris 1994 chap 6), or the Channel Tunnel where the late eighties boom in international travel allowed the continual upward revision of the revenue estimates in order to cope with the cost increases (Winch 1996), this was to the advantage of the project. More often, it is to its disadvantage.

Secondly, the complexity of client organisations themselves, and the regulatory environments in which they exist, coupled with the absence of adequate quantitative project appraisal tools, means that strategic definition of the project mission is inevitably politicised, and many project goals are the outcomes of complex negotiations and trade-offs. The case studies by Hall (1980) show how decision-making around public sector projects is a complex trade-off between political, social, and economic interests, while Law and Callon (1992) pun the description of the TSR2 as a "variable geometry" aircraft due to the way in which it meant different things to different stakeholders. More recently, such a trade-off has become even more difficult with the emergence of principled, as opposed to local loser, opposition on environmental grounds and the consequent placing of the legitimacy of existing fora for handling such decisions in question. In such cases the trade-off process itself can be a major project management exercise in its own right, as the planning enquiry into Heathrow's Terminal 5 shows. For development aid projects, such issues can be particularly difficult, and can even question the viability of project-type organisational model (Russell-Hodge and Hunnam 1998)

These problems are, perhaps, most severe in the realm of the provision of public assets, for no clear economic criteria for the supply and distribution of such assets exist (Hall 1980:189). Some projects, such as Mitterand's *grands projets* appear to be entirely politically driven (Chaslin 1985). The budgetary instability generated by financing decade long projects on annual budget rounds vitiated the US weapons acquisition programme in the 1980s (Morris 1994 chap 7), as the case of the Honeywell torpedo shows (Scudder *et al.* 1989); it has been disastrous in the case of the British Library (NAO 1990). One solution to this problem has been to privatise such projects through the development of concession contracting, which in turn has led to the rapid recent increase in the project finance market. The effect of this is that financiers become direct stakeholders in the management of the project, and the allocation of risks associated with the project a matter for complex negotiation (Beidleman *et al.* 1990). In nationalised enterprises project decision making becomes politicised through conflicting public policy and profitability criteria. In both BL and Renault, decision-making around the Metro (Willman and Winch 1985) and the Twingo (Midler 1993) became politicised as trade union concerns for job protection and the future of the company were articulated.

Purely private sector projects face similar problems. The context of the Eagle project was politicised within Data General as the company moved its research and development functions from Boston to North Carolina (Kidder 1982). Kodak's Factory of the Future project was abandoned as a coherent vision that met the interests of all the stakeholders could not be articulated (Bowen *et al.* 1994 chap 12). The London Stock Exchange's Taurus project threatened the very existence of the registrars who keep records of share deals by proposing a central register. A compromise reached in 1989 provided for a decentralised system, but at the cost of a much higher level of complexity. Coupled with regulatory demands for high levels of security, and opposition from small stockbrokers who feared the system would reinforce the dominance of the large banks, this led its abandonment (*Financial Times* 10/12/90; 12/3/93; see also Drummond 1996). As the former chief executive of the Stock Exchange stated, "Taurus meant an awful lot of different things to different people, it was the absolute lack of clarity as to its definition at the front that I think was its Achilles' heel" (*Financial Times* 3/7/95).

MOBILISING THE RESOURCE BASE

The essence of the management of projects is to manage the mobilisation of resources towards the successful accomplishment of the project mission. Those resources must be scoped, procured and motivated. Scoping is the identification of all the tasks that must be completed in order to achieve the project mission, the levels of performance required in those tasks, and the resources that will be required to complete those tasks. Poor scoping can lead to problems later on. For instance, the channel tunnel was, in essence, scoped as a civil engineering project. This was reflected in the formation of the coalition which built the tunnel - Transmanche Link - and the background of those appointed as senior project managers. This meant that the importance of commissioning the facility was underestimated - commissioning is unimportant in civil engineering projects, but vital in integrated system projects such as railways - and became a major source of the time overrun which undermined the financial viability of a project already suffering major cost overruns (Winch 1996).

Project performance is usually measured in terms of time, cost and quality, but quality in this formulation is usually defined in terms of conformance. This can be traced back to the Atlas programme, where the specification of the weapons system was separated off from its delivery, leading to a cycle of overengineering which has dogged advanced technology projects ever since (Morris 1994 chap 4). The problem also bedevils construction where the establishment of the specification by the architect or engineer is seen as a pre-project activity prior to delivery by the contractor, with similar results to those in defence. The separation of the specification of the level of project task performance from its resourcing leads to overengineering, and as a result, time and cost escalation.

The motivation of the resource bases who are the holders of the required resources is central to project performance. Relations between actors in project networks may be based upon cost-plus contracts, lump sum contracts, or incentive-based contracts. Whichever is chosen, the problem remains that of contracting under high levels of uncertainty. Cost-plus has long been favoured in defence contracts, but fails to motivate the supplier to minimise the cost of the product. Lump-sum contracts were tried under the Total Package Procurement policy launched in US defence procurement in 1966. The results were disastrous, and many were converted to cost-plus contracts as contractors sustained massive losses. The reverse of this situation occurred with the Bloodhound project in the UK - the contractor made such massive profits that the contractor was obliged to repay 85% of them after a public outcry in 1964 (Morris 1994 chap 5). Lump sum contracts made under high levels of uncertainty mean that whether price formed through a competitive tender bears a close relationship to the outturn cost is more a matter of luck rather than judgement. One solution is to leave the formation of the fixed price until very late in the project life-cycle - as happens in traditional construction contracts - and to cope with any remaining uncertainties through after-measurement. The problem with this is the longer project life-cycles, higher overall cost, and tendency towards overengineering that this generates. These problems are not restricted to inter-firm project coalitions, and many new product development projects are developing "internal contracts" between the resource bases internal to the client firm (Nakhla and Soler 1996).

Usually, some form of incentive contract needs to be established which shares risks and rewards between the parties. Just as the under the influence of Japanese production methods, transaction governance within the supply chain is shifting from transactional to relational contracting, project coalitions are seeking new ways of governing transactions. In cars there is a shift from subcontracting to co-contracting where price is no longer the key variable in the relationship but merely the starting point for it (Midler 1993; Womack *et al.* 1990). In many sectors, the traditional way to govern transactions within the project value system has been a low trust one involving complex contract forms (Stinchcombe and Heimer 1985). This has led to a pervasive problem of adversarial relations as the parties try to cope with the uncertainties of project performance within the rigidities of contracts. The response to this has been the shift to partnering, in an attempt to generate bilateral, and hence flexible, transaction governance in a higher trust atmosphere (Barlow *et al.* 1997; Garel and Kessler 1998, Laigle 1998). A remarkable example of this has been the Cost Reduction in the New Era (CRINE) programme in the North Sea oil and gas industry (www.crine-network.com; Knott 1996).

RIDING THE PROJECT LIFE-CYCLE

This is the process that traditionally formed the core of project management, and it remains central to the *management of projects*. Projects are defined in time, and the nature of the tasks to be done changes as uncertainty is progressively reduced. There are a number of models of the project life-cycle; the one offered by Giard and Midler (1993 chap 2) has the merit of clarity and wide applicability. Phase 1 is a period of concept generation and broad search - evaluating a large number of potential ways of achieving the project mission - at Ford it terminates with Theme Decision (Walton 1997). Phase 2 stabilises the project definition as one option is developed for taking forward into the next phase. Phase 3 is project realisation. On new product development projects this consists of designing the manufacturing process and getting to job 1; on capital projects, this phase continues right through manufacture or construction to the hand-over of the competed product. In both cases the exploitation process follows. Wheelwright and Clark (1992 chap 5) and Winch and his colleagues (1998) emphasise the importance of the decision-making screens which terminate each phase, and provide the criteria for the project to continue to the next – Cooper (1992) calls this the stage-gate process in new product development. Thus, the task of the management of projects is to delay decisions as long as possible during inception, to accelerate them as much as possible during realisation, and to enable clear and concise choice at project definition, balancing all the while strategy and tactics over the life cycle (Slevin and Pinto 1987). The principal paradox of the management of projects lies in this life-cycle - at inception, very high levels of uncertainty are experienced, but it is at this stage that most of the major decisions that will determine the performance of the project are taken. At project hand-over all the information that is required for the project is available, but it is too late to act upon this information.

Once a project is under way it can take on a life of its own. Drummond (1996) reports in detail how the London Stock Exchange's Taurus project became virtually unstoppable until it had absorbed vast resources. The escalation of decision-making on that project was the result of interaction between the structure of power which failed to define and sustain a clear project mission, the dynamic interplay between the stakeholders in the project all defending their own interests; and the uncertainty generated by the technological challenges of computerising the share settlement system. In such situations, project managers focus on getting the project delivered, rather than worrying about whether it is worth delivering. This encourages project managers to move to the realisation phases early in order to sink capital in the project, relying upon the reluctance of investors to admit losses and the temptation to try to reduce them by investing further funds (Bernstein 1997 chap 9; Conlon and Garland 1993). Thus the project manager of Denmark's Storebælt link believed that "we had to have the concrete on the table in a hurry" (cited Bonke 1998 : 10) before too many politicians had second thoughts, while much of the early effort in the Channel Tunnel was focused on spending enough money to minimise the risk of the project being cancelled should Labour have won the 1987 general election in the UK (Fetherston 1997).

Time compression is increasingly a major competitive capability (Stalk and Hout 1990). There are various ways of doing this, but all have the effect of steepening the angle of the project information flow S-curve. The first is to reduce the ambition of each project, while increasing the number of projects in an overall capital programme. The keys to this are the development of robust as opposed to lean designs (Gardiner and Rothwell 1985) which allow the development of families of products sharing common a common platform, and taking new technology development out of the project process, so that technological uncertainties are reduced. The case of Sony (Sanderson 1992; Stalk and Hout 1990) illustrates both these tactics in operation. Proceeding by small steps rather than big leaps leads to higher rates of innovation overall within the total programme of projects. Reducing the project life cycle in this way further reduces uncertainty as the strategic horizon is brought closer and the chances of unforeseen events overwhelming the project are reduced.

A second way of reducing elapsed time is the overlapping of project phases. Attempts in the sixties to introduce such concurrency in weapons systems acquisition led to escalating cost growth as major commitments of funds were made on the basis of inadequately defined projects (Morris 1994 chap 6), however the development of concurrent engineering techniques – Charue-Duboc and Midler (1998) review its implementation at Rhône-Poulenc – is allowing greater time to be spent in engineering development while reducing project lead times overall. Research in construction (Fazio *et al.* 1988) showed that one key to enabling such overlaps was the effective scoping of the project into relatively independent packages of tasks which could proceed in parallel as sequentially organised mini-projects - an approach known as fast-tracking. Another aid to concurrency is this increasing the bandwidth of the information flows between the upstream engineering resource bases and downstream manufacturing ones (Clark and Fujimoto 1991 chap 8, Winch 1994).

The third way is to put more intensive engineering effort into the first phase relative to the third. One of the principal differences between US and Japanese product development programmes is the timing of engineering changes - the Japanese make a lot early; the Americans make them later. The result is that American ones are much more disruptive and costly (Clark and Fujimoto chap 8). Rapid prototyping is an important way to reduce engineering changes, thereby speeding up the project and reducing total costs. On IT projects this involves making quick and dirty versions of the final product so that the client can interact with it and provide feedback on its functionality and user-friendliness. In product development projects, this involves making both physical prototypes and mock-ups which allow manufacturing to iron out manufacturability problems as early as possible (Bowen *et al.* 1994 chap 7). Similarly, Eisenhardt and Tabrizi (1995) found that in the most dynamic environments many rapid design iterations with frequent testing of proposals were required.

LEADING THE PROJECT COALITION

The management of projects literature strongly emphasises the role of leadership in the management of projects – Gaddis (1959) provides a classic statement - but the range of skills required cannot usually be contained in one person. Project leadership is usually leadership of the prime contracting or program management team. These leaders do two things - manage the project context to ensure the continued flow of funds and minimise opposition, and continually re-articulate the project mission so as to infuse it throughout the network of resource bases. Raborn used PERT to convince to convince the US Navy and Government that the project was running smoothly, not as an internal project management tool (Morris 1994 p 31). Kennedy deliberately appointed Webb as someone familiar with Capitol Hill, rather than an engineer or scientist to head NASA to ensure continuing congressional support (Sayles and Chandler 1993); Morton, a banker, was appointed to Eurotunnel to generate the commitment of the banks to funding the tunnel (Winch 1996).

Leading the project coalition is not something that can be done by edict alone. Continuous and intensive face to face communication between the members of the programme team and the project teams in the resource bases is essential to deepen understanding and reinforce the message (Clark and Fujimoto 1994 chap 9). Walton (1997) captures well the ceaseless activity required by the program manager to keep the project on course. Articulating the voice of the client and the project mission throughout the project coalition presents considerable challenge, for the resource bases rarely have a direct relationship to the client. In such networks, it is typically the product itself as the manifestation of the client's requirements that gives meaning to each project coalition member's contribution and charters the network. Thus what unites the actors on a construction project is the school or bridge which provides a source of pride one the project is over. This focus on the product can become pathological as the client itself disappears from view and the project becomes a vehicle for the resource bases' own definitions of product excellence rather than the client's, but it is principally the shared vision of the product which drives the process. Vaughan's (1996) fascinating study of NASA's Shuttle programme well demonstrates how this pathology is generated by the engineering dominated culture of many projects.

Teamworking is similarly a touchstone of the management of projects, but teams are limited in the capacity of the amount of work they can do - no authority cites more than 20 people as the optimum number for a team. All but the smallest projects are, in effect composed of a number of different teams, and the key issue is the nature of the relationship between the resource-base teams and the program management or prime contracting team. In the literature on new product development projects for new product development, the debate has been cast around lightweight and heavyweight management of projects. Under lightweight management of projects the resource bases retain full authority over resources, and the programme management team are little more than co-ordinators. Under heavyweight management of projects, the programme management team reports direct to senior management, and shares authority with the resource base managers (Clark and Fujimoto 1991 chap 9). In cell project organisation, the programme manager has full authority over the resources for the life of the project. Informal cells were known as skunk works at Lockheed (Stalk and Hout 1990 chap 4), and Kidder's study of Data General describes the classic strengths and weakness of cell organisation. Lightweight management of projects fails to effectively overcome functional barriers to lateral coordination, while the cell presents difficulties of re-integration into the overall organisation when the project is over (Winch 1994 chap 8). The evidence is accumulating that the heavyweight management of projects is the most effective form of project organisation (Bowen *et al.* 1994 chap 5). Midler (1995) traces its implementation at Renault, and it was adopted in the Ford 2000 reorganisation of 1995.

MAINTAINING THE RESOURCE BASE

Projects are about mobilising resources to meet client needs, but the stock of those resources needs to be maintained ready for mobilisation within the resource bases – it is here that knowledge is held (Nonaka 1994). In industries such as construction, the strong project orientation has beggared the resource base over the years, leading to underinvestment in resource renewal. These resources are of two kinds - human and technical. Human resources need to be recruited and developed by the resource containers - be they functional departments or specialist firms – and the demands of working project organisations can challenge traditional notions of careers (Jones 1996). Typically, these resources are high grade professional skills such as engineers, but may also include craft operatives such as toolroom workers, clay modellers, or carpenters and bricklayers. The development of such specialist skills requires a critical mass of fellow specialists to ensure currency of expertise and co-learning. Cells can lead to the decay of specialist skills and production engineers who have spent too long allocated to product development teams loose track of the latest developments in the capability of the factory (Winch 1994 chap 8). Thus it is essential that the now of projects provides space for engineers to work in a functional environment to renew their specialist skills.

Technical resources present even more of a problem. One of the principal reasons why projects fail to achieve their mission is that they attempt too much innovation. This has led many commentators to argue that research and development activities should be off-project, that the technology policy of the firm should be to develop a stock of component technologies ready for application on projects. However, it is difficult to effectively focus technology development in the absence of a known application, and there is a tendency to starve development of funds in the absence of an immediate return. One solution to this is the mounting of client-free experimental projects such as concept cars which provide the disciplines of project organisation without the costs associated with project failure (Midler 1993).

Perhaps the greatest challenge that maintaining the resource base presents is learning between projects. The techniques used for riding the project life-cycle enhance intra-project organisation learning but there is a real risk that the learning will be dissipated and lost to future projects and the same mistakes will be repeated. Winch found that post-projects reviews were rare (1994 p 100), while Bowen and his colleagues (1994 chap 9) found that on the few occasions that they were used, little learning took place. They argue that every project should have two missions - the first to successfully develop the product, and second to advance the learning of the client organisation.

Of growing concern to a number of firms – particularly in new product development - is the problem of managing the portfolio of projects. Brown and Eisenhardt (1997) argue that the key to the successful management of the relationships between projects is time-pacing - launching projects on regular cycles so that human resources transfer smoothly between assignments, and people are neither idle, nor projects starved of resources. Cusumano and Nobeoka (1998) argue that failure to pay attention to the relationships between projects can lead to "fat" designs which, in effect, reinvent solutions when they could borrow from other projects.

THE MANAGEMENT OF PROJECTS, KNOWLEDGE AND NETWORKS

The management of projects in the procurement of weapons systems has been described as "a particularly black art" (*Financial Times* 13/10/94), while car design has characterised as "a business of smoke and mirrors... a business that appeals to us for emotion" (Walton 1997 p xvii) and the relationship between effective management of project processes and overall business success remains unclear. Those that are well managed, such as Canary Wharf, can turn out to be disasters for their clients as the market for the value being created collapses, and appallingly managed projects such as the making of *Apocalypse Now!* (Bahr and Hickenlooper 1991) will continue to be runaway successes as the new value they create strikes a wide chord. Much further research is needed to unravel the complex dynamic of project processes, although a start has been made by Morris and Hough (1987); Kharbanda and Stallworthy (1983); and Kharbanda and Pinto (1996). Perhaps one way forward might be to define the mission of the management of projects as the minimisation of client surprise (Winch *et al.* 1998).

MBA teaching on project management tends to be confined to a chapter in the operations management syllabus (e.g. Slack *et al.* 1995), while research tends to be the preserve of engineering and built environment schools, yet, as this chapter has hopefully demonstrated, the management of projects is central to most contemporary business management. The *management of projects* can be characterised in the following manner:

- treating projects holistically from inception to completion, not focusing merely on the realisation phase;

- treating the front-end definition of the project mission as a strategic decision involving multiple stakeholders;
- focusing on sharing risk and reward through gain-sharing between the project coalition members;
- program managers with heavyweight status;
- time-paced management, balancing strategy and tactics through the life-cycle;
- maintaining the resource bases through capturing the knowledge generated on the project, and actively managing the portfolio of projects.

This perspective on the management of projects enables the integration of two of the major themes in the current literature on innovation - knowledge management and innovation networks. Authorities on knowledge management (Nonaka 1996) stress the role of project teams as the "field" of knowledge creation, but this perspective is limited to the single firm, while it is usually the project as a network of firms that is the field of knowledge creation where project management is the "point of passage" between the "global network" of innovating firms, and the "local network" mobilised for a specific innovation (Law and Callon 1992). This is particularly true of the complex systems industries (Hobday 1998, Miller *et al.* 1996;), characterised by emergent and systemic technologies, or in industries such as biotechnology and film where technology or taste is changing so rapidly that no one organisation can generate all the knowledge required for innovation and success (Powell *et al.* 1996; DeFilippi and Arthur 1998). Thus the project coalition is the network through which information flows when the stocks of knowledge held in the resource bases are mobilised, and hence the means by which those stocks are renewed through learning from the project experience.

The aim of this review has been to show how the *management of projects* is central to the management of technology and innovation in a wide variety of industrial sectors, and five first order business processes have been identified. On the basis of the argument above it can be proposed that there are at least two fundamental types of business process - repetitive business processes associated with the exploitation of assets, and one-off project processes which create the new value embodied in those assets. Projects are the principal means by which society deliberately creates new value, be it consumer, capital, public, or cultural assets. These assets are then exploited in another whole set of business processes of a repetitive kind, but there is no doubt that the effectiveness of these repetitive processes - which are the usual focus of attention in management research - is a function of upon the prior creation of the assets upon which those processes depend through the management of projects. It follows that the effective management of projects is central to both competitive success and the success of broader political programmes to enhance the quality of life.

However, our knowledge of the management of projects is still too fragmented. This chapter has indicated the range of issues that can be considered to be within its scope, yet the literature upon which I have drawn is written from a wide variety of perspectives which are, at times, contradictory. Yet, as I hope I have indicated, there is the possibility of generating a coherent management discipline which provides a robust framework for the better understanding of how firms and societies purposely create new value. Although this is mainly through the mobilisation of engineering resources, many projects have the deployment of artistic resources at the core of their missions – building, film, and theatre can all benefit from the sensitive application of the principles of the management of projects (c.f. Hartman *et al.* 1998). The real challenge lies in bringing finance together with engineering and artistic human resources through the management of projects to create the new values upon which society will depend for its security and success in the new millennium.

Acknowledgements: I am grateful to Andrew Edkins, David Kincaid, Christophe Midler, Peter Morris, and Chris Voss who have all been kind enough to read earlier drafts. Various versions have also been presented at *British Academy of Management* 1996 (Aston) and 1997 (London), *International Research Network of Organization by Projects III* 1998 (Calgary), and at seminars held by the ESRC's Business Process Resource Centre. I am also grateful to participants in those meetings for their contributions and criticisms. Final responsibility for the chapter, of course, rests with myself.

PROJECTS FOR INNOVATION AND CHANGE

CHAPTER 10

REFLECTIONS ON THE CHANGING NATURE OF PROJECTS

John Whittaker, University of Alberta, Edmonton, Alberta, Canada

ABSTRACT

As we have moved from building great physical monuments such as the pyramids to ethereal constructions like computer operating systems, the nature of project management changes. In pyramid construction progress could be observed, and resources could be added, substituted and transferred. In software construction progress is difficult to measure, workers often know more than their supervisors, and adding resources can sometimes extend the completion time. Further, projects that are late, with major flaws and unprecedented cost over-runs, find not only acceptance but also often market success. Despite the fact that in 1994 only nine percent of IT projects were completed on time and on budget, project managers continue to try to apply the control levers of cost, time and specification.

It is changes in the nature of the tasks that affect the nature of the management options that can be brought to bear. Through an analysis of tasks, the chapter examines the changing nature of project management.

SHIFTING REALITIES

Every now and then the world shifts beneath our feet and creates a new reality. The usual reaction is to accept that things have changed, but to continue to use the same old tools that worked in the previous world. This is not because we don't acknowledge that the world has changed -- but that these are the only tools we have; we are reluctant to discard implements that have served us well in the past.

The current project management literature succinctly outlines the concern. For example, in his book, Successful Project Management, Rosenau uses the concept of a "Triple Constraint" to organize his book. His Triple Constraint is the need for a project manager to satisfy the three independent goals of time, cost and performance. Likewise, the Project Management Institute's Body of Knowledge (PMBOK) defines project management as the application of knowledge, skills, tools, and techniques to project activities in order to meet or exceed stakeholder needs and expectations. It then goes on to elaborate that the stakeholders' needs and expectations invariably involve balancing competing demands of scope, time, cost and quality. The intent of these books is to provide a set of tools and behaviors that enable project managers to satisfy their clients by completing their projects on time, on budget, and to the required quality level. But that is not what is happening!

In the mid 1960s, in the realm of project management, there was a cataclysmic event. IBM released the 360 line of computers together with the operating system, OS 360 (Delamarter 1986, Brooks 1975). By any of the traditional measures this was a project disaster. Whereas projects are supposed to be on-time, on budget and to specification; this project was late, it was between two and five thousand programmer years over budget, and it did not perform as specified. In fact there were so many bugs and problems that IBM decommissioned (an IBM word for no guarantee) many of the promised features. This project disaster, which at the time almost bankrupt IBM, went on to become the most successful commercial product since Henry Ford's introduction of the Model T, and it permitted IBM to dominate the world computer industry for the next quarter century.

The passing years have shown us that the OS 360 system project was a harbinger of things to come. It was the first example, or at least the most dramatic, of a new type of project. A project where things can get enormously out of control, and where the traditional measures of time, cost and spec, while significant, are not the final arbitrators of project success. That this is the new reality was further illustrated by the following recent incidents. One was the shipping by Microsoft of Windows 95 -- late and with 2000 known bugs. Another was a decision of a CEO of a large systemhouse who, when told of projected cost overruns of five million dollars if they completed one of their contracts, canceled the project despite the signed contract. Another is the situation, reportedly common, of Project Managers inheriting IT and systems projects where the principal subcontractor was only part way through a fixed price contract and already several hundred percent over budget.

There are today numerous situations where the traditional controls are not adequate; where the client's specifications are not met, where our very ability to scope and estimate projects is highly suspect. In short, there are numerous situations that just do not fit the mold. It is increasingly apparent that there is more than one reality in project management and we must start to match our tools to these realities. Projects vary, so the duties of project management are changing; the world has changed, and our tools had better change too.

By considering the management challenges of some major historical projects, it is possible to discern certain characteristics within the nature of the projects some of which are supportive of current management practices, and some which are inimical. This consideration suggests that projects may, from a management stance, be viewed as falling into one of three types: Manual, Machine and Mind. The following examples illustrate.

GREAT WALLS AND PYRAMIDS - MANUAL PROJECTS

Many great historic projects were primarily the result of coordinating manual labor; bringing large numbers of workers together to create great monuments. Building the pyramids and constructing the Great Wall of China are examples of this type of project. In those projects, while craftsmanship and specialized knowledge were involved, and presumably some stone masons were better that others, the fundamental working unit was the laborer. Manual projects, from a management perspective, have a number of distinct advantages. These are:

- Just by observation the manager could tell whether or not people are working, and how well they are working.
- All the workers are capable of roughly the same amount of work. Although there will be the occasional individuals who can perform marginally faster or better than others, they are exceptions.
- A count of how many bricks were needed, and a standardized rate for laying them, made estimating the work straightforward.
- It is possible to trade off resources and time; that is the total project can generally be divided into worker days, and so a ten-worker day project can be done by ten people in one day, or by one person in ten days.

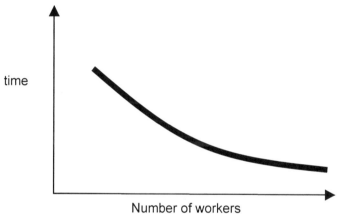

time

Number of workers

Figure 1. Relationship between time and resource for manual projects

Such labor-oriented projects are not relegated to history, but are still a very useful method of approaching many tasks. The dockside gangs of cargo handlers and the gangs of fruit and grape harvesters and excellent examples of this sort of resource usage. You hire as many people as you need, for only as long as you need them.

In Manual projects, completion dates and requisite penalties were variable. In ancient Egypt, if you did not finish the pyramid on time, it was OK since the pharaoh was already dead. However, if you did not get the Great Wall of China finished on time you were likely to be overrun by the Mongols and, as the expression goes, put to the sword. Definitely a severe penalty. Failure to get the crop in is bad if the weather is bad, not if it isn't. The penalties and consequences of not being on time vary.

The organizational structure of Manual projects is usually hierarchical, with workers organized into crews under straw bosses, foremen over several crews, and each superintendent has several foremen reporting. The span of control (number of people reporting to a boss) depends upon the nature and location of the work but in

Manual projects the crew sizes can be quite large. The principal devices and tools used by the Manual project manager are a work breakdown structure, check lists, daily task lists, and bar charts. Since, for the most part the processes are not too complex, and one task follows another and tasks are usually done by the same people, coordination is straightforward. A common strategy for dealing with prospective late completion is to "throw" resources at the project.

The issues in Manual Projects are:
- The Project Manager can see what was happening.
- The Manager can trade off time and resources.
- Resources (people) are interchangeable and can be shifted to different activities.
- The organizational structure is a classical pyramid hierarchy.
- Problems can be solved by adding resources.

But the world has become more specialized and another type of project has emerged.

MACHINE PROJECTS - NUCLEAR SUBMARINES AND CHEMICAL PLANTS

In 1957 the US Navy had 2000 sub-contractors designing, developing and manufacturing components for the Polaris Submarine System. The Navy needed a way to keep track and to calculate the influence a delay in one component would have on other aspects of the project. Also at that time the DuPont Corporation wanted to minimize the down-time when they had to take one of their highly profitable chemical plants off-line for maintenance.

The term Machine is used to delineate the second type of project. This term, not because they were no machines in building the pyramids, but rather to define an important shift. There came a time when technology, in the form of machines and their servants and the specialized skills required, determined the nature of projects. The machines could either dominate the planning process, as in the case of a crane in high rise building construction or could be the focus, the point of convergence of the project, as in the case of the Polaris submarine and missile project. In both instances, the interchangeability of resources that has characterized Manual projects no longer exists. Now different parts of the project require markedly different specialized skills, technologies, or machines and there is little opportunity for substitutions. Also, parts of the project (sub-projects) are now completed at the specialized vendors' locations, out of sight and possibly out of control.

The Machine project manager's issues are now centered around coordination and process. The concern was with insuring that the specialized machine or skill set is at the time and place where it is needed; with understanding, visualizing and controlling the complex interactions and interdependencies and with devising a means of reporting and controlling progress when the work is being performed half a continent away using a technology that you barely understand. There was a loss of direct control and a consequent increase in uncertainty. Also there was uncertainty embedded in the very nature of the tasks. Estimating becomes an area of major uncertainty as Research and Development and Maintenance type activities are difficult to scope until the detailed information (the successful prototype or the extent of internal wear) became available. It is definitely not the same as counting bricks. Further, time and money became inter-related and project management involved negotiating lateness. Now the effects can be understood and measured in monetary terms (lost profit of an incomplete chemical plant) and traded off against extra resources or efforts.

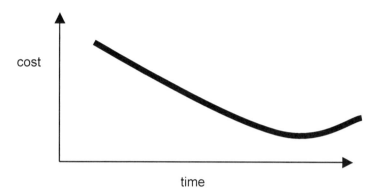

Figure 2. Relationship between Time and Cost on Machine Projects

And finally there came the realization that in some situations, the process dominates and no amount of effort can speed it up. Throwing money at the problem is not an answer. This situation, where resources are not interchangeable and a single process or piece of equipment can sometimes control or monopolize all progress on the project which leads to the classic but unfortunate relationship shown in figure 3. This situation was metaphorically illustrated in Frederick Brooks book "The Mythical Man-Month" (1975) where he writes, "You cannot have a baby in one month by putting nine women on the job."

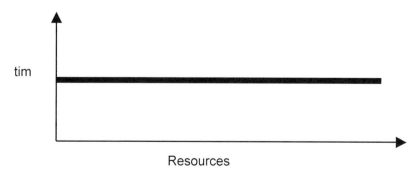

Figure 3. The Time – Resource Relationship for a Process Dominated Project

In the Machine model the organizational structure becomes a network of (sometimes very powerful) specialists (sub-contractors) or departments bound together by contracts, and coordination, measurement, reporting and monetary issues tend to dominate.

To address these issues network systems: PERT (Program Evaluation and Review Technique) and CPM (Critical Path Method), were developed. These network systems have, over the last forty years, been applied in a vast variety of different project situations--construction projects, aerospace missions, Olympic games, conference planning, book publishing, etc.-- and have proven to be very effective. In any project with a complex set of task relationships and dependencies, the only way they can be reasonably represented and monitored is with network systems.

The key points of Machine projects are:
- The Project Manager must build a reliable reporting system;
- Networks are essential to visualize and understand the complex interactions and interdependencies;
- Milestones, and summary events, are used for reporting; and
- Resources are not interchangeable and a key process or machine may often control the entire project.

MIND PROJECTS - FROM O/S 360 TO MULTI-MEDIA

Architecture, symphonies and software, are all projects of the Mind. In this model there are no longer hands, or a machine, to watch. Sometimes there isn't even a visible output. The worker is thinking! This kind of project has produced a whole new set of issues for the a project manager;

- It is not possible to tell by observation if a knowledge worker is productive, or even working! They can even sabotage projects, for example by deliberately inserting bugs, for frivolous or malicious reasons.
- Individual knowledge workers are neither replaceable nor interchangeable. Further they are talented individuals, whose agendas may differ from yours.
- The workers know more than the boss does.
- Estimating is not possible except by analogy with past projects.
- Organization incentives, groupings and policies are bizarre. Not salaries but stock options, which are sometimes worth nothing or sometimes millions, are often used as pay. There is no fixed working hours and people come and go as they please. The place of work is variable as people work at home, in cars, or at their cottages. Some commentators have applied the term, "Virtual Organization," to this new "workplace," "Anarchistic" might be a more appropriate word.

In mind projects cost and time overruns that would simply be intolerable in other project, overruns of several hundred percent, are common. The Standish Group

International reported in 1994 that only 9% of large IT projects in the US are completed on time and within budget, and that nearly one third of them are canceled prior to completion.

Some other feature of Mind Projects that affect planning, breaking the project down into activities, understanding the dependencies, and estimating the effort areas are:

- It is difficult to estimate an activity's work content since individual productivity is wildly variable and almost unmeasurable. Research has shown that one computer programmer may be as much as ten times more productive than another. There is no way to measure the productivity of someone who comes up with a faster algorithm.
- Compounding the productivity problem is the complexity issue; that is, what are the activities and the dependencies between them? What information, modules, tests and the like must be completed before something can proceed? These are extremely difficult to foresee at the outset.
- Many tasks are process dominated and take as long as they are going to take. For example, when debugging a program you test for all conditions. Problems and fixes and not visually obvious

When these features combine to create cost over-runs and slipping delivery dates, the scope for managerial intervention is severely limited. In Mind Projects adding resources can actually make a late project later. This occurs for two reasons. One is that your top-producing employees are taken off productive work and put into a training role to introduce the new resources to the project. The second is that adding resources disrupts everyone, by causing a repartitioning of the job and by adding additional communication channels.

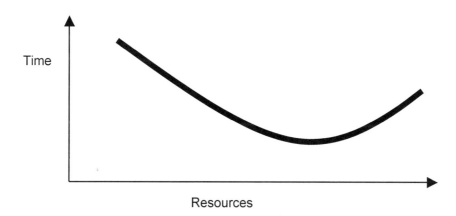

Figure 4. Time - Resource Relationship For A Project Requiring Training, Communication & Coordination

In Mind Projects the loss of key people can decimate a project schedule. When you lose an individual, you not only lose their skill; you also lose all their personal knowledge of the projects and the operating methods of the personal algorithms they have already implemented into the project. This means that normal staff turnover can badly damage the project, and the desertions that accompany a project gone bad or a company in trouble, can devastate schedules.

This was not the case with the Great Pyramids of Egypt. Partially completed tasks -- a stone moved half into position just before a worker dies of exhaustion -- can readily be completed by the next worker. Workers are also replaceable on Machine projects, although some job orientation time might be necessary. For Mind projects most of the 'deliverable' work happens only at the end. The worker may have spent months pursuing alternative design possibilities to dead ends and then produce the completed design in a matter of a week or two. It the worker is lost during the process, the replacement worker will have to revisit many of the conceptual blind alleys.

The thing that makes these Mind projects even more bizarre is the loss of control by the client. In the Manual or Machine Project, if a sub-contractor or provider failed to produce, or was overdue or over cost, the client could cancel the contract and take over the project or bring in another provider. Now, with small software teams, and projects gone bad, the clients are finding that they must absorb the cost increases, and accept the over-runs and the reduced quality, because the alternative is even worse: no system and a write-off of all the development efforts and costs expended to date.

THEORY - RESEARCH AND THE FUTURE

The world changes but people tend to carry on as if things were the same. They do not do this because they don't know that things are different--they do it because these are the only techniques they know and they are reluctant to discard a method that has worked in the past for a void (Kuhn 1962). They need new methods, methods with an underlying theory and intuitively acceptable rationale, before they will abandon the world of fixed price estimates, regular working hours and strict hierarchy based upon seniority.

Providing new tools, or the use Kuhn's term, new paradigms, is the challenge of the future.

This chapter has proposed a categorization system as a first step to embracing the challenge. The categories are not highly precise, indeed future research should further delineate and define them. They are, however, a convenient way of encapsulating many of the current agonies of project management. As long as we try to manage Mind projects like Manual Projects, with quotas and counting lines of computer code, we will fail. Likewise throwing money at a process-constrained project will not speed up anything except the consumption of money. An understanding of "what is' is a starting place for future research. The categories are intended as a start.

Historically there has been little fundamental research on project management. The literature consists mostly of anecdotal "How I did it Case Studies;" prescriptive articles of how I would do it if I had a second chance; and mathematical formulas and algorithms that don't seem to apply to well to practice. This chapter is an appeal to look beneath the formula characteristics within the projects and to the basic nature of the problem. CPM and PERT developed because the US Navy and DuPont had a problem of coordination – not because Dr. Fulkerson had developed an algorithm for network flows (1962).

This is not to say the area of mind projects is devoid of ideas and investigation. There was, in 1967, a major study of managing engineers and scientists by Pletz and Andrews that indicated Mind Project workers work best when under slight pressure. "Creative Tension," was the term Pletz and Andrews used. Then in 1981 the case study by Tracy Kidder revealed the power of esprit de corps, and introduced the pinball concept of motivation. It is Dilbertesque but it seems that the greatest reward you can give to an engineer that has just completed an impossible task is to offer an even more difficult task. The work of Total Quality Management guru, W. Edwards Deming shows us that people really want to do a good job, and will perform well if they are allowed. Concepts like empowerment and leaderless teams give us an indication of the next path but there is much that is not understood. There is still a need for much research.

So research must proceed but what, in the meantime, can project managers do? What is the result of the diverse categories of projects and how must project management adapt to deal with it?

The first step is to recognize the realities. That the nostrum of, "On time, on budget and to specification," is perhaps not able to encapsulate the complexity that is modern project management. That there are other issues. To solve them we must go out onto the firing line where the projects are and start looking. We must study the dynamics of the changed world order and ask why. Ask are there general issues or is each management situations, like the project, unique. Ask why is a Windows 95 with 2000 bugs still acceptable? Why do corporations seek fixed price contracts on projects that are impossible to conceptualize? Why do people work fourteen hour days for some projects, and not for others? What place has trust, commitment, integrity, loyalty, and leadership in the market?

These are the issues that must be addressed by today's project managers. The challenge to those with the wisdom and insight to solve these riddles is to design the tools we need for the Mind Projects.

CHAPTER 11

SUPPLY-BASED STRATEGIES
THE CASE OF THE FRENCH BUILDING CONTRACTORS

Sihem Ben Mahmoud-Jouini, University of Paris XI and CRG-Ecole
Polytechnique, Paris, France

ABSTRACT

By sector, innovation is pulled by demand expressed and anticipated by future
customers or pushed by supply. The French Construction sector is experiencing a
deep and lasting recession where the demand is not expressed anymore. How can
firms change from a demand-pull logic to a supply-push one? This chapter
investigates this question for large French building contractors.

In order to answer to this question, we analyzed innovative projects led by firms
forming a project management think-tank that was created specifically for this
research.

The author models what is a supply-push strategy in the building industry and
identifies the necessary conditions for the establishment of this strategy. She
identifies the key competencies needed for this strategy based upon six principal
dimensions and the organizational process, which allows the acquisition of these
competencies. These process are internal to the firm like networking the skills
dispersed throughout the local divisions and external to it like developing
partnerships with the various project actors.

INTRODUCTION

Project-based organizations develop specific proposals to meet the requirements of
individual customers. Such invitations to tender may be selective or broadly based.
Contracts are awarded to the best bid or to the lowest-priced bid (Cova 1990).
Bansard, Cova and Flipo (1992) have identified four situations, which differ
according to whether the customer or the supplier is anticipating the product
involved in the negotiation or reacting to it:

- The competitive bid situation, in which the customer anticipates the product and
  specifies its characteristics in a document which he submits to the supplier
  market. The supplier agrees to respond and participates or refuses to participate
  (top right-hand box (1))

- The standard goods and services market situation, in which the supplier is offering on the market a product which he has designed taking account of his customers, his competition and his own specific skills. The supplier is marketing here a product which the customer is free to choose or reject (bottom left-hand box (2))
- The situation in which each of the two players is reacting in real time to reciprocal definitions of the exchange occurring between them, with the presumption of a high degree of mutual anticipation and responsiveness (bottom right-hand box (3)).
- The situation in which the supplier and the customer are both anticipating simultaneously the entirety of the content of the terms governing their exchange (top left-hand box (4)).

These situations are summarized in table 1.

Table 1. Reaction and anticipation in the relation supplier/customer

Customer	Supplier	
	Anticipation Predetermined supply	**Reaction** Response to demand
Anticipation Proactive stance or based on experience	**Economic model (4)** Proposed supply frozen except for price and quantity	**Reverse Marketing Mix (1)** Competitive bid model
Reaction Response to supply Stimulus/response	**Marketing Mix (2)**	**Exchanges to be defined by the parties (3)**

Bansard, Cova and Flipo (1992)

OUR PROBLEM

A decline in demand has a direct impact on the activity of the firms belonging to competitive bid model (top right-had box) by reducing the level of their business. Our focus here is on the activity of these companies when demand is no longer expressed, and in general when invitations to tender competitive bids fail to arrive for various reasons. How do they react in this situation? Is it within their power to elicit business themselves or must they wait for demand to reappear ? What room do they have to manoeuvre?

The Initial Approach

Whereas mass producers tend to focus upon the marketing mix and its four components (product, advertising, promotion and presentation) to attract buyers and dictate the terms of exchange, contractors have to manage a complex interaction process leading up to, and including, an invitation to tender in order to influence demand and negotiate the terms of each transaction. Such practices are designated by the term "project marketing". This term has tended to be used in a generic sense to describe the activities and processes associated with developing a competitive response to invitations.

Project activities have the following distinctive features:
- Uniqueness: they involve different players and products on each occasion.
- Complexity: the players involved are increasingly numerous and their interactions increasingly complex.
- Discontinuity of the economic relations between customers and their contractors

Each project is regarded as an isolated market. The above characteristics lead to the fact that a good deal of uncertainty remains with regard to both of the following:
- The strategic goal or the "competitive arena" (Who will the future customer be? What will the future product be?),
- The rules of the game (When will the next project arrive? And on what terms and how?)

To the above must be added the imbalance in the relationship between supplier and customer. This is because the competitive bid situation places the supplier in a situation of informational asymmetry and submission. It is partly in response to these characteristics that such companies have developed practices directed at creating some room for strategic maneuver. The strategic maneuvers in question involve anticipating future projects and positioning the company as early as possible and as far upstream as possible in the market demand environment.

To accomplish the project marketing, Cova B. and Hoskins S. (1997) have identified two extreme approaches. The first is "deterministic", or based on the anticipation of the competitive arena and the rules of the game, and the second is "constructivist", or based on the participation of the shaping of the above characteristics. The "deterministic" approach is based on gathering, consolidation and dissemination of information necessary to anticipate future projects; optimization of competitive bidding and improvement of the terms on which the company participates in projects. This first approach is based on a relational type of strategy.

The "constructivist" approach is based on using a "creative offer" that will initiate the project and channel the demand. To accomplish this, the company makes use of its own capacity for creating offers of supply. The company thus plays a key role in the formulation of demand and response. This approach is founded on a supply-based strategy which creates market demand.

The activity of the companies is positioned at the intersection of these two approaches and takes advantage of their complementary nature.

Cova, Mazet and Salle (1994) make a distinction between three phases in the activity of such companies that correspond to the three stages of the project development:

- "Out of project": this is a phase involving relational anticipation and requiring an analytical method and an as detailed as possible representation of the local network or environment of the customer in order to enable the supplier company to position itself with respect to that network. This local network is composed by influential socio-economic players for the company's business. This phase is independent of any project. The objective is to develop a monitoring system to detect upcoming projects.

- "In-between project": this is a phase typically involving the screening (Bansard, Cova and Salle 1993) of anticipated projects and the selection and optimization of a point of entry into a given project, because contractors may enter a competitive bid in a number of ways : alone, as part of a corporate grouping, as a prime contractor in joint-venture or as a sub-contractor. This phase occurs when the contractor aims to act on the project in conjunction with the customer and his network.

- "In-project activity": this involves the submission of the bid and the organization of the technical and functional, legal and financial, policy-related and societal aspects of the response.

If we cross-correlate the two project marketing approaches with the three activity phases, we arrive at table 2.

Table 2. Project approach for each phase

Stage of project development	Deterministic Approach Anticipation and adaptation	Constructivist Approach Definition and redefinition
Project independent	Positioning in key relationship networks	Network construction Construction of a "core" supply offer to elicit demand.
Pre-tender	Project identification and screening	Project creation and risk evaluation.
tender preparation	Submission of competitive bid.	Re-definition of project.
	STRATEGY OF RELATIONAL TYPE	STRATEGY BASED CREATIVE OFFER

Adapted from Cova and Hoskins (1997)

Back to our problem
When market demand is no longer being expressed for any of many possible reasons, strategies based on relational approaches and anticipation and adaptation begin to show their limitations. This is because the projects which can be anticipated become rare. Consequently, the constructivist approach should begin to play a more prominent role in the activity of such companies. In order to develop their market in this situation, they are likely to adopt methods based on developing offers of supply which create demand. How can they do this? What leverage is available to them?

Clarifying the problem and its underlying assumptions
How can companies stimulate a renewal of market demand in this way? Of the whole range of possibilities for building such supply-based strategies, we will concentrate here on that provided by innovation and the development of new types of supply. This emphasis can be explained by the fact that we are currently in a period of history when innovation is one of the main criteria of competitiveness for a number of sectors of industry. Indeed, the capacity for development of new products and constant innovation have allowed certain companies to bring to market products which have revitalized sectors that in some cases had reached saturation. Is such restoration of demand, and such dynamism, possible in sectors in which, typically, the customer anticipates demand? How might it be possible for companies to energize the sector by reversing the normal flow, using strategies based on offers of supply which create demand?

A clarification is necessary here. When faced with a major and persistent decline in the level of activity in a sector, a range of strategies is available to companies. The main ones are:

- abandonment of the activity concerned,
- redeployment towards related or ancillary activities,
- geographical redeployment in the search for an environment more conducive to the activity,
- a proactive, innovation-based strategy directed at the revitalization of the sector and stimulating new growth, changing neither activity nor geographical location.

We concentrate below on the last of these possibilities, and explore the conditions governing the emergence of new strategies for market supply founded on capabilities for design and innovation.

Our theoretical question is therefore the following: in a sector in deep and lasting recession, and in which the typical pattern is supplier response to demand expressed and anticipated by the customer, how can a group of players working in that sector act to restore the level of activity and re-energize market demand by means of their capabilities for innovation and design?

OUR INVESTIGATIVE FIELD

The building industry
This is a sector which has been affected in France since the early 1990s by a recession linked to excess capacity. The slowdown in economic growth in 1990 led to the sharpest fall in activity recorded since the post-war reconstruction period (1950s). In addition, the forecasts for housing, which accounts for approximately 50% of all production, points to a probable decline in activity up to 2020 (cf. Figure 1).

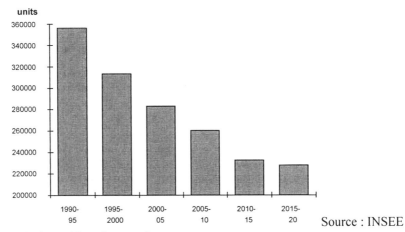

units

Source : INSEE

Figure 1. Annual housing requirements.

TheActors

The focus of our attention here is on major French general building contractors. The question posed in this study stems from an inductive approach based on a request submitted to us by a group of major French general building contractors. These contractors, which have formed a project management think-tank called GREMAP [*Groupe de Réflexion sur le Management de Projet*], enjoy the support of PCA [*Plan Conception Architecture* / Architecture Design Plan], a public body which subsidizes and channels research in the industry. The R&D managers of the above contractors expressed to us a wish to explore possible changes in project-related practices in their sector in the light of recent research in management sciences which have revealed new ways in which to manage projects (Midler 1993). Such changes have been a source of enhanced efficiency in new product development, leading to major progress in certain sectors which have gone on to build strategies based on variety of supply in order to stimulate demand. These strategies have taken the form of linking services to products, widening product ranges, increasing the use of segmentation in order to focus on tightly defined market needs ("niche strategies") and ensuring rapid turnover of new products. In these sectors, the capacity for developing new products and bringing them to market has thus become one of the principal variables in competitiveness: "the battle for better production has now become a battle for better design" (Navarre 1992). Project co-ordination on concurrent lines is an extremely significant example of these new techniques. Those requesting the present study thus saw in this stream of research a source of inspiration and of productive change in their practices. Their request was therefore to look at how new methods of co-ordination discovered in other sectors might be transferred to the building industry, where such innovations might take project management forward.

The new project management techniques were developed for the purposes of supply and product/process innovation-based strategies. However, these proactive strategies do not consist exclusively of the reorganization of methods of co-ordination. They are founded on proposed supply of new products and/or processes.

The latter are derived from skills and capacities for defining such proposals which may come just as much from internal players in the company, its engineering department for example, as from its partners. These different contributions have fed into projects and generated innovative offers which break with the past.

For this reason, we took the decision to widen the scope of our exploration from the transfer of new methods of project co-ordination as a means of implementing supply-based strategies to an examination of the other possibilities for action to promote such strategies. Our attention thus shifted from the means for implementation of such supply-based strategies to the strategies themselves. Our research therefore turned toward an examination of the feasibility of the adoption by major general building contractors of new proactive, supply-based strategies.

In our study of the feasibility of such supply strategies, we will look at the capacity for innovation required for the development of new product/process combinations. Examination of the feasibility of a supply-based strategy therefore throws a spotlight on design itself. Given this, we set out clearly below the meaning we attach here to "design" as a concept.

METHODOLOGY

In consultation with the members of GREMAP, we identified examples of innovative projects, which we then analyzed. This analysis led to the drafting of papers tabled and debated within GREMAP. During the analysis, we looked at all the players in building projects, both inside and outside the contracting company: architects, engineering firms and departments, site owners, etc.

WHAT IS "DESIGN"?

It seems to us to be important at this stage in our argument to make clear the meaning we attach to "design" as a concept, and the boundaries of building as a product. This is because design in the building industry is usually seen in terms of architects and engineering firms. In our view, design activity relates in fact to all players contributing to a building project. We include here the site owner, the contractors (main fabric and finishing work), and all the other actors. We do so because we feel, along with Simon and Schön, that design means asking questions and seeking answers both in the abstract and in pragmatic sense. For this reason, we consider that part of the actual execution of the project falls into the category of "design". Design will therefore, in this approach, include project planning, which involves the definition of the functions expected in building, the architectural and technical design, the definition of project execution and part of the building work itself. New supply-based strategies can be deployed throughout the territory thus defined. Innovation in the building industry boils down to innovating within the above boundaries.

WHAT IS AN OFFER OF MARKET SUPPLY IN THE BUILDING INDUSTRY?

Our analysis of various building projects has led us to see any building project as a combination of the five component dimensions set out below:

- land,
- functional parameters,
- technical and architectural specifications,
- specification of the process of execution of the project,
- finance.

These components are coordinated according to a mode of integration which is the sixth keystone in our model for market supply in the building industry.

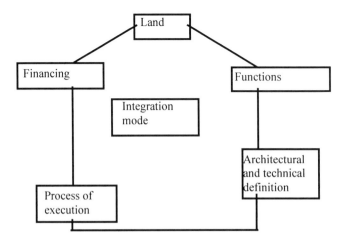

Figure 2. Model of a project in the building industry.

Both demand and supply can be expressed in these dimensions: generally, the demand precises the land (location and main characteristics), the financial budget and some functional parameters and architectural specifications.

Any project is a compromise where effectiveness is assessed on the basis of three criteria:

- the quality, perceived as the compliance of the construction's performance with that expected of it; this includes an assessment of the quality of both design and execution;
- the cost,
- the delay of the design and the construction completion .

Each of the above dimensions relates to a specific set of skills. We underline however the fact that this breakdown does not match the divisions between the areas of responsibility of project contributors, nor defined bodies of professional expertise. The question which seems to us to be pertinent and which focuses attention on this breakdown is the following: in what key ways are the three dimensions mutually complementary? What are the most productive combinations between them which would generate new synergies?

Modeling supply-based strategies

By using our building project model, as presented above, the definition of a new offer of market supply in the building industry therefore means innovating in the dimensions defined.

Over recent years, major general building contractors in France have developed a range of supply strategies based essentially on the following project dimensions: the land, the finance, the co-ordination and, to a lesser extent, the process of execution. This is so since project execution is tightly dependent on the technical specification of the building and the contractor does not contribute to this aspect of the design. For this reason, the manner in which the construction is carried out does not offer a very effective way for the generation of a new supply strategy. The limitations of the model for supply-based strategy developed by major general building contractors in France since the late 1970s, as illustrated by the diagram below, became apparent in the recession related to excess capacity in the 1990s. It was seen then that this model was not capable of revitalizing activity, nor was it capable of organizing the process of obsolescence which provides a foundation for subsequent renewal of the market. This model is based on a relational strategy involving locally-based operations, which matches contractors' decentralized structures.

It is important to be make clear that a model for supply-based strategy stems from the history of past strategies adopted by companies, from their respective structures, and from the environment in which they operate.

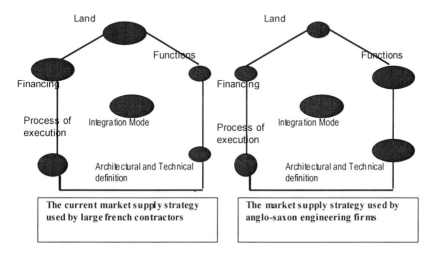

Figure 3. Comparison between the strategy market supply of French and anglo-saxon building firms.

Anglo-Saxon engineering firms which refers refers here mainly to the British and the American system, for example (cf. figure above), use another supply-based strategy matching another configuration of the capabilities for offering supply to customers on the lines of the five project dimensions. These firms in fact base their strategy on those dimensions which relate to the practical functions of their architectural and technical translation of the project, and to project co-ordination. Conversely, they do not work on the dimensions relating to land, finance or project execution.

From our model for building projects, we define a model for supply-based strategies which lies in placing the emphasis on some of the building dimensions identified above. Our exploration of the feasibility of new supply-based strategies for major general contractors leads us to seek out configurations of design capabilities different from those which have prevailed hitherto. We have identified three sets of supply-based strategies which relate to three generic types of supply and form three design capability configurations with respect to the six project dimensions. These are offers of *product supply*, *technical supply* and *co-ordination supply* .

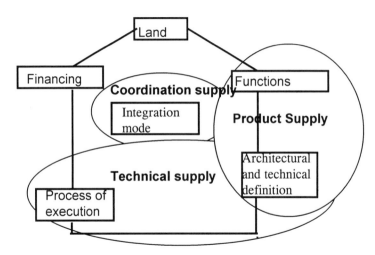

Figure 4. The three sets of supply-based strategies in the building industry.

Adopting a supply strategy in the *product supply* group means innovating in the area of the functions and architectural/technical specification of the building. The other dimensions, notably those relating to the land and the finance, remain important. Nevertheless, we do not list them among the components of the product supply offer in order to make clear the distinction between this strategy and that deployed hitherto by major general contractors.

Adopting a supply strategy in the *technical supply* group means concentrating on those dimensions, which relate to the specification of the technical aspects and manner of execution of the building. Finally, adopting a supply strategy in the *co-ordination supply* group means adopting some new way of integrating the various project dimensions.

THE FIRST RESULTS

We have analysed innovation-oriented projects in each of these generic categories: a hotel chain, service-based residential accommodation, a dry floor, an extended-range construction system, a composite wall, etc. It is important to make clear that in these projects all dimensions played important roles but in each case the focus was on one dimension rather than the others. In analyzing these projects, we sought to identify the conditions governing the emergence of supply-based strategies from the point of view of design capabilities. An initial presentation of the results shows that such offers of innovative supply originate in the capability to explore the preferred dimensions. Thus the conditions for emergence of such strategies relate to the conditions governing the presence of the design capabilities necessary for the exploration of the relevant dimensions. Given this, in order to develop supply-based strategies, it seems to be necessary to develop an explorative capability. In what ways can this be done?

One possibility would be to form skill groups for such exploration within the company. However, this method does not appear to be suitable for two reasons:

- the decentralized structure of these contractors, which stems from the need to be close to the customer base, and from the importance of locally-based operations,
- the wide variety of the skills required given the extensive territory occupied by the product as defined by us above.

Ways of building up the skills needed for exploration and for the emergence of innovative supply, which we have examined, fall into two categories.

The first involves the networking of skills dispersed throughout the local operations of contractors whose overall structure is decentralized. Such redistribution and sharing of expertise can enable certain skills to be acquired or perfected. This way forward is all the more advantageous since this is a sector in which innovations generally come about through incremental change and therefore by the making of a series of improvements.

Alongside networking, the other category of methods for forming bodies of expertise is through partnership with the various project players:

- site owners, or users, for knowledge relating to use of the construction, for example,
- prime contractors, for aspects relating to the architectural and technical transposition of project design,
- sub-contractors employed by the major general contractors and contractors handling specialist finishing work, for all aspects relating to expertise in the execution of different types of work.

These then are the methods, which have enabled the formation of expertise for the exploration of the dimensions founding various supply-based strategies.

It is important to make clear at this stage that environmental factors have a major impact. This is so because it is not enough simply to bring together the required skills for one of the two categories of approach identified above for it to become possible to implement successfully such supply strategies following the deterministic model. In particular, the regulatory and institutional context, which dominates this sector, plays a very important role. It is for this reason that strategies based on offers of new supply are implemented according to contingent patterns, which needed to be defined.

CHAPTER 12

RESEARCH ROLE IN DEFINING CUSTOMER NEEDS ON INNOVATIVE PROJECTS

Florence Charue-Duboc, Centre de Recherche en Gestion, Ecole polytechnique,France

ABSTRACT

The chemical industry studied here is exemplary, first, of a situation in which the development of new products involves a strong overlap between product innovation and basic research; and second, of detachment from the final customer or (more broadly) from the complexity of the customer-system through which the product will be processed. In this context, research management following a market-pull model and a project-management model insulating the owner from other supplier presents different limitations. Technical imponderables and market uncertainties cannot be dealt with effectively. The gap between the time required for the acquisition of research skills and the pace of change in the marketplace cannot easily be reconciled with sequential planning.

We describe the implementation of a development design model more extensively integrated with multi-functional teams. We then examine the impact of such a model on the practices of two actors involved in research and marketing. What new skills must be developed; what new coordination mechanism? To what new situations will these skills prove relevant?

BACKGROUND

The development of innovative products has long been driven by technological advances. Scientific progress achieved by research centres has fostered the planning of new products and brought about significant improvements in existing ones. New product development has thus been guided by research, with the focus on new fields which reflect acquired expertise, new findings reported in the literature, and topics studied by academic research teams. This "technology-push" strategy has undeniably made it possible to market many innovative products, as is shown by the technological progress accomplished since the turn of the century. Some developments, however, have not achieved the expected market success, and these setbacks have been attributed to flawed knowledge of the market.

In the mid-1970s, two corporate trends became apparent, the first of which was the rise in the power of marketing. As marketing skills grew, internal market analysis and responsiveness to customer expectations and segmentation grew accordingly, and centres of expertise were restructured into divisions or departments. Marketing experts, initially called upon to support product sales, were subsequently asked to define target-products for development. The second such trend was the rationalization of research operations, aimed at imposing budget limitations, often determined by a percentage of "normal" revenues for the industrial sector involved. The question then arose as to how projects should be prioritized in terms of their inherent advantages and disadvantages, and the urgency of demand for them. The by-word for the past fifteen years for research management has thus been "market-pull". The customer makes purchasing decisions, which means the customer is king, and his or her needs must therefore be understood. Understanding customer needs became therefore the task of marketing experts, and the point of departure for establishing research programs and formulating goals and priorities. This was a total reversal of the process and rationale on which new research projects had previously been based.

With ten years' experience behind us, we can now assess this new model in terms of both its positive and its negative aspects. On the positive side, it has clearly fostered a learning process, strengthening the customer rationale for product development. It has proved to be broadly applicable and effective for innovations of an incremental type, and for industries operating in proximity to the final market. On the negative side, in today's innovation-based competition between corporations, adaptive innovations, although necessary, are no longer enough to ensure a strong position in a given market (Tushman and Andersen 1986, Cohendet and Llerena 1990, D'Aveni 1994, Lynn, Morone and Paulson 1996, Chakhravarthy 1997). In addition, to satisfy new customer needs and develop the innovations they need, corporations which manufacture mass-market products are increasingly turning to sourcing sectors (Iansiti and Clark, 1994, Kesseler 1998). Finally, product-targeting errors cannot be corrected, as competitors do not give innovators a second chance. They learn rapidly from the failures of others, and are quick to offer new products of their own.

The punctuated equilibrium (Romanelli and Tushmann 1994) which alternates long periods of incremental innovation and breakthrough related to radical innovations does not seem to be appropriate to describe today's race between firms. Recent works focus on a new model of organization favouring continuous change which means the development of important innovations at a sustained rythm (Utterback 1994, Dougherty and Hardy, 1996, Brown and Eisenhardt 1997).Their focus is to characterize these kinds of organization as a whole, and they insist for example, on project portfolios and how to articulate today's developments and competencies with future innovations. Our contribution belongs to this research stream. This process has also been studied for radical innovations in Science Sociology (Ackrich, Callon and Latour 1988). They pinpoint the role of various actors surrounding the innovation and the importance of their involvement in the success. What are the implications within a firm of such theoretical results ? I focus on the process of product targeting and the early stages of design. I elaborate on the notion of the low cost probe mentioned by Brown and Eisenhardt 1997 and the probe and learn process of Lynn Morone and Paulson 1996, in defining the role and competencies of research and marketing and the way they coordinate in those very uncertain situations.

What would the ideal development-design model for breakthrough innovations be, especially at the level of industrial sourcing? This is the broad question I have attempted to give some answers to, based on research conducted at a major French chemicals corporation, for which this question is particularly relevant. This is because the specialized chemicals industry is subject to a product-differentiation strategy and most of its products are sold to processors. Finally, product-innovation and product-function innovations raise fundamental research questions. The ability to transform technical innovations into marketable products is therefore of key importance.

In the first section, I describe the limitations of the "market-pull" model, the impact of which is particularly strong because it focuses on innovations in basic materials processed by intermediate manufacturers before reaching the end-user. In the second section, I formulate a design-model which takes these limitations into account, pinpointing one specific aspect: the coordinating mechanisms which facilitate the simultaneous acquisition of expertise concerning customer needs and markets, as well as product accessibility. In conclusion, I have touched on other aspects of the model, which require clarification, so that this coordination can be implemented effectively: the internal organization of expertise; contracts and incentives for the various players; and the involvement of customers or partners.

THE LIMITATION OF THE "MARKET PULL" MODEL

First of all, I present a brief review of several defining elements in the market-pull model before going on to list the main problems involved in its implementation.

The market-pull model assumes an initial definition of the products, services, or functions to be developed; they are defined on the basis of an analysis of markets, customers, and customer needs and preferences. This model thus assumes the presence of a player with the appropriate expertise: the marketing expert. Marketing experts are expected to formulate the product-target before the initiation of the research operation required to fulfill it. The relationship between marketing and research is "contractual" in nature. Respective responsibilities are clearly delineated in a manner resembling the property-developer/contractor relationship which is characteristic of project-management models, particularly in the construction field. Lastly, the respective players in this relationship mobilize bodies of disparate expertise. Although in practice the implementation of this model does not always involve roles as contrasted and "compartmentalized" as this, a critique of the "ideal-model" appeared to us to offer greater scope for analysis.

Marketing-expert techniques and expertise

However, first let us return to the marketing experts, who are expected to use their analytic techniques to formulate specifications for the customers' dream product. The basic techniques used are market analysis and product positioning.

During the early project phases, knowledge about the product is minimal. Will this additive for paint be totally biodegradable? Solvent-free? Here, as in any development process, there are imponderables. How can traditional focus-group and survey techniques be used when no product-samples are available to quantify preferences and spot threshold effects? This is the first problem encountered when the marketing approach is used during the early project phases. It requires the development of new investigative methods, on the basis of which expertise regarding preference can be effectively built.

The second problem is that knowledge about the market is also minimal. Depending on the future properties of the product, it may or may not be useful for certain applications (as an additive for "do-it-yourself" varnishes, for instance; or, conversely, for industrial paint). Here again, market segmentation will be difficult as long as uncertainties concerning the product persist.

The third problem is to extrapolate over one, two, or several years. Let us assume that precise product and product-market profiles have been defined; the market survey then generates a sales forecast based on an analysis of today' products. By the time they will be introduced onto the market, many factors will all have been subject to change. Meanwhile, other innovations will have been introduced; new standards may have been established; the market may have been fragmented by these other innovations, etc.

Making use of marketing techniques without additional precautions and adjustments is thus particularly risky. J. M. Gaillard (1997) even goes so far as to claim that if the goal is to kill an innovation, there is no better way to do so than to conduct a market survey. He suggests doing the opposite: i.e. constructing a methodology specifically suited to these highly uncertain early phases. He bases his argument on many personal interviews and on the meticulous examination of a qualitative analysis drawn from the findings. I shall return to these findings in the second section.

Customer expertise
A second category of problems has to do with customers and their own expertise.

Breakthrough innovations are only rarely identified by asking even enlightened customers about their potential needs. Who would ever have imagined buying a glue that doesn't stay glued? And yet, this is the very property that everyone appreciates today. It was up to 3M (or, more modestly, to a researcher) to invent a possible use by consumers. Here, the issue is to invent (or crystallize) diffuse, latent, implicit needs that could be satisfied; and to construct, in cooperation with customers (by integrating them into the validation loop) a usage-value drawn from the opinions they express. This is not merely a matter of "harvesting" existing information which needs only to be tabulated.

The problems do not differ significantly even when the product under development is similar to existing products. The views of some customers will be of no use whatsoever if the product is not ready to be handled and tested. In the case of a varnish-development project, for example, the product's drying-time following application did not emerge as a crucial parameter until very late. The craftsmen at whom this product was being targeted simply assumed they would be able to apply a second coat the day after applying the first one, and did not bother mentioning this criterion. This demonstrates the vulnerability of evaluations made before the product has been tested. Some customers, on the other hand, will formulate extremely rigid technical specifications. Chemicals-industry customers, from detergent manufacturers to auto-makers, tend to present highly detailed specifications. In instances such as this, specifications based on customer expertise can also act as a brake on innovation, not because the criteria have not been thoroughly identified at the inception of the project, but because the desired objective involves too many demands. Specifications of this kind are frequently based on a technical solution to be improved. For example, when an auto-maker presents dashboard specifications independently to a plastics supplier, there is a good chance that the resulting component will be too heavy and too costly. To produce a lighter, less costly component, several points in the specifications need to be changed, and defining the margin for maneuver within which profits can be earned by both parties assumes a continuous mutual-learning process. As a consequence we can observe the formation of design partnerships

In general, customers' expertise about their own potential needs and preferences is patchy. Some customers make assumptions which they have difficulty expressing. The formulation of purchasing specifications fills in some of the gaps, but can place limitations on innovation. Meanwhile, other gaps will appear. Customers will only be able to perceive the value of an unfamiliar property, or pinpoint their preferences, by evaluating the product. It is therefore advantageous to create a market expertise which customers do not necessarily possess. It is even reasonable to claim that this type of expertise yields a competitive advantage.

Customer-system complexity
A third problem category encountered in the market analysis of products under development is the diversity of relevant opinion-sources.

For example, which opinion source should be given priority when the customer is a corporation (as is often the case in the chemicals industry)? The Purchasing Department, the R&D Department, the project teams, or the strategists? This question is particularly important, as the issue here is not to market a product, but to anticipate what will satisfy customers several months or even years ahead.

Customer-contacts can be made internally by various players: sales personnel, researchers (through technical assistance), and plant workers (through complaints). How can these various ways of approaching the customer be combined?

Furthermore, a direct customer is not necessarily in the best position to evaluate usage-relevance for the end-consumer, as there may be several intermediate stages between them. Consultants may also play a decisive role. While a direct customer might consider a specific function to be superfluous, the customer's own client might consider it crucial. A good example is a product designed to eradicate salmonella at poultry slaughterhouses. The direct customer (the slaughterhouse) might show little interest in a substance that would increase costs of a product (poultry) for which the profit margin is already very low. However, the final consumer (the purchaser of poultry in a supermarket) might be willing to pay a premium for added product-safety. If innovations are to be successful, these different rationales must be taken into consideration.

Furthermore, strategic considerations are integral to the relationships among intermediaries in a given industry. The introduction of an innovation provides an opportunity to redefine the profit margins and prerogatives of each intermediary. In the auto industry, the situation is relatively stable, but this is not the case for all industries, and particularly chemicals. The structure of the chemicals industry is complex: a customer for one type of product might be a supplier of another type, and a competitor for yet a third. To a complexity which reflects the large number of players involved is added a strategic complexity which is increasing due to current trends towards developing alliances, joint ventures, and licensing agreements.

This means that the market-testing of innovations may have an undesired repercussion: the triggering of competition.

Then again, customer interest (or lack of it) in an innovation may reflect rationales only remotely connected with the technical evaluation of the proposed product. For example, a customer might give serious attention to innovations offered by various suppliers, not because it is looking around for a new supplier, but simply because it wants to shake up its old ones. Alternatively, a customer might indicate lack of interest in a new product solely to discourage its development by a competitor of one of its own corporation's divisions, which is trailing the field. Customers might also be reluctant to show interest in an innovation due to the testing expenses involved, and to the risk that a new product still experiencing teething problems might negatively affect their brand image while at the same time providing no guarantee of long-term market penetration.

When the multiplicity of opinion sources represented by the customer-system is taken into account, the question arises of how divergent viewpoints should be analysed and rated.

The demand dynamic

The current competitive context is characterized by market versatility, rapid introduction of product/process innovations, and accelerated change in the regulations governing environmental protection (Cohendet and Llerena 1990). All of this takes place in a price-war climate. Thus stability of demand is an extremely strong assumption, rarely verified,. Examples abound of market-demand instability and the speed with which market demand shifts relative to product-development time-frames. The impact of this problem is accentuated by the fact that product/process and expertise development require a longer time-frame than that allowed by the pace of change in the market and the competitive environment.

The various limitations described above have an even greater impact on lengthy development projects (lasting several years), and breakthrough innovations usually fall within this category. Problems arise in connection with anticipating shifts in the market; with the difference between the product-functions being developed and those customers are familiar with; with the time required before a testable product can be introduced, etc. When the innovation being developed targets industrial suppliers, the difficulty in anticipating market demands increases in proportion to the strategic complexity of the industry and the interrelationships among its various players.

What kind of model can account for all these market characteristics, and for the problems involved in the market analysis of breakthrough-innovation development?

TOWARDS AN INTEGRATED PRODUCT/MARKET MODEL DESIGN

Demand instability, the inability of traditional marketing techniques to identify unexpressed needs, and the strategic complexity associated with multiple players all point to the desirability of placing the process of target-market construction in a time-frame that parallels that of the technical product-design process. In this way, the product's technical feasibility, its user's needs, and the price the latter is willing to pay can be explored in a parallel, rather than sequential fashion. Two learning processes occur; two bodies of expertise are constructed on the basis of two interdependent "objects." This is the guiding principle underlying the integrated-model design, and it is borne out by other theoretical work.

For example, research which analysed innovation processes, conducted at the *Centre de Sociologie de l'Innovation* M. Ackrich, M. Callon, and B. Latour (1988) criticizes the "linear" model which postulates a sequence from basic research to the market, successively passing through applied research, product development, and production. This work underscores the importance of achieving the involvement of the various players throughout the innovation process: future users, financiers, consultants, and production-process developers. The authors stress the importance of negotiating the technical objective with all the parties involved.

Theoretical work by Simon (1969) demonstrates that the definition of the problem cannot be divorced from the formulation of the solution. Design is a dual process which results from the combined definition of the problem and the solution. Research by C. Midler (1993) on project management has highlighted the time and cost advantages accruing from simultaneous consideration of the project's target and its technical solution (product/process).

The evolution in project management for the case studied demonstrates the emergence of this design construct, which focuses on both the relevant target and the potential products.

However, in the "market-pull" model, marketing/research coordination follows a linear sequence; and, in fact, this is also the case for the "technology-push" model. The output of the former becomes the operational input of the latter. The only difference between them is the order in which the departments intervene, and their hierarchical position in relation to each other: the one which establishes the constraints is considered to be the one in the dominant position. Coordination is greatly simplified by another point: concentration of the market interface on a single player, the marketing expert. Information thus travels in a linear manner between the firm's various departments: the players involved with internal production have as their (internal) customer a profit-centre marketing expert who oversees the interface with the post-production customer, represented by a purchasing function which, in turn, communicates with production/development functions, and so on, all the way to the final consumer. According to this rationale, marketing-department expertise is oriented primarily towards familiarity with customers, commercial negotiations with them, and prices.

Under the new model being proposed, what are the coordination modalities which will enable researchers to do their work despite the fact that no one has asked them any questions; and what will enable those in the process of formulating the questions (the market experts) to trust that their colleagues are working on solutions to a problem they have not yet fully defined?

As the process advances, coordination objectives and modalities will be specified which facilitate the parallel and symmetrical deployment of both the research and the market explorations.

A common point of departure for parallel explorations

The point of departure for an innovation project is a pathway to be explored: a silicon mastic for tools so they can be cleansed with water for example. Initial formulation of the objective is common to both the research and the marketing players, and serves as the launch-pad for parallel exploration.

The researchers will posit various technical solutions. Experiments which prove technically unfeasible are easily eliminated. Often, however, initial findings are not decisive. One approach will present certain advantages, another approach different ones. Choosing which one to concentrate on cannot be done by the researchers alone; an evaluation must also be made by the marketing experts.

In parallel, market analysis and technical exploration go forward together. The market analysis builds an initial assessment of the project's potential advantages and disadvantages. It draws in a highly traditional way on a collection of sales-volume data for the type of product with which the new development will be positioned, and for various existing products and their prices. When marketing experts are expected not only to provide volume and price forecasts, but also to supply a detailed definition of the target market; to orient development on the basis of initial research findings, and to establish compromises between functionalities, they must be able to establish a basis for providing answers to a number of diverse questions: What causes customers to prefer one product over another? Does the product under development meet all customer demands? Is it highly effective for one category sub-type but less so for another?, etc.

The above criteria assume that marketing experts will be able to embark rapidly on a broader analysis than usual: a comprehensive identification of all customer-system players, including the customer's own customers, the consultants, and the other customers of varying types (not just the largest ones); and the formulation of a methodology designed to provide an understanding of usages and preferences. Depending on the age of the operation for which the new application is intended, this knowledge may already exist; or, inversely, the market may be totally unexplored. The speed with which the project will meet the relevant target is often directly contingent on this factor.

Formulation of testing strategy: a mean of coordination

There are two goals at this stage: first, to extend knowledge of the market; and, second, to pinpoint the research effort. Considering the difficulty customers have in explaining their needs, one strategy consists in facilitating the expression of tacit needs by offering different products and collecting data concerning customer reactions to them. Marketing/research coordination operates through the adoption of a testing strategy which of course will be constructed in a linear manner. It assumes that agreement can be achieved on questions such as: Why test 2 or 3 products? What information do we expect to gain? How do we select customers for product testing? What are the major imponderables, the main factors which might cast doubt on the products?

The researchers' task is generated by the explorations carried out during the first stage, and therefore consists in identifying the different "prototypes" which will enhance understanding of the product diversity to which they might lead. The first consequence for research departments working under this integrated approach is that they must deliver prototypes quickly, organizing a research program enabling them to do so. The second consequence has to do with selection of the products to be supplied. The objective is to acquire a maximum amount of information in order to orient or re-orient the research program; and this, in turn, means a strategy of broad-based exploration. This approach is very different from the one aimed at finding as quickly as possible a product consistent with specifications fixed at the project's inception, and then conducting feasibility tests for the most promising candidate.

The marketing experts' task is to identify the firms which might be contacted for product-evaluation, and the markets in which they might be representative. Marketing experts also select the players to be involved: direct customers, customers of customers, consultants, etc. For one of the projects studied (for example), it proved possible to use the same technical concept for the development of water-based matte paint, wood varnishes, and industrial paints. For these respective applications, potential-customer lists were drawn up, and the partnership agreement covering concept evaluation was focussed in each instance on a highly specialized segment of the market.

From this stage onwards, the importance of developing the marketing and research approaches in tandem is obvious. To acquire increased knowledge of the market, it is necessary to be in a position to offer test samples in order to plan partnerships; to have access to comparative evaluations of the product relative to the competition; and to learn what the customer criteria are.

Customer evaluations: an opportunity to diversify market interfaces

Data culled from customer evaluations are an important source of information, also providing an opportunity to diversify contacts with customers. The outstanding feature of the relationship with a customer who has evaluated a sample is that much can be learned from it, but no one knows exactly what. To be sure, some questions can be raised at the outset. However, a major advantage of this type of interaction is the opportunity it provides for pinpointing important factors of which the project team may have been unaware. A risk that comes to light is far less "serious" than one that remains in the dark.

Players involved in different departments of a given firm are not always equal in their ability to recognize key points which have been omitted from the development process. Marketing experts, exercising fairly broad judgment, will be particularly sensitive to project evaluations bearing on sales volume and price. Researchers will be sensitive to evaluations bearing on technical points: for example, criteria fixed by them which turn out to be of minor importance; or criteria originally deemed of minor importance which turn out to be major. All the researchers interviewed who had had direct contacts with customers used the opportunity to fine-tune their objectives for the product under development. "When I heard the comments and questions raised by the test for evaluating biodegradability, I realized there were technical problems which needed to be investigated, and that the problem was not just a negotiating one, as had been assumed by the project's marketing supervisor." "In the beginning we were trying to make a paint with no solvent. However, it turned out this wasn't a key criterion for the customer. The product's benefits were assessed on the basis of another criterion altogether." Considering the exposure to potential information loss when a single intermediary from a single field—marketing, for example—is used, this demonstrates the importance of keeping the door open to contacts between customers and a broad spectrum of project designers.

An integrated product/market model design is one in which marketing experts no longer serve as the sole intermediaries for controlling the market interface. However, they are responsible for conducting the market-analysis process, and thus for training project players in methodology. They can explicate tacit areas of expertise and the hypotheses underlying their choices and expectations, and fine-tune project criteria. It is clear that implementation of the integrated product/market model will involve elaborating new types of marketing expertise. Researchers, for their part, must become involved in customer interaction—a situation with which they are not necessarily familiar and must attempt to gather a maximum of information for subsequent stages in the development process. One critical point has to do with problems of confidentiality, which are particularly acute in the case of complex and relatively unstable industries; or of firms that are customers for a product but suppliers through another branch of their operations; or of firms which might also be competitors, through holding-companies or subsidiaries. It is risky to foster contacts between a customer and a researcher possessing the kind of scientific, technical, or economic information a practiced interviewer might seek to acquire. This is why careful preparation of direct customer contacts is needed.

The construction of internal expertise on usage properties

Although direct contacts provide a wealth of information, they are no substitute for more carefully-calibrated demand evaluations. This is because they are extremely time-consuming—a problem for researchers who need to stay in their laboratory and focus on their experimentation to keep projects moving along. Further, customers are reluctant to make large numbers of evaluations for products under development with no guarantee that they will ever be marketed. Customers may be very interested in the benefits promised by a new product, and still consider that they have no reason to participate in its development.

"Prototypes," which are crucial milestones in the development process, will therefore be small in number. This is why it is important to identify customer criteria at the earliest possible phase in the process; to do so selectively for compromises that are difficult to establish definitively; and to arrange for taking a number of "soundings" during the life of the project in order to ensure that its foundations do not prove totally flawed in the light of subsequent developments.

The way to accomplish the above is to acquire internal evaluation techniques reflecting customer criteria. The task of the "application" research laboratories is to formulate repeatable tests for measuring product usage. The task of the researchers is to acquire a body of expertise. The fit between "application" research laboratory evaluations and customer perceptions is of course crucial. Here again, the importance of coordination between research and marketing for selecting definitive product criteria and standardized measurements becomes apparent. In addition, considering the volatility of customer preference, it is also necessary to conduct regular assessments of the tests formulated internally in relation to direct customer evaluations.

The acquisition of new research expertise

The exploration of technical solutions for improving a product feature, or for selecting products which must present very different properties for users, infers a body of scientific expertise which can link a property of measured application with physical/chemical properties. This is known as "applicability". Here again, the implementation of an integrated product/market model design system fosters the acquisition of expertise which will accelerate the process. At the firm studied, several applicability laboratories were established.

Deploying a parallel research/marketing exploration thus clarifies the contribution of both fields to the definition of the product target, while strengthening the specific expertise developed by each respective field in order to contribute to the process. I have also shown that this type of model has significant implications for both researchers and marketing experts: participation in new situations (at the customers' for researchers; orientation of the on-going research process for marketing experts); different types of intermediary production (prototypes, sampling strategy); the acquisition of new expertise (bearing on anticipation and partnership for marketing experts; with applications and applicability for researchers); and more frequent interaction between different departments, requiring the construction of intersubjectivity between protagonists.

Some consequences of the implementation of an integrated model

Beyond the emergence of coordination modalities facilitating simultaneous and convergent explorations, the implementation of this type of model raises other questions deserving of mention.

The first question has to do with project-portfolio management. If there is no business plan at the inception of the project, on what basis can the decision to launch a new project be made? How should a project be ranked in relation to other developments? Does the existence of much more reliable market forecasts for more advanced projects, or for projects reflecting a rationale of incremental innovation, threaten to stand in the way of breakthrough innovations? One strategy consists of managing breakthrough-innovation and long-term projects separately. But the prioritization of projects in this category remains a persistent problem: the development of a broad-based exploration strategy depends on the capacity to terminate fairly rapidly projects which do not generate conclusive findings during the early stages, and to transfer the teams to other projects.

The second question has to do with departmental organization. The proposed model infers the continuation of players dealing with the theme being explored and of those in contacts opened with customers. At the same time, it emphasizes the emergence and development of new expertise. How can these two rationales – specialization and project-dedicated players – be articulated? This point infers an internal organization by specialty facilitating the mobilization of a fragmented collective competence. It assumes the formulation of a profile defining players possessing the skills needed to do this, and of facilities supporting them within this dynamic.

A third question has to do with individual motivation. The linear "market-pull" model clearly establishes responsibilities facilitating the attribution of success or failure to specific players, and the corresponding remuneration. In the proposed model, this kind of responsibility attribution is not possible; but individual interest could be developed around the realization of a shared objective. Ultimately, individual commitment and internal contract could be based on the schedule enabling marketing experts to define, in stages, a precise product target, a market share, and a price. Meanwhile, the research team would base its contract and responsibilities on the strategy of exploration and of the intermediary stages at which testable "products" would be delivered to the marketing-expert partners.

A fourth question has to do with the implication of customers. Partnership strategies have repeatedly been evoked as a way to implicate customers in the design process. The development of this type of cooperation is not spontaneous, and it raises questions as to what share of the final marketable product's value-added will be attributed to each of the various intermediaries involved in its development.

In this chapter, some limitations of the market pull model are underlined especially for innovation. The main weakness of such a model for developing innovative products is the continuous evolution of customer demand and the complexity of the customer system preferences. An alternative model is elaborated where the exploration of the market and the exploration of the technical possibilities for product are two parallel and interconnected processes. Different conditions to implement such a model are developed.

A continuous coordination between marketing experts and the research team has to be structured, as the specifications of the target product remain partial and moving until late in the project. It is based on the definition of testing strategy combining sets of prototypes and sets of customer types and items to be evaluated.

This coordination mean has implications on the activity of the marketing experts. They have to conduct the market analysis not anymore sole in contact with clients. But they have also to structure the data collected by researcher as well. The researchers' activity differs also from what it used to be. They have to propose prototypes in order to define what can be done and what product the customer would prefer and not only to find the product that fits perfectly with the specifications previously defined.

Finally, new knowledge has to be developed to speed up this targeting process: in research departments, scientific expertise linking functional properties of the product with chemical of physical properties of the product or of the process.

These seem to be key points to consider in implementing the integrated product/market model design and overcome the limitation of the market pull model for innovative product development.

CHAPTER 13

INTERACTION IN THE POLITICAL MARKET SQUARE: ORGANISING MARKETING OF EVENTS

Maria Larson, European Tourism Research Institute, Östersund, Sweden and School of Economics and Commercial Law, Göteborg University, Gothenburg, Sweden

ABSTRACT

This chapter describes and analyses the marketing of a mega-event, the World Championships in Athletics in Gothenburg in 1995. Inter-organisational aspects of project marketing and co-operation between actors within a multi-project context are discussed. The literature on marketing events has a predominantly normative and practical orientation and does not contribute to a deep understanding of how the marketing of an event is organised. A theoretical frame of reference on temporary organisations and project networks is therefore used. The marketing of the World Championships in Athletics in 1995 was undertaken by a large number of actors. The actors interacted in a so-called "political market square" to further their own specific interests. Interactions in the political market square were characterised by political processes and not basically by co-operation. The reasons for this were that the actors had different goals, strategies, and target groups. Moreover, it was difficult to develop trusting relationships since the relationships were short-term. However, the relatively chaotic situation in the political market square enabled a multiplicity of interests to be promoted and considerable innovation to take place.

EVENTS AND FESTIVALS

In the past few decades, events and festivals have become increasingly popular all over the world. Events are assumed to serve a useful purpose in society since they are considered beneficial from a social, cultural and economic perspective. Moreover, hosting an event is a positive way for cities, or so-called tourist destinations, to promote themselves on a national and international market (cf. Getz 1991). In order for mega-events to become successful and gain positive short- and long-term market and economic effects, considerable resources are invested in marketing.

Until now, literature on the marketing of events (e.g. Frisby and Getz 1989, Getz 1989, 1991, 1993, 1997a, 1997b, Hall 1992, Stewart and Deibert 1993, Mayfield and Crompton 1995, McCleary 1995) has failed to allude to the problematic aspects of the marketing of events. Roche (1994: 12) points this out in his article, although he does not elaborate. The ultimately normative, practical, and "applied" orientation of the literature is aimed at diagnosing and improving planning/management practice in terms of principles and ideal models, and examples of "best practice". This limits the usefulness of the literature as a tool for the pursuit of explanatory understanding of real-world event/action production (Roche 1994: 3). Roche, on the other hand, emphasises a political approach in understanding marketing and production of events.

This chapter describes and analyses the marketing of a mega-event, the World Championships in Athletics in 1995 that was held in Gothenburg. The games are a biannual event hosted each time by a different city. For the host city Gothenburg, however, the World Championships in Athletics in 1995 were a unique, non-recurrent event (cf. Andersson and Larsson-Mossberg 1994: 2). Non-recurrent events, such as this one, are organised as projects, i.e. within a limited time frame and with limited resources.

The case is analysed from an organisational-theoretical perspective and is focused on inter-organisational aspects of the marketing work. Stress is laid on aspects concerning processes, predominantly political ones going on when actors interact. Since the study is aimed at obtaining a deeper insight into the way that events are marketed, the literature on events does not give much guidance. Therefore I have chosen to view the event as a project and to use organisational theory dealing with temporary organisations and project networks (e.g. Packendorff 1993, 1995, Lundin and Söderholm 1995, Engwall 1999, Sahlin-Andersson 1986, 1989, 1991, Sahlin 1996, Hellgren and Stjernberg 1995). This relatively new literature describes how projects are actually realised.

DEFINING THE PROBLEM

To arrange and market an event involves commitment from many different organisations and interest groups (e.g. sponsors, television networks, volunteers, tourism organisations, local authorities, hotels, and restaurants). Marketing of an event does, therefore, not only include the activities of the organising committee of the event, but also all other types of marketing performed by organisations involved in one way or another. Thus, a large number of actors create an image of the event that is expected to attract visitors. Moreover, a mega-event is a platform for firms and organisations to market their own products/services in connection with the event.

The existing literature on events illustrates the plurality of actors marketing an event to a very limited extent. Since events, and especially mega-events, depend on many actors, it is problematic to view an event as being only *one* project with *one* marketing strategy and *one* organisational structure. Since many organisations are involved, it is more relevant to speak of *several* projects, working in different ways with the realisation and marketing of the event (cf. Engwall 1999: 155). Thus, actors within an inter-organisational project network (Hellgren and Stjernberg 1995) involving several organisations market events. The actors are all working with the marketing bearing their own interests in mind. Inter-organisational projects are more complex than projects with only one actor involved (i.e. intra-organisational projects), since the number of organisations, goals, and inducements is larger. Since the objectives, goals, strategies, target groups, and modus operandi of the actors often differ, marketing in the different organisations can go in different directions that are sometimes inconsistent and even counteracting (Larson 1997). This can be assumed to lead to reduced efficiency in the marketing of the event.

Consequently, it is relevant to study the on-going processes between organisations and individuals in the project network in order to be able to describe and discuss how the marketing work of an event is executed. This chapter focuses on the overall marketing organisation of the event as a whole as well as interaction between the different actors. How can the inter-organisational structure of the marketing of an event, and the processes therein, be described and understood? How are the marketing activities co-ordinated?

AN INTER-ORGANISATIONAL NETWORK APPROACH

Many different actors in an inter-organisational network of projects, as emphasised above, market events. A network consists of positions (organisations) with links between them, which means that the positions (organisations) interact with each other (Thorelli 1986: 444). The interaction between the organisations of the network involves large-scale, mutual exchanges of resources (in one extreme) or fierce hostility and conflict (in the other extreme) (Benson 1975). Networks can be either tightly knit or loose, depending on the intensity, quality, and type of interaction between the positions. Power, i.e. the ability to influence the decisions of others, is an essential concept when analysing networks. With resources, authority, and information flow between the links in the network, it is relevant to speak of the network as political (Thorelli 1986: 444). Trust is another important concept in the interaction between the organisations.

The network concept has been used successfully by the "Uppsala School" to analyse relationships and co-operation between firms in industrial systems (e.g. Johansson *et al.* 1994). The formation of this theory accentuates *long-term* relations and mutual dependence between actors. The relationship marketing perspective has a long-term focus, too, and looks upon marketing as relationships, interactions, and networks (Gummesson 1994: 5). However, few theories and models have been developed to understand and describe inter-organisational networks of projects that focus on *short-term* relationships between actors (Hellgren and Stjernberg 1995: 377).

Hellgren and Stjernberg (1995) have developed a frame of reference to understand and analyse inter-organisational relationships in the realisation of large projects. A number of organisations with more or less conflicting objectives are supposed to co-operate within a so-called "project network". Hellgren and

Stjernberg's frame of reference is focused on interactions *between* actors (organisations) and not within organisations. Hellgren and Stjernberg (1995: 379) define a project network as:

> "(1) a set of relations, where no single actor may act as legitimate authority for the network as a whole, (2) where the network is open in the sense that there are no definite criteria by which the boundary of the network may be identified and controlled, and (3) where the network is temporally limited, dynamically changing and (partially) reconstructed from one project to the next."

The actors in a project network work under uncertainty to a large extent, since the organisations are interdependent. Thorelli (1986: 44) is of the opinion that the positioning of the organisation in the network is of great strategic importance. The relative power of an actor in the project network depends on the degree of authority (e.g. formal regulations) and how much resources the actor possesses (e.g. money, time, know-how, contacts, reputation, and trust). This leads to a situation where actors' strategies are formed in different ways also for actors with similar objectives (Hellgren and Stjernberg 1995: 179).

Hellgren and Stjernberg (1995) hold the view that processes within the project network, e.g. in the form of new actors entering or new regulations coming into force, lead to the change of power positions (changes of degree of relative authority and amount of resources). The actors' rationality also changes the network, i.e. if they act in a short-term or long-term perspective, how they model their objectives, and how they solve problems. Hellgren and Stjernberg (1995: 385) are, thus, of the opinion that process and structure interact so that structure, i.e. the relationships between the actors, the power structure, and the actors' contributions to the project network, determines the process in the shaping and implementation of the project. The ongoing processes in turn shape the structure (cf. Söderholm 1991).

Like Hellgren and Stjernberg, Sahlin-Andersson (1986, 1989, 1991) has studied processes in large projects. She states that the organising in many cases is performed in an ad hoc fashion. Pari passu with the emergence of new situations and problems, different project groups are formed. Around a nucleus of go-ahead actors, a complicated network of groups is built. In many a case it is unclear to those concerned which groups have the right to make certain decisions and act in the project (Sahlin-Andersson 1991: 45). The matter at hand, thus, creates a meeting place, an arena for action, where a number of loosely connected actors gather and/or exercise power. When many actors are engaged in the arena, the importance and the extraordinary character of the projects are strengthened (Sahlin-Andersson 1986: 174, 196).

Accordingly, literature on project networks deals with short-term relationships, and illustrates loosely coupled actors, dynamic processes, and a changing structure, whereas traditional literature on networks focuses on long-term relationships. In long-term relationships, institutionalisation processes (cf. Meyer and Rowan 1977) often take place within the network and a more rigid structure is formed. However, in project networks such as the network of the World Championships in Athletics

1995, relationships between actors are of a short-term nature. Traditional network theory is, therefore, not applicable. Instead I have chosen to use a theoretical framework on project networks, which focuses on dynamic processes rather than on structure. Moreover, literature on networks as well as events mentions the political dimension of organising. This chapter aims at rendering the political aspect more explicit.

The actors that marketed the games operated within a project network that can be characterised as open, and consisting of short-term relationships and dynamic processes (Larson 1997). Co-operation between actors may, which is considered to be desirable by most researchers on the subject, be problematic in this situation. In the following section, aspects of the World Championships in Athletics 1995 will be described and analysed using the perspective discussed above.

CASE STUDY: THE WORLD CHAMPIONSHIPS IN ATHLETICS 1995

The Case
The World Championships in Athletics 1995 (WC) were organised in Gothenburg, Sweden. The games are one of the largest mega-events in the world. Thousands and thousands of people invaded Gothenburg in August 1995 to watch the competitions and to take part in the festivities arranged in connection with the event. The realisation of the event was assigned to a project organisation, i.e. the Local Organising Committee (LOC), which assumed the operative responsibility for the event.

The principal actors involved in the strategic and operative marketing activities of the WC were the LOC and Göteborg &Co (the tourism organisation responsible for the so-called destination marketing of Gothenburg). These organisations had different functions. Göteborg &Co answered to the municipality of Gothenburg as far as marketing the destination Gothenburg was concerned. The task was to market the region of Gothenburg, co-ordinate marketing and information activities, and initiate and co-ordinate activities in the city during the days of the event. The LOC, on the other hand, was appointed by the Swedish Athletic Association (and they in their turn were controlled by the International Amateur Athletic Federation, IAAF) to market the event as the mega-event in sports of the year. The LOC was established in 1992 and Göteborg &Co built up its project organisation at about the same time. Accordingly, the project work was performed during a period of time of about 3 years.

Eight months prior to the staging of the WC, a qualitative case study was made which included 25 in-depth interviews with individuals working with the marketing of the event. Furthermore, participant observation and collection of documentation (e.g. marketing plans and notes from meetings) were accomplished. I concentrated the case study on the LOC and Göteborg &Co, since they were the dominant organisations working with the operative marketing of the event. Other actors were studied, but not as exhaustively.

The Inter-Organisational Structure of the Project Network

Many different actors took an active part in the mega-event, from the large sponsor company Telia to the small petrol station near the arena where the games took place. There were actually no restrictions as to the number of actors or type of actors that could join the project network of the WC. Although there were formal restrictions on for example sponsor activities, companies found ways around those restrictions. Therefore, every actor who in any respect took part in the marketing of the WC had opportunities of creating a strong position in the project network. As a consequence, new actors who emerged in the WC project had as good chances as the already present actors to capitalise on the event. Most actors had the opportunity of leaving the project network at any time. Thus, the WC project network had an open structure. However, there was a time-related limitation, since the games would take place at a given point of time and afterwards the network was dissolved.

According to Hellgren and Stjernberg (1995: 385), the structure of the project network exerts an influence on the implementation processes of the actors at the same time as the processes in turn have an influence on the structure of the network. Structure and process interact, leading to a constantly changing project network. (Please read the objectified structure of the event, i.e. how the individuals interpreted the structure. The structure was a social construction that was perceived differently by different individuals.) This interaction can be discerned in the marketing work of the WC project. At the time, when the marketing of the event was initiated, the actors (the International Amateur Athletic Federation, the Swedish Athletics Federation and the municipality of Gothenburg) and their working structure, i.e. the relationships between them and their respective procedures, naturally influenced the marketing process. The regulations and contracts that these actors had bargained for affected the scope of action of other actors. E.g. the marketing work at the LOC was, from the start, governed by contracts between IAAF and ISL (the international sponsor agency) and between ISL and the sponsors. These actors acted within the scope of permanent organisations with a solid organisational structure with fixed procedures and often long experience of marketing of events. Therefore, they had the opportunity of directing certain processes to their advantage.

However, as new actors entered the WC project network, the balance of power changed. The municipality of Gothenburg, Göteborg &Co, and the LOC negotiated with ISL and tried to handle ISL's power position (e.g. ISL's strong demands for outdoor advertising space in Gothenburg). The ongoing processes in the different projects and interactions between the actors restructured the project network. Accordingly, the WC project cannot be perceived as a unity closely joined together, but as an arena for several, loosely linked actors and activities (cf. Sahlin-Andersson 1989: 27) in incessant change.

Marketing Actors in a Political Market Square

Figure 1 below shows the project network including the actors involved in marketing the event. The complexity of the project network makes it impossible to give a fair picture of the actors, their relationships, and power positions. Only a few actors are presented; those who appeared most clearly in the study. The two main actors responsible for the operative marketing of the event are presented in the large circles in the model, whereas other actors are shown in the small circles. (The circles are equally sized disregarding actors' difference in power position in the network.) The figure shows the network at a certain point of time, i.e. the spring of 1995. Since there was a continuos change of involved actors during the progress of the WC project, a different picture would have appeared at another point of time. The lines in the figure illustrate the interaction between the actors. Thus, the central and the peripheral actors can be distinguished.

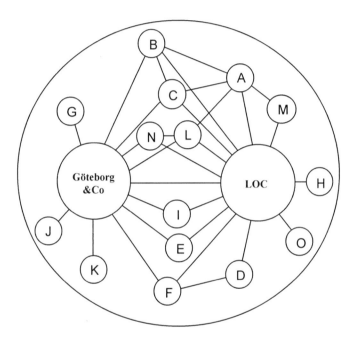

Figure 1. Marketing actors in the project network of the World Championships in Athletics 1995

A: ISL
B: IAAF
C: The municipality
D: Advertising agency
E: Niclas Josefsson AB

F: G-P (newspaper)
G: Liseberg (amusement park)
H: SJ, The Swedish State railways
I: Landvetter airport
J: Next Stop Sweden (tourism org.)

K: The Export Council
L: Telia (sponsor)
M: Reebok (sponsor)
N: The WC Academy
O: Lynx Promotion

"Political market square" (Larson 1997) is a metaphor for the project network. "The market square" is the arena in which actors (i.e. actors that had a conscious intention of participating in marketing the WC) acted in order to contribute to the marketing of the event. The WC project was in a way an opportunity to take advantage of. Certain actors were involved for several years, while others were engaged for a shorter period of time; i.e. they withdrew from the market square when they were no longer interested in participating. The political market square suggests that actors had different interests (expectations or goals) in participating. In interaction with other actors, they tried to attain their own goals by increasing their influence and strengthening their positions in the market square. No individual actor in the market square had a stable position of power (cf. Hellgren and Stjernberg 1995: 390). Therefore, there were conflicts, power games, and tough negotiations between actors.

Mega-events are especially exposed to political games between different actors (Getz 1991: 152, Hall 1992: 84, Roche 1994: 6).

> "The potential result is a public relations contest among various interested parties, rather than co-operation and integrated planning." (Getz 1991: 152)

> "Hallmark events are not the result of a rational decision-making process. Decisions affecting the hosting and the nature of hallmark events grow out of a political process. The process involves the values of actors (individuals, interest groups, and organisations) in a struggle for power." (Roche 1994: 6)

The political games took place because actors sometimes tried to control other actors, i.e. they strove to be in the centre of the project network and to make strategic marketing decisions. Since actors could not act as an authority for the entire project network, actors entered into alliances with other actors with similar interests. In other cases, actors acted with nothing but their own interests in mind, i.e. they ignored other actors. Therefore, to some extent, anarchy prevailed in the political market square. The actors were so absorbed in their own activities and in looking after their own interests that they, under certain circumstances, did not pay attention to regulations and norms that were in force in the project network. One example: the WC-Academy (the student organisation) used the WC logotype without permission from the LOC. This was not appreciated by the LOC. However, the WC-Academy had nothing to lose, since the organisation was dissolved after the event and nobody was left to be held responsible.

In sum, actors within a so-called political market square marketed the WC project. The interactions between the actors were characterised by political processes. The actors could jointly have decided on the most effective way of marketing the event in order to co-ordinate marketing activities accordingly. Below the difficulties of achieving co-ordination and co-operation will be discussed.

Co-operation between Marketing Actors
The above section described the marketing of the WC event as a political process. It was difficult to reach a compromise between the different interests of the actors. Consequently, co-operation between the marketing actors of the WC event did not function in a satisfactory way.

> "In general, the contact between Göteborg & Co and the LOC has been very poor."

"More co-operation would be useful."
"In broad outline, co-operation has been good but, of course, there have been different opinions and sometimes things were not working smoothly."
"Göteborg & Co should try hard to co-operate for combined forces."
"If you would want to focus on highlighting the city of Gothenburg, more co-operation is needed...."
"Co-operation, my foot! Everybody is looking out for number one, including the chaps at Göteborg & Co."
(Quoted from interviews with the marketing personnel at Göteborg & Co and the LOC)

It is easy to see why co-operation did not work smoothly; the fact is that the two organisations did not really market the same product. Göteborg & Co marketed the destination in the first place and the LOC marketed the event. Therefore, both organisations had different objectives and addressed themselves to different target groups, i.e. Göteborg & Co prioritised tourists, while the LOC prioritised the local people since it was easier to sell tickets to them than to non-locals. The organisations acted with their own objectives in mind as starting-points and, therefore, the strategic and operative marketing efforts of the organisations moved in different directions. Thus, owing to the intention of the actors to strive for their own objectives, conflicting targets can be perceived as a hindrance to co-ordination (cf. Sverlinger 1996: 86). However, in the case of the WC project, the organisations' aim for different market segments can be seen as complementary rather than competitive, because the large scope of the project renders it possible for many market segments to be targeted. Aiming at a large number of target groups can be self-reinforcing for an event as a whole.

Sahlin-Andersson (1989: 64-65) is of the opinion that organisations participating in a project cannot erase their differences; they try to run the project together despite different points of departure, interests, norms, and contexts and, therefore, the situation is complex. According to Getz (1991: 152), the only sensible way of solving this is to:

"...demonstrate that working together maximises the degree of every stakeholder's goal attainment. Only if all parties have an equal share in the planning will effective planning result."

Sverlinger (1996: 45), too, maintains that co-ordination is of decisive importance for the efficiency of a project.

"By co-ordinating the actions of several individuals, the result becomes of greater value than the sum of the acting of the individuals alone."

However, establishing a co-ordinating agency for the WC project would not have made a difference, since it is difficult for such an agency to obtain legitimacy to exercise authority over the other actors in the project network. Moreover, it would be difficult for such a body to look after the interests of all actors.

Axelrod (1984) states that co-operation is possible without the existence of common objectives, friendship or a central authority. According to Axelrod, the most effective strategy for interaction between actors is always the one based on reciprocity. However, when contact between individuals is expected to cease in the near future, the incentive for co-operation diminishes:

> "No form of co-operation is stable when the future is not sufficiently important in relation to the present." (Axelrod 1984: 111)

Accordingly, the fact that the WC project was of a temporary character might have led to the actors not giving co-operation high priority.

Trust is an important concept in successful co-operation. Mayer, Davis & Schoorman (1995) define trust as believing in and being willing to depend on another party. To be able to co-operate, the parties must trust each other, but generally it takes time to develop mutual trust (Norbäck 1978: 255). Since the marketing activities of the different actors went on for a relatively short period of time, the actors did not have time to develop trusting relationships. Instead, some actors distrusted each other and power and control, to a degree, replaced trust. However, co-operation between Göteborg&Co and the LOC improved as time went by. The relationship developed into a more long-term one and actors trusted each other (cf. Ford 1990: 49), and were able to improve co-operation.

Another reason for the actors' reluctance to co-operate could be that co-operation might restrict the individuals' freedom of action. As actors interact, ties, influences, and dependencies are developed that stabilise the course of the processes. However, this ties up the actors and restricts their possibilities to act on their own (Sahlin-Andersson 1989: 150). In this way, co-operation can be a threat to the freedom of action (cf. Trägårdh 1997: 51). Since liberty of action is the very essence of marketing events (Larson 1997), it is natural that the individuals oppose potential restrictions in this respect.

Yet another obstacle to co-operation was the temporary organisations' lack of time and resources. Since it is often strenuous to co-operate and to reach a compromise, the limited time and resources for marketing the event might have led to the actors' not prioritising co-operation. Furthermore, the fact that no major crises arouse may be an explanation why the WC-event actors did not co-operate. When everything runs smoothly, there is no urgent need for co-operation.

Consequently, the interaction between the actors in the political market square was not characterised by a high degree of interchange and co-operation. There were political games including conflicts and counteractions. Some actors did not interact at all, since they did not see any advantage therein. Instead, there was some kind of co-existence (Trägårdh 1997), i.e. the actors neither competed nor co-operated but had a weak form of fellowship which was reinforced by their complementary market groups. Thus, some actors co-existed, some were in conflict, and a few co-operated.

To Co-ordinate or Not?

The study on the WC event showed clearly that the marketing was not co-ordinated to any appreciable extent. A common view on co-ordination is that it brings about organisational acting towards common goals (cf. Sverlinger 1996: 45). An event as a whole might, however, lose on too much co-ordination. Since a mega-event like the World Championships in Athletics incorporates many different actors with different interests and goals, every kind of adaptation to common goals involves a choice of perspective (e.g. increased tourism or commitment to sports and athletics). Instead, it is possible that the very purpose of such a large event is to allow scope for many different goals and perspectives. This in turn can lead to innovations and changes in different fields. An example of such innovations is the WC Academy's work in information technology, which led to the establishment of a successful IT-company.

A project such as an event allows scope for the participation of many actors with *many different purposes and perspectives*. In a more rigid and closed project network with for instance a governing and co-ordinating agency that would limit the number of actors and their marketing orientation (i.e. a hierarchy), the number of purposes and perspectives that would benefit from the marketing of the event would not be as large. If the intention were to achieve market effects in as many fields as possible, such an agency would not be effective. Thus, the loose and changing organisational structure of an event renders it possible for a dynamic and heterogeneous network of actors to appear. The plurality of actors makes it possible for a great variety of goals to be reached, a multiplicity of market segments to be targeted, and many marketing activities within different fields to be carried out.

However, in a dynamic and heterogeneous project network, the concentration on each individual perspective is limited. The marketing actors, in a way, compete for peoples' attention. Moreover, the various goals and marketing strategies of the actors may also be inconsistent in such a way that the actors counteract each other (for instance, the LOC sold tickets chiefly to the local people, whereas Göteborg&Co preferred to try to attract more tourists to Gothenburg). Thus there is a balance between the advantage of having a multiplicity of goals and perspectives and the advantage of concentrating the resources available to a smaller number of purposes. For instance, if the municipality had had more influence on the activities of the LOC, the goals of the municipality would have been reached to a higher degree. However, in such a case it is possible that the chances would have been reduced for the perspectives of sports as an institution to be promoted.

Consequently, more co-ordination of the marketing work in a project network leads to a situation where relatively few perspectives are focused on (where the investment in one perspective is relatively large). On the other hand, when the actors of the network act in a free arena of action, i.e. in a so-called political market square, the event marketing contributes to promoting several perspectives (where the investment in each of the perspectives, however, becomes comparatively smaller).

This section has described and analysed the inter-organisational structure of the WC project network, the processes therein, and co-operation and co-ordination of the marketing of the event. Below, the findings of the above discussion are summarised and a conceptual model is presented.

CO-OPERATION AND MARKETING CO-ORDINATION IN A POLITICAL MARKET SQUARE

The inter-organisational marketing of the World Championships in Athletics in 1995 proved to involve a vast number of actors and activities and, therefore, it was difficult to give a comprehensive and clear picture thereof. The event can be described as a *project network* consisting of a number of independent projects with different aims and marketing strategies. A metaphor for the arena in which the actors interacted is *the political market square* (Larson 1997), which is characterised by political processes and changing structures.

The processes that were going on in the form of interactions and activities changed the structure of the network and the positions of the actors in the network. Consequently, the project network changed during the course of the marketing process in an iterative process owing to the fact that actors entered and disappeared and that the absolute and relative importance of the actors changed in the course of time. Accordingly, there was not, at the inter-organisational level for the implementation of the event marketing, any fixed structure that limited the actors' freedom of action. Regulations or contracts that were drawn up between parties could be interpreted differently and were sometimes deliberately ignored. The event was used as a tool for actors in achieving individual goals.

There was a low degree of interchange and co-operation between actors concerning the marketing work. The difficulty in co-operating can be explained by the fact that every actor aimed at different goals in his/her operations. In such a situation, it is difficult to tactically limit the number of actors engaged and to operatively co-ordinate the actors' different activities, i.e. to create a hierarchy. Another explanation could be that the temporary character of the project network prevents *development of mutual trust in the relationships between the actors*. This is due to the fact that the operative implementation of the event is going on under a limited period of time; the actors act within temporary organisations, which are dissolved after the event. Yet another explanation of the difficulty in co-operating is that co-operation implies *restrictions on the actors' liberty of action*.

Co-operation is generally seen as something desirable that makes the most of the resources used. However, co-operation could give rise to a situation where the actors limit each other's freedom of action or where certain actors succeed in negotiating a position of superiority, i.e. the project network approaches hierarchy. When the actors organise themselves as a hierarchy instead of acting in a political market square, the consequence might be that the activities are directed at looking after just a few interests. Consequently, the effect of co-operation (i.e. co-operation leading to hierarchy) is not entirely positive. On the contrary, liberty of action in the political market square and the presence of many actors lead to effects and innovations in many different fields.

Moreover, a large project such as the WC has the potential to attract many different target groups that are complementary and mutually supportive. Accordingly, co-operation leading to co-ordination of the marketing is not needed. Instead, co-ordination can, seen from this perspective, be regarded as inefficient.

The table below illustrates two opposites; hierarchy and political market square, which represent different structures of a project network. The table summarises the result of the WC study by including the main issues analysed. The results of the study show that actors in a political market square marketed the WC event (see the right part of the model). The hierarchy is presented as a hypothesis of the situation in a project network with a rather rigid and tightly knit inter-organisational structure. The hierarchy model can be applied on the perspective on marketing events presented in Getz's (1989, 1991, 1993, 1997a, 1997b) normative models.

Table 1. Characteristics of Project Networks - Hierarchy versus Political Market Square

	HIERARCHY	POLITICAL MARKET SQUARE
Inter-organisational structure	Closed and rigid, tightly knit actors	Open and changing, loosely linked actors
Marketing processes	Institutionalised	Political and dynamic
Relationships	Long-term	Short-term
Trust	High	Low
Liberty of action	Low (a few leading individuals/actors make the decisions)	High (for the individual/actor)
Co-ordination	High	Non-existent or low
The effects of marketing the event	Few perspectives are promoted, comparatively large investment in each perspective	Many perspectives are promoted, comparatively small investment in each perspective

IMPLICATIONS AND FUTURE RESEARCH

An event is not a phenomenon that can be formed in advance. On the contrary, it grows by interaction between people who are genuinely attracted by the idea of achieving something unique. An event is subjective in a sense that the actors have different expectations, purposes, and interests when participating. The overall marketing of an event has, all in all, many nuances, and it aims at looking after the interests of many parties. An event could be said to be a social construction of individuals, constantly changing in interaction with other actors and individuals in a so-called political market square. The creation and the marketing of the event product can, therefore, not be defined and planned with a strict "goal-means" approach, i.e. with traditional marketing theory as a starting-point, since the prerequisites in the environment and the expectations of individuals change continuously over time. It can better be described as a dynamic process, involving a large number of people and organisations, formed by peoples' expectations, actions, and subjective interpretations.

The findings in the case study of the WC project network are focused on process aspects, and the changing nature of the project, and not as much on structural aspects. In a projectified business world with focus on innovations and change, a research perspective focusing on processes would be more rewarding in terms of gaining increased understanding of problems in project organising. Since literature on projects (as well as literature on events) has not largely focused on processes, such as political processes, more research is needed.

The results in this chapter are based on a case study of the World Championships in Athletics in 1995. The event was (for the organisers and Gothenburg) a non-recurrent, unique event, i.e. it was a project performed only once. It was also a mega-event – the largest event ever organised in Sweden. Consequently, for a better understanding of project networks, case studies on small, repetitive projects would be fruitful.

PEOPLE'S PROJECTS

CHAPTER 14

LEADERSHIP FEARS AND FRUSTRATIONS IN PROJECT MANAGEMENT

Kam Jugdev, IBM Canada Ltd.

Francis Hartman, University of Calgary

Janice Thomas, University of Calgary

ABSTRACT

Leadership literature has repeatedly identified the visionary, team building, communication and conflict management skills required in project management. Although many authors focused on noble leadership traits and characteristics very little research has been evident on the fears and frustrations project managers experience.

Project managers function in high-stress environments and are responsible for ensuring that the technical aspects of the project are on track (e.g. cost, scope, quality, safety, and risks). In addition, they are responsible for managing the interpersonal dynamics within cross-functional teams and with senior management.

The research objectives of this study were to have project managers identify common project manager fears and frustrations, prioritize them and provide recommendations on addressing the challenges.

The authors used the Delphi technique to survey a sample of experienced project managers in the Oil and Gas and Information Technology industries. The survey results confirmed the existence of fears and frustrations and related them to project critical success factors.

INTRODUCTION

Project managers work in complex knowledge-based environments and face numerous responsibilities and challenges. In part, the following characteristics of high technology companies compound their challenges: work complexity, evolving solutions, innovation, teamwork and group decision-making, complex support systems and highly complex forms of work integration (Thamhain 1996). Although a considerable amount of research has focused on noble leader traits, very little research has been conducted on project manager fears and frustrations. Not only must project managers ensure that the project is on track in terms of cost, scope, quality, safety and risks etc., but they must also manage project interpersonal dynamics.

This chapter presents the findings of an exploratory study in a relatively uncharted area. The authors identify and prioritize determinants of project manager fears and frustrations by means of a Delphi approach and present recommendations on addressing the issues. The chapter begins with a literature review on leadership in project management.

LEADERSHIP: THE ROCK ROAD OF PUTTING THEORY INTO PRACTICE

Current literature indicates that project management involves two essential dimensions, a technical one (hard skills) focusing on planning and scheduling tasks and an interpersonal one (soft skills) dealing with behaviors, attitudes, communication abilities and leadership (Geaney 1997). Leadership can be defined as "an exercise of influence resulting in enthusiastic commitment by followers" (Yukl 1989).

Traditional definitions of leadership involved the heroic traits of setting direction, making decisions and energizing troops whereas the more recent transformational era defines them in post-heroic terms e.g. the leader as designer, steward and teacher (Senge 1990). Transformational leaders are expected to "inspire and intellectually stimulate employees to perform beyond normal expectations and personal self-interest to achieve challenging group goals" (Keller 1995: 41). Descriptions like this can be quite intimidating because of the lofty expectations and noble attributes ascribed to leaders. In addition, it is the rare leader who can inspire everyone involved on the project (Keller 1995).

Along with the leadership responsibilities, project managers face challenges in leading cross-functional teams within matrix structures. They often have little span of control over team members who report to functional heads (Kezsbom and Donnelly 1994). Consequently, they require additional skills of teamwork, leading by example, providing training, practicing empowerment and sharing leadership (Lewis and Bloom 1993). The concept of shared leadership can be difficult to practice because project accountability and responsibility generally rests with one person - the project manager. Kezsbom (1994) indicated that project managers might find it difficult to adopt participative leadership styles partly because of limited resources, demanding schedules and cost restraints. Project managers may unwittingly discourage involvement due to defensive behaviors such as limiting input and ignoring what they hear, especially in high-stress project conditions.

Effective teams involve synergy and empowerment is required to attain this (Bellinger and Beyerlein 1995). It is up to the leader to share the power. However, creating high performance, empowered teams are a resource intensive, time consuming undertaking because the process involves trust, change and taking risks. Such daunting responsibilities can be stressful, especially when the job of a project manager also involves responsibilities of pressing deadlines, cost constraints, customer issues, teams and senior management demands, to name a few.

Leadership capabilities become critical as the interpersonal dynamics become more complex. Kezsbom (1992) noted that the top three categories of conflict on projects were related to goals and priority definition, personality conflicts and communication and information flow. Bates indicated that leaders should learn to negotiate around and through potential conflict (1994). As corporate change agent, project managers understand that buy-in from stakeholders is critical. However, since participants may not readily table their agendas for any number of reasons, this can be both frustrating and hamper project progress.

Kezsbom (1994) wrote about the need for a supportive organizational environment, senior sponsorship and a clear, shared vision. Winkler (1996) indicated that "commitment and leadership must come from the top" (pp. 59). However, senior managers are in stressful, demanding roles themselves. This, along with competing priorities and the interpersonal relationships at the senior level (politics) may result in inconsistent support for project managers.

Considering the responsibilities and expectations placed on project managers, none of the articles addressed the personal fears or frustrations that must be an unsettling and very real part of the role. However, in keeping with the theme that project managers must be noble leaders, the articles supported education and training to help achieve this. Geaney (1997) observed that soft project manager skills could be learned by emulating mentors and taking courses. Santo (1997) indicated that the test of good managers appeared to be linked to education. Morrill noted that project managers should know their strengths and weaknesses and address their limitations to be more effective (1996). According to Morrill, when project managers do not appreciate the value of the human relations responsibilities of their role, "they manifest disdain for continuing education, entropy sets in and each project leader becomes worse than his predecessor" (pp. 23). Saia (1997) recommended that companies develop internal programs to foster professional growth. For these approaches to be successful, the premise that must first be accepted is that the interpersonal dimensions of leadership are vital to project success.

A partial assumption in some articles seemed to be that the root cause of project problems was the project manager. In order to improve project success then, the implication is that the project manager should take courses and learn to be more effective. However, as indicated by Pinto and Slevin (1987), critical success factors for project implementation are broader than the abilities of the project manager. Their 10 factors contributing to project success were: project mission, top management support, project schedule / plans, client consultation, personnel, technical tasks, client acceptance, monitoring and comments, communication and troubleshooting. The authors suggested that these categories be kept in mind in relation to developing effective leadership capabilities. The writers of this chapter suggest that if some project manager fears and frustrations relate to critical success factors, then addressing the fears and frustrations may enhance project success. This brings us to some of the literature on personal fears and frustrations in relation to project management.

Suarez (1993) emphasized the importance of paying attention to fear because of its negative effects. Fears in the work place were associated with position, power, authority and psychological and social factors. Ferris (1997) criticized the formal study of leadership for not placing enough attention on the nature of personal fears that lead to stress. His research indicated that those with psychological hardiness characteristics of a commitment to tasks, internal locus of control and an ability to see challenges as opportunities were better able to cope with stress. Ferris (1997) also noted that those with high self-esteem and confidence might be better able to cope with stress. Ferris proposed that leaders feared leadership failure or feared how they might react in stressful situations e.g. fear of not behaving nobly or with competence. These fears could cause them to temporarily be unable to act or make mistakes in judgment. Common coping mechanisms included taking control, escaping (take a vacation, move to another project), and symptom management (exercise, healthy habits) strategies. These strategies were only part of the solution though, since leaders were further stressed because of a strong sense of responsibility and sensitivity on how others perceived them.

Gemmill and Wilemon (1994) studied the interpersonal concerns project managers had in relation to teams. Their findings were that project managers' main frustrations in leading teams included a lack of team member involvement, not reaching consensus, inability to influence team members and an inability to influence the organization. The most commonly reported fears of being a project manager included dominating teams, making mistakes, losing team control and having an apathetic team.

The authors recommended that project managers *and* senior management challenge processes, inspire a shared vision, and enable others to act and model the way. Leaders were encouraged to develop norms on the acceptability of discussing difficult team issues. In turn, this should create a culture of open trust and support team performance. However, for any of this to occur, project managers needed to acknowledge their team-related fears and frustrations first. Furthermore, fears are not unique to a few. This brings us to the research conducted for this chapter where the writers explored fears and frustrations beyond teams, at a project level.

METHODOLOGY: THE FIRST STEP IS ACKNOWLEDGING THAT FEARS AND FRUSTRATIONS EXIST

The Delphi technique enabled the writers to collect preliminary information on a topic that is relatively new to project management research. Pre-tested self-administered surveys were used to systematically identify and categorize the feedback provided. Three iterations of the Delphi were used and are referred to as rounds one, two and three in this chapter.

Calgary, Alberta is renowned for its Oil and Gas industry. The initial contact names compiled for the surveys represented project managers in the Oil and Gas and Information Technology (IT) industries. Forty-one participants working on Oil and Gas (O & G) and IT projects were selected through the purposive sampling technique (Fink 1985). The questions were not asked in reference to particular projects but were focused on the topics of fears and frustrations. In the surveys, fears were defined as states of dread, apprehension, alarm, agitation or anxiety caused by perceived or real dangers. Frustrations were defined as factors that kept one from attaining a goal or finishing a project. Participants were asked to identify and describe the major fears and frustrations they had experienced in leading projects. Then they were asked to describe how the fears and frustrations affected the project (e.g. in terms of scope, quality, cost, time, safety, etc.) as well as from an interpersonal perspective.

The results from round one were used to develop 9 fear and 10 frustration categories. For round two, the participants were asked to confirm that the material was an accurate reflection of their views and were asked to rank the fears and frustration categories using a priority grid (Bolles 1994). The grid enabled participants to compare pairs of fears or frustrations before ranking them. In round three, participants reviewed the group's prioritized fears and frustrations by project type (O & G or IT projects) and were asked to confirm whether they agreed with the rankings and if not, were asked to modify the order.

RESULTS: FEARS AND FRUSTRATIONS ARE REAL BUT CAN BE MANAGED

On the average, 27 participants participated in each survey for a response rate of 66%. 12 (44%) worked on IT projects and 15 (56%) on O & G projects. 23 (85%) men and 4 (15%) women were involved. In terms of age, 2 were under 35, 10 between 36 – 45, 13 between 46 – 55 and 2 were over 56 years. 6 (22%) had under 10 years of work experience, 14 (52%) had between 11-20, 6 (22%) had between 21 – 30 and 1(4%) had over 31 years of experience. 18 (67%) had a university degree, 6 (22%) had a graduate degree and 3 (11%) had either a technical diploma or college certificate.

The high response rate was attributed to the reminder calls made approximately two weeks after each survey distribution. Since the writers were conducting exploratory research on qualitative determinants of fears and frustrations, the findings were analyzed for the aggregate instead of by O & G or IT projects. In addition, the sample size was too small for any industry analysis to be representative. The one industry specific difference noted related to safety. Safety was a higher priority for the O & G group but lower on the list for the IT group.

Results on Frustrations

For all three rounds, participants provided extensive written responses to the open-ended questions. The comments provided in round two confirmed and supported the opinions provided in round one; by round three, no new themes were identified by the participants. In response to the question on the major frustrations project managers experience, the majority of comments in round two related to changing expectations, expectation mismatches and unrealistic expectations. The lack of alignment between setting expectations and the realities that ensue were reflected in such comments as - "You think you have support and commitment (buy-in) but soon find out you don't". Other comments emphasized that the end dates or price for projects never changed but that expectations did.

Participant feedback on how frustrations affected the project in terms of scope, quality, cost, time, safety etc. follow: client dissatisfaction, staff turnover, stress, reduced morale, micro-management, job dissatisfaction and miscommunication. Regarding the question on the effect of these frustrations on the project from an interpersonal perspective, insights included the following: poor communication, strained relationships, low morale and productivity, lack of support, "finger pointing", conflict, tension, lack of respect, perfectionist behavior, burnout, lack of trust and reduced customer satisfaction. Some also described how the frustrations magnified defensive behaviors in project managers. Some commented on the impact of the frustrations at a personal level in terms of balancing work, domestic, social, professional demands, time and energy. In the written comments provided in round three, participants indicated that they agreed with the rankings. The following comments were offered: communication should be moved up on the rank order, the rank given to senior management depended on the company you worked for, senior management support was vital and human resources were market dependent.

Results on Fears

In round two, the written comments related to personal failure, failing others as well as the fear of making decisions without all the facts. One participant commented on the fear of having no fear. Another stated that we fear what frustrates us. The range of comments reflected the pulls that exist on project managers i.e. commitment to the project vs. detachment from the project, authority and responsibility vs. letting go, personal values vs. project values, customer expectations vs. marketing expectations and personal expectations vs. team and senior management expectations. Some participants viewed client, senior management and other stakeholder expectations as being beyond the control of project managers. They described project managers as being sandwiched between the customer and senior management. Although the frustrations were described as being beyond their control, some participants still described project problems as indicative of a fear of personal failure.

When asked to describe how fears affected the project, the comments related to the project manager. For example, the project manager may micro-manage, be indecisive, make wrong decisions and lose credibility with others. The participants appeared to take many of the project-related problems personally as noted in the following comments: I will be labeled a failure, I could lose my career, and people may question my abilities. Several mentioned that fear could actually be a positive experience because it enabled them to work and try harder. They described it as unavoidable but indicated that it enabled them to put proper safeguards in place. In round three the respondents offered the following comments on fears: client expectations and senior management are high sources of fear as are schedules, junior project managers may experience more problems with self esteem, project managers fear losing command status, people experience anxieties, worries or concerns but not fears (a denial comment). Some of the participants indicated that the rankings were "similar" to theirs and that the order "felt" right.

FEARS AND FRUSTRATIONS RELATE TO PROJECT CRITICAL SUCCESS FACTORS

In the course of the three rounds, 5/10 frustrations and 7/9 fears remained at the same ordinal position. The degree of consensus between the second and third rounds indicated that the Delphi had been effective in prioritizing fears and frustrations. Fears and Frustrations as the study participants perceived them are shown in Table 1 and compared to Pinto and Slevin's (1987) critical success factors. Client Expectations were the primary source of frustration and Schedules / Budgets / Estimates the main source of fear. Other similarities between the lists of fears and frustrations were that Client Expectations and Schedules appeared at the top of each list, Project Teams appeared in the middle and Senior Management near the bottom. There also appeared to be some rough correspondences between the lists of fears and frustrations as compared to the critical success factors developed by Pinto and Slevin (1987). These are marked with symbols in the table.

Table 1. Prioritized Fears and Frustrations as Compared to Pinto and Slevin's Critical Success Factors.

PRIO-RITY	FEARS	FRUSTRATIONS	PINTO & SLEVIN'S CRITICAL FACTORS FOR SUCCESSFUL IMPLEMENTATION
1	☒ Schedule / Budgets / Estimates	♦ Client Expectations	♦ Mission
2	♦ Client Expectations	♦ Scope	☞ Top Management Support
3	Technology / Functionality / Equipment	☒ Schedule	☒ Schedule
4	Failure / Inadequacy / Self Esteem	☺ Human & Physical Resources	♦ Client Consultation
5	☺ Project Team	☒ Budgets and Estimates	☺ Personnel
6	Fear of the unknown	☺ Project Team	Technical Tasks
7	☞ Senior Management	E Communication	♦ Client Acceptance
8	Safety	☞ Senior Management	Monitor and Feedback
9	Other	Quality	E Communication
10		Other	Trouble Shooting

NOTE: The areas of commonality between Pinto and Slevin's (1987) critical success factors and the lists of fears and frustrations are marked with symbols.

Often described of as consisting of Time, Cost and Scope, the traditional project management triangle (PMT) was also compared to the top three project manager fears and frustrations of this study. As shown in **Diagram 1**, the comparisons indicated areas of commonality between the two.

In rounds one and two, some of the written comments reflected the tendency to support and use single completion dates and budgets. The participants also commented on their fears and frustrations when these deadlines and time commitments were not met. The ability to agree on manageable target budgets and date ranges may enable project staff to address these concerns more effectively.

The literature review had discussed personal fears in the work place and the results of this research placed Failure / Inadequacy / Self-Esteem 4th on the list of fears. This report confirmed that issues around self-confidence were of concern to the project managers surveyed. In part, despite the years of experience participants had to develop personal esteem and confidence, personal failure still appeared to be a fundamental source of fear. The writers queried to what extent the participants and others continued to see project failure as a reflection of the project manager failing, despite the number of other factors that influenced project failure and appeared to be beyond their control?

Diagram 1. Prioritized Fears and Frustrations Related to the Project Management Triangle

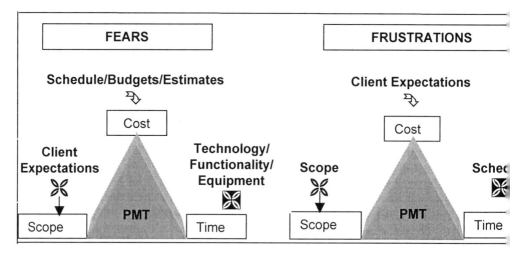

Note: The apexes portray the three dimensions of the PMT and are shown in the boxes. The top Fears and Frustrations as identified in this study are related to the PMT dimensions and marked with a ↳. The PMT dimensions that relate to the Fears and Frustrations are identified with the arrow.

In the frustrations PMT, elements of Scope and Time related to the personal frustrations of Scope and Schedule as identified by the participants in these surveys. In the fears PMT, elements of Scope and Cost also related to the personal fears of Client Expectations and Schedules / Budgets / Estimates. If fear and frustration have negative impacts, effective personal and interpersonal coping strategies can potentially enhance project implementation success.

CONCLUSIONS AND FURTHER RESEARCH

To summarize, this chapter has described the noble leadership expectations placed on project managers. In a rapidly changing environment, with project expectations being frequently modified, project managers are expected to be effective leaders multi-tasking the technical and interpersonal roles of their positions. Is it any wonder then, that project managers might experience fears and frustrations in relation to their roles? However, the literature review indicated that this area has not been extensively researched other than in relation to teams and personal fears in the work place. This chapter involved qualitative research into the area of project manager fears and frustrations and was based on three Delphi surveys.

As this is initial exploratory research and due to the sample size, the results should be interpreted cautiously. A limitation of this study is that the survey focused on participants in Calgary, Alberta, Canada. In addition, the study grouped fear of Schedules / Budgets / Estimates together when in hindsight, it would have been prudent to separate schedules from costs. Areas for future research relate to surveying a larger sample size and analyzing the results for industry specific trends. As a result the chapter should be interpreted in the context of being a local pilot. Nevertheless, the preliminary nature of the chapter enabled us to identify improvements and revisions to the methodology for further research.

The literature review and comments from the participants indicated that when critical success factors were not met, project managers were viewed as responsible. However, the nature of organizational structures (e.g. functional and matrix) and issues that related to team dynamics, conflict, communication, senior management support and client expectations also contribute to these challenges. Furthermore, attitudes of "finger pointing" project managers to "make things right" or recommending that they attend workshops to improve their leadership capabilities may not address the root causes of problems. In addition, some project managers may deny that they even experience fears or frustrations, thus limiting their abilities to manage them effectively.

The causes of project problems are often rooted in project critical success factors and those of the PMT, not just the abilities of the project manager. This chapter has identified commonalities between the fears and frustrations and project critical success factors. Personal fears and frustrations can have negative effects on the individuals involved as well as on the project when coping techniques are not as constructive as they could be. The negative effects can be seen in stress levels as well as decision-making abilities and interpersonal dynamics. Thus, we can pose the question "To what extent can we improve project success by addressing project manager fears and frustrations?"

To begin to address this question, the following ideas are offered for consideration. We can:

- Begin by heightening awareness among essential stakeholders, clients and senior management that the onus for project success is a shared responsibility.
- Discuss how fears and frustrations negatively affect the project and relate to success factors so that effective strategies can be developed.
- We can ensure that expectations are better managed from the *onset* and that processes are in place to support project managers when stakeholders change expectations.
- Examine our organizational structures to ensure that project managers have responsibilities that are aligned with their accountabilities in relation to functional managers.
- Learn to improve our abilities of getting to the root causes of project problems instead of addressing symptoms or "finger pointing".
- Ensure that there is organizational support as well as appropriate avenues for project members to discuss and develop effective personal coping strategies on fears and frustrations.

In addition key project participants are encouraged to work together on improving alignment between stakeholder expectations. Hartman (1998) offers such a set of tool and techniques (S.M.A.R.T.© Project Management). These strategies enable organizations to define success from the perspectives of key stakeholders, identify key result areas, understand and evaluate risk and develop flexible delivery strategies. Most of the items that contribute to Project Manager frustrations have independently been identified in other research. Drawing on this, industry practices that address these frustrations, and other work, S.M.A.R.T.© Project Management has been developed. This approach has now been tested on several hundred live projects with results that support the contention that project managers fears and frustrations can be reduced.

Effective Project Management is a shared responsibility and vital to organizational success. This chapter has presented initial strategies for improved coping mechanisms with fears and frustrations. With the appropriate support from Senior Management and stakeholder participation, project managers who ensure that critical success factor related fears and frustrations are discussed and addressed in open and constructive ways can enhance project success and minimize these fears and frustrations.

NOTE: Details on the survey are available upon request to kjugdev@ca.ibm.com

CHAPTER 15

IMPROVING CROSS-CULTURAL PROJECTS THROUGH BETTER COMMUNICATION

John B. Kidd, Aston Business School, Birmingham, United Kingdom

Paul C. Robins, Aston Business School, Birmingham, United Kingdom

ABSTRACT

The trend for businesses to become global is widespread and with it has come the need to manage cross-cultural projects. This adds to the difficulties project managers already face in achieving successful outcomes and some authors suggest that particular combinations of cultural groups are sufficiently different to make close harmonious working impossible. We argue that good communication is a pre-requisite for successful projects and that communication difficulties already account for many project failures. This chapter considers how the situation may be improved by improving communication and examines the guidance to be obtained from cross-cultural studies. It examines client-provider relationships in projects and the key processes of projects in which communication must be of high quality. The analysis provides a model of project processes that accounts for the recognised difficulties and provides a framework for the examination of a range of cross-cultural studies. It is suggested that the approach taken here, while not eliminating the difficulties altogether, may considerably ease them. In the process, areas for further work are identified.

THE PROBLEM OF PROJECT FAILURES

There is ample evidence showing that many major projects fail - sometimes due to poor management and sometimes due to poor specification or both. For example in the early 1980s the UK's Department of Social Security planned to install 40,000 terminals in 1000 local government offices in order to reduce operating costs and increase customer service levels. Planning and design took place through 1982-85; the Government announced further details in 1985; implementation was due to begin in 1987 with 1992 being the target completion date. The outcome was very different; there was a sour industrial relations climate and costs went out of control and there was a shortage of internal IT staff leading to the hiring of many external consultants adding greatly to overall costs. At a late stage government plans changed, leading to significant project revision although outright abandonment was avoided. These difficulties, which are of course well known to project managers, were shown to be due to poor consultation between all parties and a widespread lack of knowledge and understanding of the deliverables (National Audit Office 1989).

This example emphasises the fact that the task and the working environment of project managers are seldom simple and smooth. Project managers must make many kinds of decisions throughout the life of a project and most of them are intended to reflect or support the goal of the project. Many things conspire against the project manager having a clear basis on which to make these judgements, even if initial ideas were committed to paper. People (clients or customers) change their ideas, difficulties or opportunities arise or misunderstandings come to light. Overcoming these obstacles requires that the manager communicate with (talk to, discuss, ring or email) whoever it takes. In particular, projects tend to fail if all parties do not understand its nature in detail; a general idea is not enough. Effective communication also depends on a shared understanding at a broader level; participants must have similar perspectives or 'world views' to be certain that ideas are reliably exchanged whether they refer to a project deliverable or a project activity. Such understanding is particularly unlikely to occur amongst people of different cultures without taking special steps to create it. We do not yet know, in detail, what these steps are but this chapter examines the basis on which they may be developed.

We will not consider issues that are in the realm of the strategic evaluations and therefore particularly germane to client concerns. For example there are many academics who now look to Transaction Costs as a theoretical base upon which to predicate their discussions of new ventures (essentially based on Williamson 1975, 1985) and we assume there is a project to manage. This locates our concerns well past those appropriate to the Transaction Cost school. Similarly there is much written on Agency Theory (see Baiman 1982, 1990, and Brickley *et al.* 1996) and the study of the actors in the contractual situation: these ideas attempt to control project managers' 'freedoms' through a finely worded contract. Although one might view the latter as a mechanism for enforcing reliable or practical communication we shall take a wider perspective. In a similar vein, there are others who will see the project management issues as one within Stakeholder Theory (following Freeman 1994, Mitchell *et al.* 1997) which can be considered under three headings - descriptive, instrumental and normative. Taking the latter, the normative approach simply leads us to conclude there is a legitimacy in the various and specific stakeholders in the project, and that management has a function which is specific yet intertwined among the various actors. In this we concur but wish to examine the situation in more depth.

Project Management: The Product and the Process
Much of project management literature is concerned with the 'product' and the tools of the trade are designed to ensure that projects are successful in terms of the output,

bearing in mind the need to control the duration and resource use (Meridith and Mantel Jr. 1995). Since the late 1950s considerable progress has been made in developing such tools which include many attempts to refine supporting software. These focus on time, cost and quality of product, which have become the principal performance measures of projects, particularly in the UK. Even so, difficulties remain as clients demand that projects meet their functional specification while being at one and the same time rapidly completed at low cost and to high quality standards. naturally this demand creates conflicts for the project management team. However, the advances in the performance of the tools mean that if clients and project teams utilise subjective probabilities elicited in an appropriate way (Kidd 1975), processing them with appropriate software will ensure the client is suitably advised on the strategic implications of (a) the whole plan and (b) of the impact of 'small' changes that tend to creep into projects (Kidd 1987). The elicitation is difficult to make and requires careful consultation to attend to the basis of their estimation (Pearl 1988). We also note there is now a tendency for manager/clients to plan their own projects. This possibility arises from the ready availability of project management software that is increasingly easy to use (cf. Microsoft Project within Microsoft's Office Suite). We suggest this tendency towards self-programming is a false economy as it is difficult to merge the roles of client and project manager satisfactorily (Kidd 1990). However, the focus in this chapter is with the processes that give rise to project characteristics referred to above.

In essence it is a process in which practitioners seek to balance incommensurate goals so that the client and project manager can agree about the nature of the project to be undertaken. Arriving at this position requires negotiation, a process that is inescapably bound to communication. The most important target of such negotiation is the establishment of an agreed definition of the goal or outcome of the project and this is perhaps the greatest challenge as so many things depend on its outcome. The topics discussed is broad and time scales considered may be long into the future which means that many apparently peripheral issues may influence peoples ideas. Reaching an agreement might be viewed as resolving jointly the form of expression and the details of a description of a target state that is accepted by all. This focussed aspiration cannot be achieved without shared understandings that enable the participants to verify that the interpretation given to the expressions that constitute the goal definition are indeed properly shared. Developing this understanding requires many additional interactions which are both more varied and detailed than those concerned directly with the goal specification. While the definition of the project in terms of what the client will accept and how the project team can provide is clearly the primary outcome of the communication there remains the need for quality assurance; the participants have to arrive at the position where they can be confident that their ideas are truly shared. Groups of people with similar backgrounds and from the same culture have many fewer difficulties achieving this than is the case when people from widely different cultural backgrounds are concerned.

As the project progresses other decisions gain in importance and although they may be viewed as more operational they too depend on good communication and to some extent put the earlier process on test. Failure of communication and understanding early in a project's life may be manifest as difficulties in later stages. Briefly we summarise the life of a project and indicate the contribution of communication processes: essentially we see the client wishing to be given a 'golden egg' and to this end has proffered the project specification with this as its aim. In many cases of course the aim, encapsulated in a brief, is unclear to the potential project manager and subsequently may be found to be unclear to the client. The negotiation process may seek to disabuse the client of their wish - either because 'golden eggs' do not exist, or because the project team can't deliver such a high specification outcome and wishes to agree on a more achievable deliverable. Later negotiations may concern more practical matters such as agreeing to make the eggs smaller in the face of a large rise in the price of gold for example. However, had the project manager fully understood the significance of the size of the eggs then such a suggestion would not have been made. Instead the possibility of them being hollow might be explored.

This view of the Project Process is compatible with that of Cash *et al.* (1992). They relate the risk of the project to the knowledge base of the technology in focus, to the project size, and to the project structure. They equate highly structured projects (which we would interpret as well defined) with reduced risk. They hint at our target - the necessity to employ a process where all involved come to the same vision, possess the same models and perceptions of the situation, and thus have the same aspirations for the dynamics of the project.

Communication in Projects
There have been many studies of 'interpersonal' communication, networking, and the way that these support knowledge acquisition. However, here we focus on the process of sharing ideas utilising a model that was originally concerned with digital transmission systems. The message or idea is initiated by a conceptual process, transformed (coded) into words (signals) and transmitted by being spoken, for example. Reception of the message and thus of the idea depends first on the message being heard, and then on being interpreted to recreate truly the message and idea. The meaning of the received message and thus the idea that is transferred depends not only on what was received but also on the mental framework of the receiver. The later determines the context in which the signal is interpreted.

Clearly effective communication requires that the coding and decoding of messages is compatible; this includes translation from one language to another, or in technological terms using compatible communication protocols. Naturally all modes suffer from the effects of attenuation when the quality of the signal carrying the message may be compromised, and for this reason mechanisms to detect the need for a repeat sending of the signal are important. However, the transfer of ideas also depends on the compatibility of the forms of expression and the way they are interpreted. Ensuring compatibility involves the sender making judgements about the interpretation process likely to be used by the receiver and vice versa. We illustrate this with an example:

... in the early days of the Americans attempting to arrange contracts in Japan it was alleged that these hurrying visitors (being so predicated upon their cultural background) often came away firmly believing that they had a deal arranged. The Japanese, they said, had said "Yes!"

In fact it was the translator who accurately translated the Japanese language from '*hai*' into '*yes*'. Here the Japanese negotiators were using this word only to indicate ... 'please continue the conversation we are listening'. We understand that most nations and individuals have particular verbal and non-verbal ways to indicate this request. Thus we see here the CODE< >DECODE aspect has worked without attenuation, but the contextual aspects have not. Thus the US negotiators came away with the wrong message.

Unlike long-lived organisations, projects need to establish contexts, or a common understanding, as an integral part of their processes, and to do so quickly before many outcome-determining decisions have been made. Our aim is to provide suitable support for this. Even where the project team is chosen for their previous experience (a process that acknowledges the importance of contextual understanding) there remains the need to adapt to each new situation. We view one of the primary benefits of the Soft Systems Methodology proposed by Checkland (1981) to be its potential for developing a sound basis for communication. Its formal exploration of 'rich pictures' and the explicit attention to the perceptions of people when developing 'root definitions' serves to provide a common context for message exchange. The drawback to such an approach is that there may be significant learning involved before the methodology can be used effectively and there remains a tendency for people to view the exploration phase as something akin to 'navel contemplation'.

We plan to provide guidance on ways of improving specifically cross-cultural communication that is, as far as possible, methodology independent. We believe that this must be based on a formal recognition of the culturally determined mechanisms that operate during communication, and that the most significant of these is the contexts or world views that govern the coding and interpretation of messages. We are in the process of reviewing current knowledge in the area with a view to identifying possible methods of providing support. The creation of practical guidance and useable tools is still some way off but the following sections outline the direction our work is taking.

Our clear aim is to be culture independent. Many researchers have researched the Japanese joint ventures and have reported great differences in attitudes, skills and managerial predilections between national staff and Japanese staff in enterprises: in the UK see for instance - Oliver and Wilkinson (1992), Hunt and Targett (1995): or from a European perspective - Shibagaki *et al.* (1989): and internationally - Kopp (1994), Durlabhji and Marks (1993). Pucik (1997) has referred to the 'conflict' that occurs when organisations decide to move from competitive collaboration to collaborative co-operation - once again his example is focused on early Japanese practices.

COMMUNICATION AND CULTURAL BACKGROUNDS

Individual Characteristics: Time-Frames and Contexts

While we may speak of cultures that collide, it is people who communicate. Hall (1976) argues that the most natural time frame for people is that which accords with nature: being determined by the rise and fall of the sun, and weather patterns. He suggests that the industrial revolution that began in England is to blame for the development of monochronic (M-time) persons from otherwise polychronic (P-time) persons. The former have been trained to live by linear time whereas the latter live by more natural rhythms. The majority of managers and workforce in the European/North American regions, work in M-time: they are grounded in this heredity and tradition. This creates psychological tensions since their mode of work is not in accord with their 'body clocks', nor of those 'clocks' with whom they may work - if they are from a different culture, working in P-time.

The monochronic person emphasises schedules, segmentation of activities, and promptness: M-time is almost 'real' - they say that "time may be wasted/lost/saved" as though it were a real commodity. The M-person will compartmentalise his/her life and accept the schedule as sacred and unalterable so yielding to an ordered life-style with clear priorities. The polychronic persons on the other hand are characterised by being at the centre of many simultaneous events and by their great involvement with people. They focus strongly on the completion of human transactions irrespective of any on-going schedules (such as they are). P-time is *experienced* as being much less tangible than M-time: in this sense it cannot be lost. The P-person can jump from one point to another in a seemingly random way, rather than accepting that time is understood to be a road along which the person travels without deviation.

Hall (1976) also discusses the nature of *context*. He suggests one function of culture is to provide a selective screen between man and the outside world. This screen protects the nervous system from 'information overload', which when transgressed can lead to many disorders ranging from 'cognitive dissonance' to full mental breakdown. People handle some of these overloads by delegation, while organisations must employ other methods to improve their capability. Ashby (1956) in his 'Law of Requisite Variety' states that "only variety can overcome variety or complexity". Thus more complex situations need more complex systems as solutions to remain viable (Beer 1972, Espejo and Harnden 1989).

Hall suggests one method of coping with complexity, or working in a different world, is to 'pre-program' individuals through "contexting". Herein a person should learn to recognise a complex yet novel situation and have access to methods to cope with it. Discussing with a mentor is an example of how one might learn to deal with context overload, a practice firmly established in Japanese firms that supported lifetime employment principles. In these firms there is the *sempai-kohai* approach where a superior has the responsibility for the development a junior staff member. This serves as a mechanism for a junior member of staff to learn how to interpret messages or instructions with precision and appropriateness - in some respects it is an apprenticeship.

Messages exchanged within projects may be categorised as high context (HC) or low context (LC) messages. High context messages are those in which most of the information is already held by the recipient, so the message itself can be brief: it consists of an abbreviated signal that can be given meaning by the understanding of the recipient. A low context message is more explicit carrying with it what would be background understanding in a HC message. Therefore it tends to be verbose. Business communication should therefore attempt to be compatible with the intended audience. We note from the work of Hall and others, that the Japanese, Arabs, and Mediterranean persons in Europe (in fact, Latin persons in general) all have large family or family-like networks having close personal relationships and they are habitual HC message users. They keep themselves informed through their network. In contrast US, United Kingdom and Swiss persons are LC (as are most northern European persons) and they will compartmentalise their personal relationships, their work, and their day-to-day life. LC persons will often need a full briefing from his/her support team including the provision of contextual information. Therefore much time may be required to reach a co-ordinated decision with an LC team compared to that required by an HC team.

This creates further issues. Advisors to a CEO are "gate keepers", since they not only filter information but do so according to their personal view of context though this may not conform to that of the CEO, the organisation in general, or the supplicant attempting to make a case to the CEO. Furthermore, a low context CEO sees only the LC persons relevant to his/her day's work, all of whom must be on the appointment schedule. In addition 'modern management methods' tend to force everyone into low context since they attempt to make all facts and aspects of a situation fully explicit and transparent. Little account is taken of what people may bring to a situation. We note that few consultants will take (or be given) the time to become fully contexted in the environment of their new task simply because in the client firm will not often wish to pay for this 'time wasting' activity - yet we think it is vital for the well-being of a project. A further implication of this short-term viewpoint is the observation that very little credibility is given to the implementation of a complex solution: solutions have to be self-evident, simple and thus low context, especially in a mixed HC/LC world (Salter and Niswander 1995).

Towards Team Learning

We note that Argote and McGrath (1993), and Huber (1991) to some extent, postulate learning to be at the level of the individual thus organisational learning may only be achieved if somehow individuals transcend their individuality and look for organisation-wide data, assimilate its nature and store their results in accessible rules and procedures. Persons joining the firm later will be able to access these rules and so quickly perform at the level of the organisation's norms. On the other hand,

Nonaka and Takeuchi (1995) have defined a four-stage dynamic pattern of organisational learning - wherein an individual's learning is merged with that of others over time in an unending spiral. He considers there are four stages in the knowledge conversion process linking one person to another as the awareness of learning is developed within the firm. A brief description of Stage 1 follows:

> … herein basic knowledge exchange is obtained by direct appreciation - being an apprentice is a good example. Knowledge is acquired from the master, not through abstract language but by observation, imitation and by practice. Nonaka notes the meetings held by Japanese firms, often outside the premises, to undertake 'brainstorming'. Herein there is a sharing of the realities of life: drinking, eating, generally chatting and experiencing communal bathing in a hot spring - it gives a 'throw-back' appreciation of the one-time good life in Japan, it relaxes and in so doing allows deeper communion.

Bartlett and Ghoshal (1989) have also stated firmly that a firm wishing to move into the Transnational phase must allow its staff to participate in a great deal of *socialisation* (our emphasis), see also Kidd (1998). March (1991) has emphasised that organisations should not only socialise their members but also learn from them. Furthermore, there is a role for humour. Bateson (1972) has described the process of making a joke as a three-fold process: first the surface telling exchanges the information content, the second phase links the background information which is implicit, and finally, the point of the joke creates a paradox or an unexpected viewpoint by means of which a context creating leap is enacted.

These ideas identify a potentially significant problem for project teams whose organisation is essentially ephemeral. We have no quantifiable way of establishing whether a project team has become fully contexted. At first sight it looks as if they need LC methods although they may work in HC or mixed environments.

Quantifying Culture

There are very few measures of 'culture' that might be adopted to guide interactions across cultural boundaries. One seminal study (now based on 110,000 respondents in over 50 countries) was undertaken by Hofstede (1980, 1991) with partial replications by Hoppe (1993), McGrath *et al.* (1992) and Trompenaars (1993). These indices may be summarised as follows:

> Power Distance (***PDI***): Some societies like hierarchies, and other wish all to be as equal as possible. There is also an aspect of interpersonal independence in this measure, in which a tall hierarchy will be said to maintain a high PD index.
> Uncertainty Avoidance (***UAI***): Some societies prefer few rules, less stable careers, less fixed patterns of life; i.e. more uncertainty and risk than others would like.

Individualism (*IND*): Some societies like to see individuals express themselves, while others wish for collectivism, having close relationships that even extend to permitting the firm to look after one and in return expect one's loyalty.

Masculinity (*MAS*): The more 'masculine' a society the more it values assertiveness and materialism. It cares less for the quality of life or concern about other people, ie the more caring or 'feminine' aspects.

Confucianism (*CD*): This dimension relates to the long or short-termism of the society. A long-term person can be thought of as being persistent, being thrifty and who orders relationships by status, and who looks to maintain this order.

It is gross to consider that all persons of a given country may be typified by one set of characteristics, yet Hofstede's research offers powerful comparisons which, in turn, lead to interesting conclusions about the ways in which *individuals* may or may not work with each other. A partial set of Hofstede's data is shown in Table 1.

The Power Distance (propensity towards hierarchy) and UAI (tolerance of rules) are the two Indices which relate most to work-based behaviour; the other three incline towards societal behaviour. We see that in this selection, France is the most bureaucratic (likes tall hierarchies) and has high rule observance. Its nationals would not work well with the English, for example - though they should be in accord with the Japanese (giving attention to meticulous detail and being logical). Collectivism (an inclination to work together as a group) is assessed by the Individuality index - the Japanese and Asians are all, in general, more collective than the Occidentals.

Table 1. A Selection of Country Index Values

Country	PDI	UAI	IND	MAS	CD
France	68	86	71	43	*
Spain	57	86	51	42	*
Japan	54	92	46	95	80
Italy	50	75	76	70	*
US	40	46	91	62	29
Netherlands	38	53	80	14	44
Germany	35	65	67	66	31
UK	35	35	89	66	25
Sweden	31	29	71	5	33

Source: Hofstede 1991   * data not yet collected

Finally we note the Confucianism index which links many Oriental attitudes such as patience, the respect of elders, and upholding the family. In this sample data set only Japan has a high score, though China scores a maximum 100. In contrast, the United Kingdom and the US both have low CD scores (short time-frames) implying a need for instant action and in a financial sense, looking to short-term returns on investment.

There is a clear suggestion of potential Oriental/Occidental conflict at many levels within these Indices when we consider the need to converse between client and consultant to establish the nature of the 'golden egg'. Following Kidd and Kanda (1997) we may presume that in Japan the HC managers and workers are well informed about the 'inside department' contexts and thus do not need many formal meetings to discuss them, whereas in Britain, the managers being LC persons frequently find that data is not fully available and formal meetings are needed to collect and exchange it. Further, British organisations often use formal Job Descriptions which both limit the scope of managerial interactions and institutionalise formal meetings. Thus when there are mixed culture groups with and without job descriptions there are boundary definition problems which cause incomprehension between all parties. Changes take place sometimes due to prevailing economic conditions, rather than in the base cultural norms. For instance - frequent formal meetings in Japan would indicate a breakdown in the Japanese-ness of Japanese work arrangements. Indeed changes in Human Resource Management practices in Japan indicate a 'hollowing out' of their work-force leading to the assignment of role-specialists rather than generalists - see Steffensen and Dirks (1997). Naturally this will also lead to a breakdown in their formal mentoring process, as the superior-subordinate relationship may not be guaranteed 'for life'.

CONCLUSIONS AND FUTURE RESEARCH

We have found little to suggest that our view of the culture-crossing problem is exaggerated. We see that to avoid failure project teams need to be HC but their ephemeral nature means they typically start LC. The clear need is for guidance on selecting teams that can become appropriately HC quickly, for the identification and development of mechanisms that stimulate learning in this area, and for ways of ensuring the process of becoming HC is properly managed. The required mechanisms must be designed to help project workers minimise the time taken to learn a new context. Analysis of the literature, such as that presented above shows us some of the possibilities although the practical requirements of project management add complexity to the research that remains to be done.

In the short term, project teams in mixed cultural environments must consider devoting time to becoming contexed. Staff profiles should help to select the team (especially if an effective way of assessing context learning ability is available). But the first activity of a project, we suggest, should be a period of intensive socialising and brainstorming. This step is particularly important if team members are to work remotely (an increasingly likely eventuality in an age of networked computer systems). This may go some way to overcoming the dehumanising tendency in computer communications. We also see value in the development of a model to enable people to discuss (and ideally assess) cultural issues concretely in much the same way as the model at the heart of Transactional Analysis (Berne 1979, Harris 1973). Its aim was to help people discuss feelings and behaviour in concrete terms: our aim is to help people discuss cultural issues of a new project in similarly concrete terms. Thus learning about 'the team' being developed may occur in parallel with learning about the business or goals and processes of the project. We regard such learning difficult to acquire, particularly in the hurly-burly of day-to-day management where adequate time may not be allocated or made available. We may find a basis for the model in the categories of Hofstede, but the means of providing practical utility in a project environment remains a challenge that will be addressed in future work.

CHAPTER 16

ON THE FAMILIARITY OF STRANGERS

Magnus Gustafsson, Research Group for Project Based Industry, Åbo Akademi University, Finland

ABSTRACT

Inter-cultural communication is often considered complicated and a source for many problems in international business. Yet, looking at international project industry one can but wonder at how well projects are seen through, even though they involve the most difficult conditions, forcing people from the most differing cultures together. Instead interviews with managers from over 60 countries show issues such as trust and commitment play an important role in international business. Trust is here seen as the way the words and actions of other people and organizations are interpreted. To understand the complexities of intercultural communication, it is argued, it is necessary to look beyond the very physical act and look to its interpretation and the intentions ascribed to it.

THE INTER-CULTURAL PROBLEM

Inter-cultural communication is often treated as problematic with differing habits and business practices seen as complicating business and communication. For this purpose bookstores and libraries are filled with information on how to behave with foreigners, what one should know of their culture and warning of cultural shock. For example, one author advises people dealing with Taiwanese not to point their shoes at them while talking to them and not to pat them on the head (Example given by Johan Galtung in a lecture held at 14th Nordic Business Conference, 14.8 1997, Bodø, Norway). To really get to know the other culture and avoid catastrophes, people are often advised to spend more or less a lifetime studying, and preferably living, in that culture before interacting and doing business with them. This, of course, will cause a problem in the project industry (and most international trade) where there simply is no time for practice. However, looking more closely at how managers describe international business, a more complicated picture emerges. Not only do most business deals, despite the dark forecasts, go quite well with companies from different cultures happily cooperating, it actually seems as if the problems interacting with "strange" foreigners were smaller than those arising with "familiar" foreigners.

TRUST

To understand inter-cultural communication the question of interaction in general has to be addressed. Managers often stress the importance of trust. Trust is seen as the very base for all forms of economic enterprise, the very aspect that makes cooperation possible. Trust is important throughout the business process, from the time before the contract to carrying through and managing the continued relationship. Trust is often seen as a prerequisite for business as such; if the parties involved do not trust each other then there will be no business. The bigger and more complicated the enterprise, the more important is trust.

Olli Lagerspetz stresses that trust is not a conscious expectation. It can rather be seen as a tacit demand in the relation between two people where the one placing the demand (the trusting party) seldom – perhaps never – is aware of the demand. The trustee, on the other hand, feels the demand in the form of an obligation or a sense of duty. The trusting party remains unaware of the demand as long as it is fulfilled. It is not until the demand is not fulfilled, that the trusting party becomes aware that such a demand has ever existed. At this point he will try to explain what has happened, <u>what</u> the other one really has done and <u>why</u> - two aspects that are closely knit, which will be shown later on.

The idea of a tacit demand can seem strange, almost as something mystical. There is, however, nothing strange or mystical about a tacit demand. Our opinions of people are mostly formed by their actions. What a person does, adds to the general picture we have of him or her: what they usually do, if they are nice, sporty, lazy, intelligent, etc. These opinions do not have to come from eye-to-eye situations. We learn about both individuals and whole groups of people from others, before we meet people from that group. These opinions are often, rightly or wrongly, called prejudices. However, even in these cases learning is based on people doing things.

Perceiving something means comparing something against a ready set of assumptions. Ludwig Wittgenstein (1992) stresses that understanding takes place against a sort of pre-understanding, *pre* in the sense that the understanding existed before the subject to be understood was perceived. Thus we judge the world according to how we think it is. Whether the world really is this way does not matter, Collingwood (see Janik, pp. 96-100) talks of absolute presuppositions, that is, although mere assumptions, they are nevertheless seen as self-evident and cannot be seriously contested. The point is that these are the assumptions that perceptions are judged against and understood.

Thus, following the logic of Wittgenstein, our view of other people is formed by their actions, but our view of people influences the way we perceive their actions. What we have here seems like a chicken-and-egg sort of problem. The circle is however not fully closed, but forms a type of spiral over time where each interpretation influences the view, which in turn forms a basis for the next interpretation. Thus when an act is judged it is in relation to all other, previous acts that have formed the view. Acts that are in coherence with the picture strengthen it and are in a sense not noticed. However, an act that does not fit the picture can have a different effect depending on the circumstances. Isolated by itself, the act is viewed as a mere aberration. An overall positive image does not necessarily fall on *one* single negative incident, after all, accidents happen and we all have our bad days. This can clearly be seen in the way the customers interviewed describe their relation to the supplier.

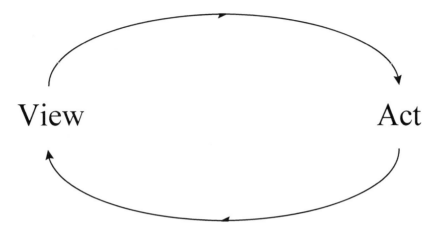

Figure 1. The circle of sense making

The circle of affirmation and reaffirmation means that our impressions of others are quite stable. To challenge a view the incident has to be seen as more than an aberration. When this happens there will be a qualitative shift where the absolute presupposition about the other party suddenly changes. A change like this can have dramatic consequences and undoing the damage done (in case it is a change in the negative direction) can be very hard, as it once again becomes a question of changing an absolute presupposition.

THE MAKING OF A DEAL

The role of trust is decisive if there is to be any kind of deal. This concerns both large and small companies (see Gustafsson 1996). If the other party is not trusted, then there will be no deal. Managers therefore often spend a lot of time getting to know the other party both as a person and as a representative of a company. This can be done in many ways. Although it sounds like a cliché, the ways of getting to know each other often involves sitting in karaoke-bars in Asia, playing bridge with Americans (or actually visiting the other one's family) and burning your skin in a sauna in Finland. However, it is not the karaoke that is important, it is the social interaction, getting to know each other. Managers often stress that this form of interaction in *non-business surroundings* works as a way of in a sense showing your true self to the counterpart. This can be clearly seen in the studies conducted by the Research Group for Project Based Industry. The studies consist of over 1000 interviews with managers involved in project industry either as buyer or seller, coming from over 60 different countries. The project deliveries discussed here often involve delivering a fully operational power plant out in the jungle where there are no roads. Under these circumstances you probably want to know the person you are going to do it with.

The relation does not have to be face to face. Interviews with managers involved in international project industry show that reputation and references play an important role in business. Both buyers and sellers stress this. It is therefore usual for the parties involved to contact other partners, so as to get to know the counterpart by getting to know their *friends*. Reputation can therefore be said to be the collected experience of all those who have been in contact with a certain company or person.

A deal can be said to consist of two parts: a written contract and a mutual understanding. When the deal is done it is based on the mutual feeling that the counterpart has the will, skill and proper understanding of the undertaking agreed upon, that is he trusts the other party (see Gustafsson 1999). The formal written contract can then be seen as the manifestation and specification of this agreement, a form of memo over all the details included, and becomes and therefore secondary or at least contingent on the existence of the understanding.

This is of course common sense; you can not very well make a contract if you have not agreed on the subject. However, it is important to remember that the formal contract is the only part and first sign of the deal that those outside ever see. There is however, a long process of interaction preceding the contract that is almost invisible to outsiders. As an outsider one should not be fooled by this fact. One should remember that one, by definition, understands and knows less of the relation in question than those in it do. They are making the deal, based on a relationship that more often than not is very long.

In interviews, managers often stress that a written contract without trust is no more than a scrap of paper and forms no basis for a continuing relationship. This goes against neo-classical economic theory, according to which man is a self centered, rationally acting opportunist who cooperates only when it benefits him. Cooperation in this view arises only when the benefits of cooperation outweigh the benefit of defection. Once the benefit of defection is greater, economic man will immediately defect, because that is the rational thing to do. Thus the actor in these theories is always convinced, that everyone else is like him - self centered, rational and opportunistic. To protect himself against the other party's defection, economic man, Ouchi argues, writes a contract specifying who is responsible under what circumstances and stipulating sanctions against the one that breaks the contract. These and other sanctions are thought to deter each party from defecting.

However, neo-classical thought has been much criticized. Martin Hollis argues that the theory as such is not logical; the behavior of A is dependent on the behavior of B, which in its turn is dependent on the behavior of A.

> "There is no coherent way of working with strategically interlocked probabilities."(Hollis, p.83)

Charles Perrow follows the same line when he argues that theories like transaction cost economics only account for the possible defection of one party.

"The possibility that the capitalist (principal) might lie to the workers about profit levels or threats to lost business, falsify the records of their outputs, endanger agents' health, all to extract more profit, or simply shirk her responsibilities is ignored or swept aside by mentioning that a firm will protect its reputation." (Perrow, p.227)

However, the strongest argument against neo-classicism comes from interviews with those actually doing the business. Managers often stress that no contract can be complete; it is by definition impossible to cover all contingencies. Thus, if you do not trust the other person, you will always feel that there will be some hole left in the contract for him to take advantage of. No contract can safeguard against the threat of defection.

REALIZING THE ENTERPRISE

Although the selling/commitment stage is crucial for any enterprise to be started, realizing the project is none the easier. Managers often see the realization of the enterprise as a prelude to next deal and thus part of the groundwork for the next sale. When realizing a project just about anything can happen, deliveries might be delayed, ships sink, even the ground can give in if it has not been properly insulated. Problems can arise in even such small transactions such as when buying breakfast from McDonald's. No matter how well everything is prepared there will always be problems of some kind; they cannot be avoided. The question therefore is not so much how to avoid problems, but rather how to solve them and prevent them from growing into bigger, much more serious ones.

An example of problem handling is the two power plants in the jungle of Borneo I visited a few years ago. At mine A there had been just about every sort of problem with the power plant. There had been fires, electrical cables melting, spare parts delivered all the way from Europe falling from ships, and these were just the major incidents. At mine B there had been only one minor accident during a test run. Nevertheless the people at mine A were very happy with the supplier of the plant, while those at mine B were extremely unhappy. The difference lies in how the supplier had behaved. At mine A the customer felt the supplier had done his utmost to solve the problems. That there had been problems was just natural. Technology is limited. It was all just accidents. In the end the customer trusted the supplier. However, at mine B the customer felt neglected. The customer and the supplier did not agree as to the cause of the problem. The customer blamed a certain failing part, while the supplier kept repeating that the problems were only because the customer did not know how to run the plant. The customer felt the supplier did not pay any attention to his opinions. In the end the cause of the problem was found, and the customer was proved right. However, by this time the customer felt that the supplier was only interested in getting the money and did not take responsibility for the things supplied. The problem was now much bigger. The customer did not trust the supplier.

CONTRACTS

The question is whether a formal contract would have helped in either of these situations. One could of course imagine a contract stipulating that the supplier would be responsible for any technical problems arising. However, this would probably become far too costly and would anyway not prevent the very existence of technical problems – they do not depend on the human will. It is even harder to imagine how to prevent lack of compassion by contractual means – you cannot force someone to care. However, an even more interesting example of contracting can be seen in the power plant sold from Europe to Southeast Asia. The plant was to consist of 15 units of a certain model B18. (Both the number and model-insignia of the engines have been changed.) The plant was to be delivered quickly; it was one of the central conditions and one of the main reasons why the supplier had won the contract. There was however a problem. It was impossible to deliver all the units from the main factory in Europe within the stipulated time frame. To solve this problem the supplier decided to take some of the units from an assembly plant in a third world country.

Contractually this was not going to be a problem, the contract did not specify that all the units had to come from Europe, it only said 15 units of B18. There was however a problem, the units from the non-European assembly factory were of much lower quality than those from the main factory. The supplier was well aware of this and decided therefore not to mention it to the customer. After all, the units looked the same on the outside and you could always hope they would work this time. When the customer noticed this they became furious, and felt cheated.

> "I personally feel lousy about that. We subsequently found out that some of the [units] are coming from [the other country]. We thought that [they] should have been more forthcoming and told us."(interview with customer)

Would it have been possible to avoid a situation like this? At first glance the answer might seem clear; it would have been enough to specify in the contract where the units should come from and the matter would have been settled. However, this answer is valid only with the knowledge we have from hindsight and the question should rather be why this was not written in the contract. The answer must simply be that the customer did not imagine such a thing could happen. Note, the customer did not feel that the probability for cheating was small or negligible; the thought simply did not arise. If the customer had thought it possible for the supplier to deliver units from another factory, then they would probably have included that in the contract.

The customer could be criticized for being careless; he should have taken the possibility into account. However, in that case it can be asked whether there are not many other things the customer should have anticipated, things that did not happen but which could have happened. However, it is reasonable to assume that if the customer had felt the deal indeed was so risky, there would have been no deal as such. After all, there are enough risks in the project industry as it is - there is no need to gamble.

The companies who did this deal both have a long record in their business. One can assume that they accounted for the risks they saw in the deal. That it did not go as planned simply shows that we cannot see into the future. There is a difference between taking a risk and running a risk, which Lagerspetz stresses. Risk is a subjective feeling and strictly objective risk very seldom exists. Wittgenstein (1992) points out that all doubt is based on certainty, doubt cannot exist by itself, there has to be a reason to doubt. When it comes to personal relations they are subjective and specific to the parties involved, therefore no form of objective risk is applicable in this context. Thus, if party A does not doubt the good will of party B and vice versa, the question is whether there exists any risk. As such it is questionable to what degree an outside observer can ascribe characteristics not accepted by the actors involved in the situation or whether it should all be seen as a misunderstanding of the language game that the relation forms (Wittgenstein 1992).

The difference lies in what one is afraid of. There exist no objective criteria for what is and is not dangerous. Fear is in the eye of the beholder. People who are suspicious of everyone are called paranoid while those who are never suspicious are called naïve. However, when judging the course of events one should be careful not to call the paranoid careful just because he was right for once. Or *vice versa*.

Getting back to the example it should be pointed out that neither the customer nor the supplier felt a more specified contract would have helped. Both thought that the key to avoiding the problem would have been more openness and communication. The supplier excused itself by arguing that it would not have acted as it did, had it not been for the schedule, which was more or less impossible to fulfill. The customer used the same reason to excuse the supplier. As such it was not so much the fact that they had delivered the wrong units, but rather the fact they had tried to conceal it, which angered the customer. In the end one could say the supplier admitted its mistake and ended up paying quite a lot for upgrading the engines.

THE INTER-CULTURAL PROBLEM

The problems of communication and business take a further twist when the parties involved come from different cultures. Francis Fukuyama discusses social capital, the prevalence of common virtues and norms, spontaneous sociability, the ability to form new associations and act within the norms of those associations. Fukuyama (see also Casson) stresses that social capital and trust varies between cultures, and that some societies show a greater tendency for association than others. The preferred form of association also differs; in some societies kinship forms the core of association while others have strong voluntary organizations with the family playing a relatively minor role.

Fukuyama accordingly divides the world into high-trust societies and familistic societies. Examples of high-trust societies are Japan, Germany and the USA, while Chinese societies and Latin societies such as France and Italy are examples of familistic societies. According to Fukuyama, familistic societies show a lesser degree of trust, which can be seen in a lower degree of spontaneous sociability and self-organization. People in familistic societies tend to organize along family lines, and show a low degree of voluntary association. High-trust societies on the other hand show a higher degree of organization along non-family lines. A high degree of unionization and large publicly owned firms - neither of which is very common in familistic societies - is typical for them.

Thus, trust can be seen in the forms of organization. In a familistic society, kinship is seen as committing. A greater responsibility is felt towards kinsmen than towards non-kinsmen. In high-trust societies, on the other hand, kinship is of less importance for trust. Instead, other forms of identification, such as clubs, union membership or common hobbies might play a greater role. Birgitta Forsström discusses the relations between expatriate Finns (high-trust) working in China, and their local Chinese (familistic) counterparts. One of the problems in the relations between Finns and Chinese was the question of employment. According to the Finns involved, the Chinese tradition of employing and taking care of relatives was highly immoral, and nepotism was seen as a problem plaguing many organizations in Asia. The Chinese on the other hand found the Finns callous, lacking in compassion and simply immoral, since they did not understand that relatives had to be taken care of. This goes for other societies too, I have many times heard Finns and Swedes bitterly complaining, "the only thing that counts here is kinship, they're all related."

Conflicts like these arise, because the absolute presuppositions vary from culture to culture. The problem is deepened by the fact that, in a conflict like this, neither side has to be wrong. What is right and wrong depends on the moral framework, and thus both parties were, according to their own views, right. Inter-cultural communication can therefore be very complicated. Unfortunately importance of kinship is just one of many aspects where the absolute presuppositions vary from culture to culture.

FOREIGNERS ARE STRANGE

Thus it would seem that the bigger the cultural difference, the bigger the problems. There is, however, one aspect that rescues the situation and that is the very fact that the parties involved belong to different cultures; that they both are foreigners or at least strangers to each other. When meeting a Finn a Chinese person will immediately notice: aha, he looks different, he talks and dresses differently. He is definitely different from me, he is definitely not Chinese - and vice versa. With this as background he will not be surprised if the Finn behaves in what would seem like a strange manner for a Chinese person. Foreigners are, in a sense, expected to behave strangely - or at least no one is surprised if they do. Their actions are seen as acts of a foreigner. In fact the strangeness of their actions is part of what makes them foreigners. As such the words: foreigner or stranger implies *not like us, someone whose manners one does not know.*

A common feature in projects involving people from what can be seen as very different cultures (for example Finns and Pakistanis or Finns and Chinese) is the propensity to explain and excuse the other party's bad behavior as a cultural misunderstanding. Thus, for example, Pakistanis (Pakistan is an Islamic republic with a predominantly Moslem population) were not upset with the Finns getting drunk. Although public intoxication, and drinking alcohol as such, is seen as negative, the behavior of the Finns was not considered offensive, but rather as part of their culture and thereby excusable. In an inter-cultural context the perceived cultural difference explains, or excuses the behavior of the counterpart. Thus foolish behavior is seen as merely a cultural misunderstanding, rather than as a personal trait. As a side note it could be pointed out that it is possible to buy alcohol in Pakistan provided you show your passport and sign a paper confirming that you do not belong to the Islamic faith, this I know from personal experience. One should also not assume that the reaction would be equally benevolent in other cultures.

In fact it seems as if differences in culture tend to cause much bigger problems when they are not perceived. Finns often complain of that Swedes are unreliable and that everything has to be written down. I recently encountered another example where a Finnish executive complained how hard it was to do business with Australians.

> "We thought Australia would be an easy country to do business in. After all, we thought, well perhaps one looks at it in a more European way. But it is very difficult, a very difficult country." (interview with supplier)

The Finnish representatives responsible for Australia and Southeast Asia did not expect the cultural differences to be as big as they were. What they saw was a White, Anglo-Saxon, Protestant culture, a culture very reminiscent of their own (more or less). The impression was accentuated by the fact that every one else in the area, as the manager saw it, was very different. This of course influenced both their actions and also the way they interpreted the Australians' actions. Because they did not perceive a cultural difference, neither the Finns nor the Australians applied excusing inter-cultural context to the interpretation of the actions. This had important implications to the relationship. If there is no excuse for the other party's behavior it means that the perceptions is that it is the person himself who is at fault.

Thus one could say that inter-cultural problems tend to be minimal when the perceived difference between the cultures is bigger than the actual difference. In this kind of situation both parties expect communication to be complicated and misunderstandings to be frequent. The guard is therefore raised and more caution is exercised towards both one's own judgments and actions (judgments are of course also actions). The problems will arise when the perceived cultural difference is smaller than the actual cultural difference. In this case possible bad behavior will not be excused as a cultural misunderstanding (which it might very well be) but rather be judged as lack of respect or compassion, a personal trait. To put it simply: inter-cultural differences become problems only when you think they do not exist.

CONCLUSION

Should we then ignore advice on how to behave when meeting people from other cultures? Of course not, on the contrary, a great deal of attention should be paid to the advice being given. It is the content of the advice, which is misinterpreted either by the reader or by the author. Most books on inter-cultural communication focus very much on different acts, on what to do and what not to do. For example, people often advised that when in Japan they should hand over their calling cards, holding them with both hands, rather than with just one hand. These are however nothing but cheap tricks and are quite meaningless when it comes to actual inter-cultural communication.

As such it can be questioned whether cultural knowledge by itself is of any benefit. The key to successful inter-cultural communication is not how well you know your counterpart's culture or how many cheap tricks you know. As such there is a very narrow limit on how much cultural knowledge one can have. The way of handing over calling cards, or your table manners (with sticks, by hand, spoon, fork and knife, or only fork) are only external minor manifestations of cultural differences. The real differences are much harder to pinpoint. As such it is by definition almost impossible to gain a thorough knowledge of the other one's culture, because it would mean questioning just about everything one holds as self-evident. Even then it might not help. Just because two people are from the same culture, it does not mean there will be no conflict.

When managers discuss international project industry, they often describe actions in terms of courage, generosity and respect. Actions such as these are different in the sense that they are not economically rational. Courageous, generous or respectful behavior cannot be explained in terms of the actor's own benefit, these are actions that specifically lack benefit for the actor. These actions are done because of the counterpart, the object of the act. The difference lies again in intention of the act. Whether you hand over your business card with one or two hands will neither save nor destroy the business deal. It is why this is done that matters. One way to do it is to show the counterpart that you respect and value him, and that you therefore have taken the time to learn his culture. In this situation cultural knowledge plays a positive role by showing respect. However, if this is not done in earnest, if the act is performed merely as a cheap trick to woo the counterpart, then it will in the best case be meaningless, in the worst case it will seem disrespectful. One could of course argue that the intention of the act would be concealed. However, intentions are manifested in action and an intention that was never manifested in either word or action would in fact be like the private language Wittgenstein (1996) discusses – it would not exist.

What therefore matters in inter-cultural communication is not the amount of cultural knowledge or the number of tricks you know. What matters is the behavior as such, taking the responsibility which is yours (courage), not being greedy (generosity) and simply respecting your counterpart for whom he is, not what he is. In this context cultural knowledge can become a tool. However, if the behavior is cowardly, greedy or disrespectful then the cultural knowledge will be seen as merely cheap tricks, used not for whom the counterpart is but merely as an instrument to reach some benefit.

Moreover, explaining somebody's activities as being "just cultural", denies that person his or her personality or individuality. This means that he or she is not met and treated as an intentionally acting person, but instead as one subconsciously driven by "cultural forces". The concept of "culture" when used as an explanation or description of the other, denies him or her of the capacity of intentional conscious deliberation, and thus easily becomes an attitude of utter contempt. Cultural knowledge, used without proper consideration, will therefore easily turn on its user, and probably do more harm than good to the relationship.

As for not patting Taiwanese on the head, the idea seems so ridiculous it would be more interesting to know which group the text was addressed to, i.e. in which culture it would be considered acceptable, and not condescending, to pat adult people on the head. As a Finn I would also advise people not to pat Finns on the head, you might get a black eye, unless you are lucky, and only confirm his view that foreigners really are strange, although many of them can be quite nice.

CHAPTER 17

EMPIRICAL EVIDENCE OF PEOPLE AS DETERMINANTS OF PROJECT SUCCESS

Thomas Lechler, IBU, Karlsruhe University of Technology, Germany

ABSTRACT

In this chapter the impact on project success of human factors and factors related to project form will be compared by analyzing 448 projects from a wide spectrum of German industries. Questions about how to plan and organize projects play a dominant role in many discussions about project management. In contrast empirical studies indicate a strong influence of human related factors. A framework of eight success factors derived from a meta-analysis of 44 empirical success factor studies is used to analyze the question which of these two factor classes is more important for project success. The question will be answered in consideration of causal relations between these factors. These causal relations are important for more accurate estimates of the impact of various factors on project success. Using a confirmatory LISREL-Analysis, the empirical results shed new light on the discussion about success factors. In contrast to conventional wisdom they indicate only weak influences of the formal aspects on project outcomes. On the other hand the results strongly recommend the growing trend to recognize the "human" side of project management as crucial to project success.

PROJECT MANAGEMENT – A MATTER OF FORMALISM?

Both researchers and practitioners discuss the use of tools and organizational standards for successful project implementations with the same intensity. Maybe it is because these topics are relatively accessible for the discussions. Which manager does not like to mention that the implementation of a new concept, or the use of a certain tool, has led to a successful project outcome? Which consultant does not like to talk about his invention of a tool or concept that "guarantees" the success of a project?

This often practised simplified analysis of the causes of project success explains why project management is mainly seen as a formal, tool based concept. Sometimes the perception of project management is even taken so far that the critical path method is regarded as a synonym for project management. But it is basically a contradiction itself, because projects are in general innovative, complex, and time restricted. The course of a project is uncertain and often experiences considerable changes. Therefore, a purely formal, rule-bound approach reaches its natural limits. Nevertheless there are a lot of innovative and successful projects! Obviously project success is also influenced by some other factors. The capabilities of the people involved in solving extraordinary and unforeseen problems are an important key for project success (Pinto 1986, Pinto and Slevin 1988a, Zielasek 1995). However, discussions about the human aspects of project management are less prevalent and intensive. An explanation might be that the human-related factors are a complex topic and the development of solutions is significantly more complicated than to develop concepts which solve formal quantitative problems.

It is interesting to mention that the empirical research more often analyses the human factors of project management than the formal factors. The discrepancy between the empirical research and the conceptual and practical discussions about project management leads to the question we want to address empirically: which role do the human and formal factors play for project success? Another weakness of the actual discussions is the single level causal view of the effects of success factors. Mostly causal relations between success factors are overlooked. The view that success factors have only a direct impact on project success is too simple and could lead to wrong conclusions. To get more precise insights, we consider causal relations between the individual success factors as well. This approach allows us to analyse the direct, and also the indirect effects on project success at the same time. To summarise the analysis is based on the two assumptions that the success factors of project management show causal relations and that the personnel factors are most important for project success. These hypotheses are tested with a confirmatory LISREL analysis of 448 projects.

In the first step, a framework of eight theoretical key success factors of project management are suggested. This framework was derived from a comprehensive meta analysis of the empirical research on success factors of project management. The framework also contains the basic causal structure between the eight factors. After a brief description of the research design and the sample, the influence of the formal factors of project management are tested separately with a simple correlation analysis. Finally, the third step is a synthesis of the formal and personnel point of view. Success factors of both groups were empirically checked, in term of their interaction. The main conclusions and look to further research steps are given in the last part of this chapter.

THE CONCEPTUAL FRAMEWORK

In a comprehensive meta analysis of 44 empirical success factor studies, which investigate more than 5,700 different projects, 11 key success factors of project management were identified (Lechler 1997: 77). It is interesting that these studies prove that the formal factors of project management, including different aspects of project planning, control and organization, have less influence on project success than human resource factors. More important for project success are the characteristics of the involved people and their behaviour. The results verify the hypothesis that the people are the most important success factors for projects.

Furthermore the actual empirical research could be characterised as mainly exploratory with a focus on the discovery of key factors that are not yet taken into account. However, the possibility of causal dependencies between the key success factors is rarely considered (see Murphy *et al.* 1974 for a notable exception). Projects are complex and interdependent processes. For this reason, success factors cannot be assumed as independent in their influence on project success. This leads to the second hypothesis: the success factors are causally linked to each other.

Out of the 11 identified success factors, the eight most often analysed (top management, project leader, project team, participation, planning and control, information and communication, conflicts, change of goals) were chosen for this empirical analysis. These eight factors are summarised into three categories (People, Activities, Barriers) described below. These categories are ordered in a conceptual framework, which describes the basic causal structure for the joint analysis of the factors. The eight success factors are defined and measured as follows:

People Category:
The factor *top management* includes direct support as well as the general interest of top management in an individual project. It is measured with a Likert scale consisting of four items.
The factor *project leader* refers to the formal authority of the project leader. It is measured on a Likert scale with four different items. This factor does not describe the personal characteristics of the project leader, it describes a formal aspect of the project organization. In our sense this factor belongs to the formal aspects of project management.
The factor *project team* describes the task, administrative, and self-management know-how of the project team. It is measured on a Likert scale with three different items.

Activities Category:
The factor *participation* refers to the direct and indirect involvement of the project team in the decision processes of the project. It is measured on a Likert scale with four different items.
The factor *information/communication* describes the formal information system as well as the effectiveness and efficiency of communication, both formal and informal. It is measured on a Likert scale with eight different items.
The factor *planning/controlling* focuses on the intensity and effectiveness of activities concerning planning and controlling the project as well as the use of planning and controlling instruments. It is measured on a Likert scale with seven different items. This factor describes the formal activities of planning and controlling. In our sense this factor also represents the formal aspects of project management.

Barriers Category:

The factor *conflicts* pertains to both the intensity and the kind of the conflict (i. e., goal conflict, conflict of interests, conflicting perceptions, conflicting assessments/evaluations). This factor also assesses both conflicts within the team as well as with selected people outside the project team (i. e., top management, line management, customer). This factor is aggregated from four conflict factors, which are each measured using Likert scales consisting of from six to eight different items. *Changes of project goals* refers to the extent or importance, as well as the frequency of changes. It is measured with 2 items.

Project Success Category:

Project success is a subjective evaluation of the project's outcomes. The determination of project success is a very complex and multidimensional issue. Evaluations of project success may vary greatly depending on individual perspectives, reference criteria, the point in time, as well as the object itself (de Cotiis and Dyer 1979, de Wit 1985, Pinto and Slevin 1988b, Gemünden 1990, Hauschildt 1991). Because the present analysis examines the differences of the total impact of the people and formal related factors it is sufficient to use an overall measurement of project success. The original, more detailed framework, recognizes the multidimensional nature of project success by the three dimensions of project success efficiency, effectiveness and social success (Lechler 1997). In this research, a project is considered successful if the people involved and the customer are satisfied with the process and the results. The overall project success is measured with a Likert scale consisting of four items.

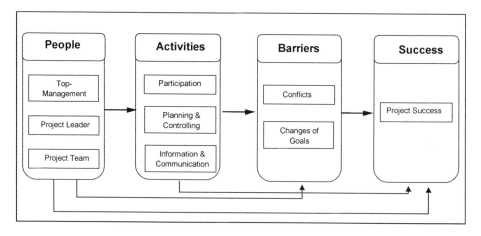

Figure 1. The Conceptual Research Framework

The conceptual framework categorises the factors and relates them in a certain causal structure. The relations between these different groups of factors represent the main hypothesis of this investigation. They are based on the following assumptions:

All the success factors have a direct positive or negative impact on overall project success.

The people category influences activities and barriers. These influences are based on the assumption that the people involved in the project will mark it with their own characteristics and that these characteristics are relatively stable during the course of the project.

The activities category also influences the barriers. It is assumed that the activities cause or prevent barriers i.e., conflicts or changes of goals.

Also, within the categories, the factors are causally related. These dependencies are discussed in the empirical analysis, so a theoretical deduction is not provided here (Lechler 1997: 109).

RESEARCH DESIGN AND SAMPLE DESCRIPTION

The data for this study were gathered in a survey. The questionnaire was developed by using fifty items which were originally developed by Pinto (1986) (see also Slevin and Pinto 1986). These items were translated into German and some were restructured to new factors. All items are measured with a seven point rating scale ranging from strong agreement to strong disagreement. The questionnaire was distributed to members of the German Project Management Society (Gesellschaft für Projektmanagement (GPM) and to large industrial companies. After the initial contact by telephone, two questionnaires were mailed out to each respondent, asking them to report on one project they regard as a success, and one project they regard as a failure (Rothwell *et al.* 1974). This method was used in order to achieve high variance in the variables concerning project success. Additionally, it diminishes the possibility for an unbalanced sample, dominated by successful projects. The data collection effort achieved an overall response rate of **43%**, resulting in a sample of **N=448** projects. The sample consists of **257 successful** and **191 unsuccessful** projects. The largest group responding to the questionnaire were project managers (46%). The other groups were managers of technical (19%) or commercial (18%) tasks. The group "others" (26%) consisted mainly of external consultants, who had co-ordinating, consultative or leading functions in the project.

The sample is relatively balanced concerning the kinds of projects included. About 26% of the projects in the sample are machine tool, engineering, plant construction or building construction projects. Development projects made up about 26% of the sample and includes projects for product modifications, product enhancements and the development of completely new products. A further 24% are software projects. The category "others" consists predominately of concept studies, tests or organisational redesign projects. The broad variety of projects shows that the concept of project management is being employed in all industries (including services). Also the similar distribution of the different types of projects precludes a bias caused by a certain type of industry or a certain type of project. The sample is qualified to prove the two hypotheses that the success factors are causally related and that the capabilities and behavior of the people are more important than the more frequently discussed formal aspects of project management.

EMPIRICAL FINDINGS

The Influences of Formal Project Management on Project Success

Due to the dominant topic of the discussions but the weak and rare empirical tests we analyse in the first step the influences of the formal aspects of project management on project success. The following table includes the used items of the questionnaire and their correlations with the overall measurement of project success. The table also includes the correlation of the factor 'project leader' and the factor 'planning/controlling' with project success.

Table 1. Correlations of formal aspects of project management with project success (* level of significance < 1%; n.s. = not significant).

Items used in the questionnaire	Correlation with project success
There is a company wide project standard in form of detailed guidelines	n.s.
There was one department to support all important project activities.	n.s.
The projects were supervised by a project steering committee.	n.s.
The project priorities were specified and changed by a committee	n.s.
Projects were coordinated by an interfunctional multiproject control committee.	n.s.
The appropriate technology (equipment, training programs, etc.) has been selected for the project.	.38*
Project management software assisted in project planning	n.s.
Project management software assisted in supervision and control.	n.s.
Multi project management was done with the help of project management software.	n.s.
Communication channels were defined before the start of the project.	.42*
All proceedings, methods and tools used to support the project worked well.	.61*
Factor: Project leader	.47*
Factor: Planning/Controlling	.59*

The topics of discussion in most project management discourse suggest that formal tools and standards are of primary importance to project success. But the correlations shown clearly paint a different picture. Standards and organizational issues such as centralized support or steering committees, have no influence on project success. But appropriate project specific actions, for instance the use of planning tools, the definition of communication channels or the formal authority of the project leader, characterise successful projects. At first glance, the results support the main hypothesis, that the possibilities to reduce risk and uncertainty in projects through formal tools are limited. Most of the correlations are not significant. The results could be seen as a first support of our hypothesis that people-related factors are more important.

Interaction between Success Factors
The second step of the data analysis represents the synthesis of the two points of view, so the influences on project success will be analysed under the interaction between personnel, formal and process based success factors. For this step the data analysis was conducted using the LISREL-Approach (Linear Structural **Relationships**). LISREL is a statistical method, that allows simultaneous analysis of hypothetical causal relationships for a number of variables, while still accounting for possible shortcomings in measurements (Jöreskog and Sörbom 1989).

Building the empirical model of success factors using LISREL was carried out in three steps (Bagozzi 1980, Anderson and Gerbing 1988, Bollen 1989, Fritz 1992, Soni *et al.* 1993). In the first step, a confirmatory factor analysis was calculated in order to verify the measurement of the various constructs. The second step involved the separate analysis of the detailed structure of causal relationships within the three groups of factors (*People*, *Activities* and *Barriers*) as well as their respective impacts on project success. The third step integrates the models developed in step two to get the full model. Recognizing the issues involved in evaluating linear structural equation models (Bollen 1989, Mulaik *et al.* 1989: 432, Medsker *et al.* 1994, Fritz 1992: 127), a comprehensive sequence of checks was developed and employed.

Table 2. Global Fit Indices

Degree Achieved 100%					
χ^2	$= 2750.25$	GFI	$= .979$	PGFI $= .860$	$t = 105$
df	$= 756$	AGFI	$= .976$		$t^* = 861$
χ^2/df	$= 3.64$	RMR	$= .059$		$t < t^*$

To evaluate the model from the statistical perspective we used several global fit indices. The estimated model shows an adequate fit if the GFI (Goodness of Fit Index), AGFI (Adjusted Goodness of Fit Index) and the PGFI (Parsimonious Goodness of Fit Index) reaches values approaching 1. These indices are measures for the discrepancy between the hypothesized and the estimated causal model. The derived model of success factors meets all evaluation criteria and shows good to very good fit indices. The model can be therefore seen as an accurate base for valid statements (Lechler 1997: 257).

The path diagram in the following figure shows the ways in which the eight success factors influence project success. The coefficients (path coefficients) above the arrows describe the strengths and the directions of the influences between the factors. With one exception (top management -> goal changes) all of the shown coefficients reach the significance level of 1%. The magnitude of the estimated coefficients represents the importance of causal interactions of the success factors and supports the second hypothesis.

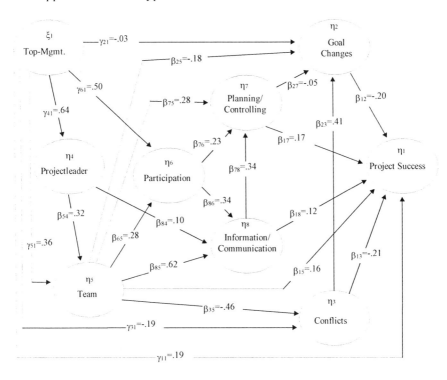

Figure 2. Path Diagram of the Empirical Model (Level of Significance < 1%)

The individual success factors exert their influence on project success in different ways. This is explained below.

Top management directly promotes project success as 'customer' and highest organizational authority ($\gamma_{11} = .19$). Through transferring formal authority to the project leader ($\gamma_{41} = .64$) and by influencing the design of the project team ($\gamma_{51} = .36$), Top management provides the organizational environment for the successful completion of the project. Top management also impacts the process directly through the participation factor ($\gamma_{61} = .50$). The considerably high impact of top management on project success can also be interpreted from a more critical point of view, as this could indicate an overly strong involvement of top management in the process of the project itself.

The *project leader* exerts influence over the information/communication factor (β_{84} = .10). The impact of the project leader on planning/controlling, however, was not supported by this data. Thus this hypothesis has to be rejected. Additionally, there was no significant direct influence of the project leader factor on project success, so that this hypothesis had to be rejected too.

The *project team* is the main driving force for project operations and thus directly promotes project success (β_{15} = .16). A good team actively utilizes its decision making authority (β_{65} = .28). Its know-how leads to better planning and more adequate and flexible controlling of the project (β_{75} = .28) in addition to improved information flows/communication within and outside the team (β_{85} = .62).

These data do not display a significant relationship between *participation* and project success, so that the hypothesized direct impact is not supported. However, the strong influence of participation on communication (β_{64} = .32) gives evidence to the assumption that participative leadership enhances the formal and informal exchange of information within the project. Additionally, the project team participating in project-relevant decisions does improve the quality of planning and controlling (β_{54} = .29).

Out of the group of *Activities*, the factor *information/communication* shows the strongest direct impact on project success (β_{16} = .13). Its influence on planning and controlling (β_{56} = .20) documents the importance of free information flows on that success factor.

The direct impact of *planning/controlling* on project success is surprisingly low (β_{12} = .10). This result contradicts the widespread opinion that planning/controlling is one of the most important success factors. The relatively weak influence could be attributed to high levels of uncertainty, that force the project team to take 'ad hoc' actions as reactions to ever changing situations. In such cases, the need to react may outweigh the benefits of the preset project plans. Another explanation for this weak influence could be that the project team does not take the plan seriously, in which case the plan would serve as an alibi.

The strong negative impact of *conflicts* on project success demonstrates the significance of effective conflict management to projects. Often times the causes for conflicts come from outside 'the project'. For instance, differences between project and line management over authority as well as political activities are frequently being carried into the project from outside. Conflicts are particularly likely to occur in so-called 'weak' project organizations, where project decisions have to be approved by numerous departments and hierarchical levels. Additionally, projects in these organizations are more apt to experience high personnel turnover, which, in turn, may increase the chances for changes in goals (another obstacle to project success).

The second *Barrier*, *changes in goals*, also displays a strong negative impact on project success. Because of complexity and uncertainty, project goals are often difficult to determine. However, our data document that a lack of continuity in goals is significantly related to unsuccessful projects. Our research also suggests, that the potentials for conflicts and changes in goals are built up before project start, and thus are difficult to control during the course of the project.

The Impact on Project Success
The main hypothesis we want to address in our analysis is the question of whether the human side of project management is more important to project success than the formal side of project management. To answer this question more accurately the causal relations between the success factors have to be considered. But in the first step it has to be proven that the model really involves success factors of project management. As the amount 59% of explained variance in the dependent variable project success shows the success factor model displays considerable explanatory power. With the help of this model it is now possible to compare the effects on project success of the "human" factors against the ones for the "formal" factors.

Factor	Effect		
	Direct Effect	**Indirect Effect**	**Total Effect**
Top Mgmt.	.19	.41	.60
Project Leader	-	.18	.18
Project Team	.16	.36	.52
Participation	-	.10	.10
Planning/ Controlling	.16	.01	.17
Information/ Communication	.12	.06	.18
Conflicts	-.21	-.08	-.29
Goal Changes	-.20	-	-.20

Figure 3. The Influences on Project Success

The results of this investigation show the people involved as the primary success factors of projects in general. If a project lacks top management support, or if the project team is not qualified enough, then the chances for a successful project are fairly limited. These deficits can not easily be compensated through *Activities* such as planning & controlling or communication & information, as these themselves are results of people's abilities. Overall the weak total effects of the formal authority of the project leader (.18) and the planning/controlling factor (.17) on the one hand and the strong influences of the top management (.60) and the project team (.52) on the other are clear indicators that verify our main hypothesis: that the human side of project management is more important than the formal aspects.

CONCLUSIONS AND FUTURE RESEARCH

The empirical test of the eight factor model supports our two hypotheses. The consequences deriving from this analysis are obvious. In the future, if the effects of single key success factors are estimated, it is necessary to take into account causal relations to other success factors. The big differences between the effects concerning project success in between the studied key factors are surprising. Contrary to the main topics of practitioners' discussion, human factors are very important to the success of a project. Of course the design of the study has its limitations. First of all it is not possible to test variations of the factors over time or bi-directional causal effects. To get more valid data a longitudinal approach might be useful in the next step. Also contextual influences like the situation within the firm and the characteristics of the project have to be considered in future analysis.

The present results also raise some questions. Which actions can be taken to make success more likely? The results we have on hand suggest that right before the beginning of a project, the course should be set. In cases where no adequate team is available, or top management has no personal interest in the project, it makes more sense to move the project start to a later point in time. Otherwise the probability of failure is too high. The way this phase is set up, should not depend on chance or on the generally tight conditions. This leads to the question: how could the front end of the projects be organised? Is it possible to develop tools or heuristics to support these activities?

Future discussions about successful project management should focus on the human aspects. The questions must shift from the selection of a specific tool to questions of how projects could be managed more effectively on the human side. The uncertainty of many projects sets limits to rigid formal approaches. More relevant questions are how the conditions of a project have to be designed and which actions have to be taken to encourage teamwork in order to increase the abilities of the involved people, and motivate the collaboration of the different participating parties in the project. The questions are how to motivate people working at the same time in two or more different projects? Are virtual teams a useful approach or are they only buzz words?

CHAPTER 18

BUSINESS IN THE FUTURE AND THE NATURE OF PROJECTS – RESEARCH ISSUES

Francis Hartman, University of Calgary, Canada

Rolf A. Lundin, Umeå School of Business and Economics, Umeå, Sweden

RATIONALE

A clear message in the various chapters of this book has been the need to understand the essential nature of the organizations that sponsor projects and the temporary teams that deliver them. Projects are no longer a prerogative of the world of technology. The use of project terms, habits and practices has extended well beyond technology-based ones. Project management has also grown from its beginnings in scheduling techniques as seen with PERT on the Polaris Project in the 1950's, into a significantly more sophisticated skill set. This set of skills encompasses not just project management tools but also deals with the business and social context of projects. The relationship between organizations that sponsor projects and the teams that deliver them is of significant importance to the efficacy of the projects themselves. We can see these relationships continue to evolve. The differences between the two groups are diminishing as the organization adopts project tools, project teams adopt more process thinking and both become more socially aware. The growth in social awareness generally and triumph of the individual in particular was predicted by Naisbitt and Aburdene (1990). In projects we see this emerge as a part of evolving project management practices. At the outset we saw project management as essentially a tool-based discipline, with a heavy focus on scheduling and other techniques. The next stage in the evolution of project management was growing awareness of the need to address process issues, such as team effectiveness and how to move from a plan to action by the team members. A strong task orientation remained. Since then business context and relevance has been added and the newest dimension has been attention to the social issues that are essential to project success. These social issues are early manifestations of what Naisbitt and Aburdene predicted. In this chapter one view of what the future might hold is presented. Within this future context, the nature of projects and how they come into being is considered.

With a view of what future projects will bring, we can see the challenges that such projects will face. Some are old problems. Others are new ones. Either way, better solutions to the old and new approaches to deal with the new are needed. This points the way to where project management research needs to go over the next few years.

In writing this end-piece to the book, we have taken a deliberately provocative look at where the future might lead. The intent is not to seek total agreement, but to stir the thinking of readers of this book. In this closing chapter of a book that presents some of the current evolutionary thinking of specialists in the project management arena, we hope to help open the door for the next generation of research thinking.

ESTABLISHED TRENDS

One of the most obvious trends in the management of projects over the years has been the shift from a purely internal (largely tools-based) view of project management to one with a greater business context. This was explained as an analogy to an inverted black box (Lundin and Söderholm 1998). [This particular paper highlighted the introverted and business-blind nature of many projects]. Growing awareness of the business context was then followed by increased awareness of the social framework in which projects take place. This is still emerging, with European thinking seemingly leading that in North America. We could debate the drivers for this trend. Is it competitive pressure, a shift in the mind-set of younger people entering the project world with greater awareness of and sensitivity to the environment? Perhaps it is simply a growing competence in or an awareness of the need for effective management of projects? Whatever the reason, the horizon of the project has expanded. As this horizon moved beyond the immediate project, business competence to address the host organization's needs has become a needed skill set for project managers. The next shift has been to the general environment in which the host organization operates. This shift seems to have introduced greater social awareness in the management processes of the more effective project managers.

This move from the tools-based mentality of the fifties to the broader view of project management seen today has been slow. In some practice areas, it seems almost to have stagnated. There are many project managers that still believe project management can either be bought in a shrink-wrapped software package for about $500, and others who expect to be fully trained in the relevant knowledge and competence in a few-days long seminar. It is worth giving this some thought. What is the cause of this? And is it a good thing or a bad thing? Is the reliance or at least a propensity to use tools only a search for a Project Management panacea?

We see companies discard one scheduling package in favour of another on a regular basis. Others will have several different packages in use. Some will consider use of the package equivalent to project management, while others will recognize the need for "something more" – but may not be too sure what that other stuff is. At the other end of project management maturity, sophisticated and well-integrated approaches are used that address all aspects of the project. Project Managers come from all walks of life. They have highly varying qualifications for the position. The certification that is available from PMI and IPMA arguably covers part of the skills, knowledge and competencies required of project managers. (The PMI certification has a different focus to that of IPMA, though). It is logical therefore to assume that the project management profession – if there is such a thing – remains both fragmented and incompletely defined. In such an environment will there not be a tendency for people who have achieved some form of recognition as a project manager to protect the turf on which they have established their career and position? If this is so, does this mean that we are building a high degree of inertia into the growth of the profession – at least with the people who are potentially threatened by growth or redefinition of what project management is really about?

While the project world has moved to a broader view of what management of temporary teams to deliver specific needs, so the more conventional management view has moved closer to a projectized approach. Even management thought leaders like Tom Peters (1992) now predict that projects are the wave of future management. Here is what Peters says (1992: 222):

"Arguably, project work was the norm before the industrial revolution. Most activities took place in small, independent shops, and craft and craftsmen were the company's centerpiece. The industrial revolution changed all that....we are arguably returning to the craft tradition. *The essence of craft is the project.* It may turn out that the 150 years from Dickens to 1980 will have been an anomaly. What's normal, on the job or off, will end up being craft, learning, adding value – i.e., the project."

The convergence of traditional management and project management is clear. The speed at which it will occur is still open to discussion. We believe that it will happen very much faster than most management researchers and academics are prepared to accept. Our experience suggests that students in management programs are gravitating towards project management courses rather than the general management ones. Special lectures and short courses on how to use project management techniques to do better in their studies have also taken hold in at least one institution. Interestingly, these short sessions are consistently identified in student evaluations as the highlight of the program within which they participated in that session. And students tend to have a nose for smelling the future. If we see this trend and believe in it, and if we also agree with Peters' observation, then we are left with a really big question.

This question stems from the youth of management as a discipline. It is younger than the 150 years since Dickens. *Have we developed general management theory based on such an anomaly?* Is project management what real management is all about and we are only just starting to realize this?

Naysayers will, of course, hit the Achilles' heel of this view very quickly. The weak point is that project management also started on the wrong foot – with a focus just on time management. It is slowly moving towards a broader view that goes beyond the project itself and addresses issues of the host organization and – in most advanced applications – also society.

This is another interesting observation: there is the growing awareness of the need for a holistic view of what truly effective project management is about.

Specifically, balancing technical, business and social criteria and needs in delivery of projects appears to be a theme touched on directly or indirectly by other authors in this book, and rightly so.

On a broader horizon than just the world of projects we see many things that are changing the way in which we do business. There is both convergence and fragmentation. We see this in the way companies and nations are evolving. While some splinter into smaller groups (fragmentation), others join forces to take on larger competitors or to cut competition out altogether (convergence). Mergers (convergence) and spin-offs (fragmentation) are taking on new meaning. Cisco is funding telecommunication start-ups in Europe in order to create a market for its data switching products (convergence). Hewlett Packard has a long tradition of sponsoring bright ideas from within and helping the inventors spin off new companies (fragmentation). A newer phenomenon is now referred to as coopetition (convergence of fragmented organizations?). This is the joining of forces between normal competitors in research, product development, manufacturing or marketing within non-competitive arenas. The definition of what is competitive and what is not is constantly being redefined too. As is the definition of what "core business" is all about. As little as five years ago, companies would not have considered outsourcing their Information Technology (IT) or Information Systems (IS), as this was a central part of their core business. This was how they handled corporate information – and was part of their competitive edge. Today, outsourcing IS and IT functions is commonplace. Interestingly, it is a significant source of "projects" as the function is transferred to management by a third party. The relationship between IS/IT service vendors and their clients must be an interesting one to study from the perspective both of relationships and projects. We also see a growth in the use of alliance or partnership arrangements between organizations. These may be project-specific or longer-term business ties based on a symbiotic relationship. These shifts are reported in various ways, including the work of the Cost Reduction Initiative for the New Era (CRINE) out of the UK and its Norwegian equivalent NORSOK. In the construction industry we see Alliances and Partnerships being studied. The Construction Industry Institute (CII) has issued a number of reports in this area over the past few years. Current studies by Andrew Pettigrew and his colleagues confirm projectization and outsourcing as important (cf. Whittington *et al.* 1999). Is there a pattern in all of this? Here is one interpretation.

We are likely to agree on a few things:
- Globalization is making labour markets both more accessible and more affordable as work is moved to the lowest cost producer regardless of location
- The Internet and e-commerce is shrinking the global village in ways we had previously not though possible. Just one of the dimensions being shrunk is productive time, as work can now be spun around the world and three sequential eight-hour shifts can be created to work on material that can be moved on the Internet.

- One obvious commodity is knowledge. Another is software (arguably a specific form of knowledge). And there are more.
- Businesses are taking advantage of this technology because they need to respond to growing pressure on:
- time to market,
- shrinking product half-life (Like radiation of nuclear material, half the value of a product to the producer erodes rapidly first. The product's half-life has been reached when half that value is gone.)
- rapid innovation,
- falling production costs,
- innovations in product distribution,
- the need for smarter and more cost effective marketing,
- finding the specialized expertise needed for the tasks in hand

All of these pressures are making the business of managing a business more fragmented and more demanding. The fragmentation is created largely by the need to combine a growing number of expert or specialized contributors – often from different organizations, and sometimes geographically distributed – to achieve an integrated end product. Increasingly the world of business is looking more and more like a war where the battlefield is survival, battles are fought as programs and the skirmishes are won or lost as projects. This analogy holds as we look for advantages through alliances, need specialist units to help address particular situations and require logistics to bring materials and people to the battlefront and sustain them there. In essence our armed forces need to win projects. That takes planning and good leadership in a world of chaos.

WHAT THESE TRENDS MIGHT MEAN – PLANS FOR THE PAST AND KNOWLEDGE FROM THE FUTURE?

The trends we are seeing can be viewed in many ways. Converging technologies, for example are leading to greater specialization. We are creating new expertise and, therefore, more experts. The same task that needed one (relative) generalist a decade ago will need several specialists today. The driver for this is burgeoning technology. The growth of technology is exponential. The US Patent and Trademark Office issues about 22% more patents in any year than it did five years earlier. This trend has been fairly constant since 1975 (Taylor and Wacker 1997) The number of electronic components in commercial aircraft have doubled between 1950 and 1970 Between 1970 and 1980 they doubled again (Augustine 1997). Using these examples and others as a basis for estimating and projecting technology growth, the number of types of different artifacts that exist roughly every three years (1999 – estimates, there are no real figures). Understanding these new artifacts – many of which are hybrids of earlier technologies, such as the Palm Pilot VII Personal Assistant which combines handheld computers with cell phone technology and the Internet, requires increasing specialization. It also requires increasing amounts of technical and other coordination. Survival in managing a business that produces such artifacts on a commercial basis means, more and more, managing in bite-sized (byte-sized?) pieces rather than in a continuous and increasingly bewildering and unmanageable stream. Some of the fall-out of this technology boom is also interesting.

We are developing many jargon dialects. These are making effective communication more difficult. Cultural differences are linked closely to language, so likely we are developing sub-tribes with their own language and traditions. Cell phone technology would not have solved the problem faced by the builders of the Tower of Babel. No matter how good the telecommunications technology, we can only communicate effectively if we speak the same language. Let us pause here for a moment and consider what is changing. We have just discussed increasing numbers of technology artefacts. As these grow in number, we do not increase our vocabulary in tandem. The lag in language development generally means we re-use words but with specific meanings. The line between language and jargon (Craft language or tribal language) is becoming harder to define or see. Language has become a problem that needs to be addressed by management. Communication is at the heart of effective project management.

Speed to market, innovation and finding the right expertise all points to better management of the supply chain. Possibly it also points to better understanding or even re-definition of what a supply chain really is. Supply chain management is more than managing a supplier or a customer. It is all about managing part of a value chain. And to do that we need to understand the chain beyond where it impinges on our projects, because then we can understand our partners' behaviours better. This is important because it is within an effective and synergistic value chain that we fine the expertise we need, and therefore the innovation that keeps us all competitive.

Such chains are as strong as the weakest link: what are the options? In putting our value and supply chains together we have traditionally done so based on best short-term value. This manifests itself in the form of competitive bidding and fixed price contracting. It is unlikely that this mindset will be the right one in the next millennium. Not only that, but we have worked at protecting our own organization at the expense of our value chain partners. The resulting continuous shifts in allegiance and in business arrangements are less than efficient. The Japanese model has been more effective. Reworked and modified, this partnership model has emerged in Europe through the NORSOK and CRINE initiatives in the North Sea. These initiatives have achieved significant breakthrough project performance compared to previous similar projects in the same industry and geographic areas. Spurred by these and by other drives, others have and continue to challenge traditional contracting methods and processes in search of better performance.

Not a new idea, distributed teams have been around on projects since Rome sent troops out to conquer the world. There are earlier examples too. What is new is the technology that speeds up all that is associated with projects. This means there is less time to plan, respond, adapt and understand what is going on. The technology side again, offers solutions that bring new management challenges in their wake. A response that seems to be emerging is a tendency to adopt fast-moving and flexible organizational structures. Regardless of the labels and macro structures under which these form there seem to be a conglomeration of lots of small teams with a high degree of autonomy. Decentralization is also a feature. If history is to repeat itself, we need to eliminate central control if we are to survive. As Dr. Ralph Levene pointed out while presenting one of his 1999 PMI Symposium papers (Levene 1999), every empire's demise was preceded by heavy centralization of the "corporate" operation and control.

One of the drivers behind a wish to centralize or decentralize is power. If knowledge is power, we need to seek the source of knowledge in organizations – at least the knowledge that adds intrinsic value. We find this in innovation and ownership of intellectual capital. Who innovates? Who owns intellectual property (IP)? Who really adds value to what? How long does that value have value? These are burning questions in today's world. And there are no burning answers for them yet. The ownership of IP is a growing issue as companies collaborate on product development. The complexities of doing business are increasing too it seems.

What this means to projects is that the projects we manage are more complex. Our solution to added complexity in projects has, traditionally, been to make the management of those projects more complex. That option has pretty well been exhausted, so we need a new and different approach. This is one arena in which the research gladiators must fight and win. If we are to identify trends and then learn from them, we need to understand where these trends are taking us. Let us summarize what we have so far.

Technologies are merging. This means that in the producers of this technology need to integrate more components than ever before. This is increasingly craft-like, to use Peters' analogy. It is also more demanding in management of business relationships between the producers of components and the integrator as well as between the integrator and its customer. Often customers are service providers such as banks, insurance companies, retailers, telecommunications companies and other utilities. These service providers need to understand technological development and then select, adapt and use the right ones if they are to remain competitive. E-commerce is opening doors of business opportunity that we did not even conceive could exist scant years ago. Creation of new technology, its manufacture, marketing, adoption and adaptation and finally its use all generate projects.

These projects are more complex than ever, involve more diverse organizations and individuals, a broader span of expertise and greater geographical dispersion than ever before. For illustration, we have picked just one, but perhaps the most critical, aspect: communication. Language is increasingly becoming a barrier to effective communication because we do not mean the same thing when we use specific words. The areas that need to be researched are growing faster than the capacity to research them. And they are growing even faster when compared to the ability of frantically busy practitioners to address the issues that these changes are bringing about.

The result of this is that there is a shift in how practitioners and researchers need to work together. More specifically, it is the project management researchers that need to do the work. It is the practitioners who need to help identify the priorities and be willing to learn from the findings of researchers

THE IMPACT OF FUTURE CHANGE ON PROJECTS AND THEIR MANAGEMENT.

Anything that purports to sustain or add value to a business is a step. Steps have a start and a finish. Invariably, such steps are constrained in terms of the resources and available time that they have to be completed. That is the common basic definition of a project. It follows that projects are the only kind of value-adding business venture. (Hartman 2000)

Managing projects well is what every venture needs to do for survival. Be it a government agency, a business or a not-for-profit organization. All of these projects are unique in that they have different goals and objectives. The question to ask is: "Are these projects unique at every other level, or can we share ideas and processes, methodologies and knowledge between them?" We know we can. But at what level is this useful and when does such sharing reduce in relevance and value?

Here is another view of this issue. Projects differ in two fundamental ways. The first can be classified as nature and the other as class. The nature differences lie in the specific intent, culture, language and technologies that the project will operate with and under. The differences in this category are what make all projects different. The class of project can be defined in a number of dimensions. These dimensions set out the key variables that guide how we manage the project. All projects of the same class will likely benefit from the same management approach. Classification of projects has been part of a study by the Project Management Institute. So far this has not yielded any significant results. Other studies are searching for a set of measures that define the management needs of projects. Hartman's current study is still too new to have delivered any useful results. Promising indicators suggest that at least five and possibly six dimensions need to be considered. These are:

- impact (a measure of relative size and sponsor anxiety)
- complexity (a measure of the number of different disciplines and therefore communication challenges involved)
- uncertainty (a measure of how well and confidently the end outcome of the project can be defined at the outset)
- attractiveness (a measure of how keen people will be to be associated with the project)
- urgency (a measure of the degree(s) of constraint placed on the project).
- Risk (if this turns out to be truly different to uncertainty in how it affects projects, will affect the degree of control that there is to be had on a project and its outcomes)

The idea behind this set of dimensions is that between them they cover the main measures. Individually or in combination, they address most of the variables that define the class of project that we need to manage. The labels can undoubtedly be improved. Each dimension specifically affects a set of project management criteria, and so the criteria can be "scaled" up or down to suit the specific needs of the project. The use of a particular set of tools, processes and competencies to manage a project is likely more dependent upon the class as opposed to the nature of a project. Understanding the nature of a project remains of vital importance, however, as this affects language. Language affects credibility. If we do not speak the tribal language for a particular project, we will be assessed as not understanding the business. If you are not familiar with – and ideally steeped in – the culture of the project's industry and sponsor organization, you are seen as an outsider and therefore less competent than those within the tribe. Is this manifestation of protectionism not a natural phenomenon that we see repeated at many levels in business and society?

If this turns out to make sense, we still need to understand the best way of tackling the organization of project teams. Do we follow the military model of regiments with specialist troops? Should we look at the medieval model of trade associations or unions? Are tribes a better model for tomorrow's project teams? Should teams be static or ever changing to suit the needs of the project? The answers to these questions do not lie just in organizational design. They are influenced by many other factors. Just two of these are the use of monetary currencies and other internal exchange of value systems and the need for technical specialization, and the half-life of the knowledge needed. The brave new world we face tomorrow will impact projects in innumerable ways. Half the challenge is to understand what those ways might be.

OLD PROBLEMS AND NEW CHALLENGES

We still have not solved the old project management problems of delivery to meet expectations of stakeholders for performance (quality and cost), time, money and safety. These chestnuts still need research attention. But the search for solutions cannot wait for understanding of the process, because the processes being used are changing faster than researchers can properly study them. Faster paced and more innovative approaches to project management research is just one of the challenges that we face. In Chapter 1 we elaborated on this.

In the absence of evolution we face revolution. The new challenges that are being put to project managers and their teams are arriving faster than the relatively small group of specialist researchers in this field world-wide can even hope to consider. We cannot rely on evolution alone, but must expect revolutionary ideas to emerge and to be tested on real projects.

The new problems for project managers are cross-cultural and cross-disciplinary in nature. Some of the new ground rules for project managers include managing projects with high uncertainty, living and operating in a digital world that few manager really understand, dealing with new demands for tracking and auditablity, addressing social constructs, continuous learning and disenfranchisement of segments of the team and of the population.

FUTURE RESEARCH NEEDS IN PROJECT MANAGEMENT AT THE LEVELS OF PROJECT, ORGANIZATION AND SOCIETY

What do we really know today about tomorrow's projects? We are challenging and re-building such old concepts as CPM scheduling and the Work Breakdown Structure. If we redefine projects, do we redefine Project Management? What is the real value of conventional project management in tomorrow's unconventional world? If everyone needs to be a project manager, how do we make them one? Will we need to rely more on self-managing teams? Will we have to share power more?

Traditions have served over the years to help stabilize society. We accept them primarily for this purpose. How can we hope to understand traditions if they now live in a world that is made up of a vast collection of the temporary? If we need stability in our lives so that we can make at least temporary sense of what is going on and what we are trying to achieve, can we do this by using projects to set our strategy? Is setting of strategy for a corporation or a government not just another project? Can we use projects to help us understand strategy?

As we near the end of this chapter and of this book, we find more questions than answers and more answers than the facts can really support. The best research in project management today seems to be founded on cooperation between practitioners and researchers. There remains much to understand and more to do. A closing message for this book may be that there is an eternity of study to undertake, but we must choose our topics carefully if we are to help make projects more successful and better in the future. The selection of research topics jointly by researchers and practitioners is probably an important step in achieving a sound portfolio of research topics. Rapid research also requires collaboration between practitioners (who own the "laboratory" and the data) and the researchers who must make sense of the data and test their findings in the laboratory. If the collaborative research at the University of Calgary is anything to go by, the yields to industry are significant.

Ackrich, M., Callon, M. and Latour, B. (1988) "A quoi tient le succes des innovations?" (Why are innovations successful?) *Gerer et Comprendre*, No. 18 & 19.

Alvesson, M. and Lindkvist, L. (1993) "Transaction costs, corporate culture, and clans," *Journal of Management Studies.* Vol. 30, No. 3, pp. 427-452.

Anderson, J. and Gerbing, D. (1988) "Structural Equation Modeling in Practice: A Review and Recommended Two-Step Approach", *Psychological Bulletin*, No. 3: pp. 411-423.

Andersson, T. D. and Larsson-Mossberg, L. (1994) *Forskning om VM i friidrott 1995 (Research on World Championships in Athletics 1995)*, Göteborg: Handelshögskolan vid Göteborgs universitet.

Andres, A (1992) *Mondeo: the Story of the Global Car*, Luxembourg: Word Publishing & Publicity Consultants SA.

Anell, B. (1985) "Exercises in Arbitrariness and Ambiguity: A Study of Twelve Cost-Benefit Analyses of Industrial Disinvestment Decisions." *Accounting, Organizations and Society*, Vol. 10, No 4, pp. 479-492.

Anell, B. and Persson, B. (1982) *Förändringsbenägenhet hos tjänstemännen vid SSAB.* (Change propensities among white collar employees at Swedish Steel Inc.) Linköping University.

Anell, B. and Persson, B. (1983) *Avveckling av verksamhet.* (Terminating operations) Linköping University.

Anell, B. and Persson, B. (1984) *Munksjökoncernens omstrukturering 1 - Vaggerydsfallet: Fabriknedläggningars orsaker och deras konsekvenser för individ, företag och lokalsamhälle.* (Restructuring the Munksjö conglomerate 1. Causes and consequences of closing down) Linköping University.

Anell, B. and Persson, B. (1985) *Företagsledning i krissituationer: Munksjökoncernens omstrukturering och finansiella rekonstruktion* (Managing in crises. The financial and organisational restructuring of the Munksjö conglomerate) Linköping University.

Anell, B., Lindell, P. and Persson, B. (1982) *Förtidspensionering på grund av arbetsbrist: Effekter för den enskilde.* (Early retirement: Consequences for the individual) Linköping University.

Applebaum, E. (1987) "Restructuring work: temporary, part-time and at-home employment," in H. Hartmann (ed.) *Computer Chops and Paper Clips*, Washington: National Academy Press.

Archibald, R.D. (1992) *Managing High-Technology Programs and Projects,* 2nd Edition. New York, NY: Wiley. (1st Edition, 1976).

Ardrey, R. (1966) *The Territorial Imperative*, New York, NY: Delta Books

Argote, L. and McGrath, J.E. (1993) "Group Processes in Organisations: continuity and change". In Cooper C L and Robertson J T (Eds), *International Review of Industrial and Organisational Psychology,* New York: Wiley.

Argyris, C. and Schon, D.A. (1978*) Organizational Learning: A Theory of Action Perspective*, Reading, MA: Addison-Wesley.

Arthur, M. B., Claman, P. and DeFillippi, R. (1995) "Intelligent enterprise, intelligent careers," *Academy of Management Executive*, Vol. 9, No. 4, pp. 7-22.

Arthur, M. B., Hall, D. and Lawrence, B. (1989) *Handbook of career theory*, New York: Cambridge University Press.

Arthur, M.B. and Rousseau, D.M. (Eds.) (1996) *The Boundaryless Career. A New Employment Principle for a New Organizational Era*, New York: Oxford University Press.

Ashby, W.R. (1956) *An Introduction to Cybernetics*, London: Chapman and Hall.

Augustine, N. R. (1997) *Augustine's Laws - Sixth Edition*, Reston, VA: American Institute of Aeronautics and Astronautics Inc.

Axelrod, R. (1976) *The Structure of Decision: The Cognitive Maps of Political Elite*, Princeton, NJ: Princeton University Press.

Axelrod, R. (1984) *Från konflikt till samverkan (From conflict to co-operation)*, Stockholm: SNS Förlag.

Bagozzi, R. (1980) *Causal Models in Marketing*, New York: John Wiley and Sons.

Bahr, F. and Hickenlooper, G. (1991) *Hearts of Darkness: A Filmmaker's Apocalypse*, Hollywood: Blue Dolphin/Zaloom Mayfield/Zoetrope.

Baiman S. (1982) "Agency Theory in Management Accounting: a survey", *Journal of Accounting Literature*, pp 154- 213.

Baiman S. (1996) "Agency Theory in Managerial Accounting: a second look", *Accounting, Organisations and Society*, Vol. 15, No. 4 pp. 341-371.

Baldwin, C.Y. and Clark, K.B. (1997) "Managing in an Age of Modularity." *Harvard Business Review* (September-October):84-93.

Bansard, D. (1991), "L'offre en milieu industriel : des typologies aux stratégies", *Working paper 91/30 (juin), Institut de Recherche de l'Entreprise, Groupe ESC, Lyon.*

Bansard, D., Cova, B. and Flipo, J.P. (1992), "Le marketing de projet: de la réaction à l'anticipation", *Recherche et Applications en Marketing*, vol VII, N°4/92.

Bansard, D., Cova, B. and Salle, R. (1993), "Project marketing : Beyond Competitive Bidding Strategies", *International Business Review*, Vol2, N°2.

Barker, J., Tjosvold, D. and Andrews, I.R. (1988) "Conflict Approaches of Effective and Ineffective Project Managers: A Field Study in a Matrix Organization", *Journal of Management Studies*, 25(2):167-178.

Barley, S. (1986) "Technology as an Occasion for Structuring: Evidence from Observation of CAT Scanners and the Social Order of Radiology Departments", *Administrative Science Quarterly*, 31:78-108.

Barlow, J., Cohen, M., Jashapara, A. and Simpson, Y. (1997) *Towards Positive Partnering*, Bristol: Policy Press.

Bartlett, C.A. and Ghoshal, S. (1989) *Managing across Borders: the transnational solution*, London: Century Business.

Bates, W.S. (1994) "Strong leadership". *Computing Canada*, Vol. 20(22), pp. 32.

Bateson, G. (1972) *Steps to an Ecology of the Mind*, New York: Ballentine.

Beckman, S. (1979). "Immunization - In Defence of Status Quo." In Persson, B. (ed) *Surviving Failures. Patterns and Cases of Project Mismanagement*, Atlantic Highlands, N J.

Beer, S. (1972) *The Brain of the Firm*, London: Allen Lane.

Beidleman, C.R., Fletcher, D. and Veshosky, D. (1990) "On Allocating Risk: the Essence of Project Finance", *Sloan Management Review* 47 .

Bellinger, R., and Beyerlein, M. (1995) "Teams, as seen by electrical engineers: Linking up cuts design cycle and boosts quality, but does it save money?" *Electronic Engineering Times*, no. 859, pp. 59-61.

Belous, R. (1989) *The contingent economy: the growth of the temporary, part-time and subcontracted workforce*, Washington: National Planning Association.

Ben Mahmoud-Jouini, S. and Midler, C. (1996), *L'ingénierie concourante dans le Bâtiment, Synthèse des travaux du GREMAP*, Editions du PCA, Paris, 230 pages.

Bennis, W.G. (1968) "Beyond Bureaucracy", In W.G. Bennis and P.E. Slater (Eds) *The Temporary Society*, New York, NY: Harper & Row, pp. 53-76.

Benson, J. K. (1975) "The Interorganizational Network as a Political Economy", *Administrative Science Quarterly*, June, pp. 229-249.

Berger, P.L. and Luckmann, T. (1967) *The Social Construction of Reality: A Treatise in the Sociology of Knowledge*, London, UK: Penguin.

Berne, E (1979) *Games People Play*, Harmondsworth, Middlesex, England: Penguin Books.

Bernstein. P. L. (1996) *Against the Gods: The Remarkable Story of Risk*, New York: John Wiley.

Bittner, E. (1967) "The Concept of Organization", *Social Problems*, 32:172-186.

Boklund, A. (1996) *Att överskrida och bevaka gränser*, (To cross and defend boundaries, in Swedish) in Sahlin, I. (Ed.) Projektets paradoxer, Lund: Studentlitteratur.

Bollen, K. (1989) *Structural Equations With Latent Variables*, New York: John Wiley & Sons.

Bolles, R. N. (1994) *The 1994 what color is your parachute? A practical manual for job-hunters and career-changers*, Berkley, California: Ten Speed Press.

Bonke, S. (1998) *The Storebælt Fixed Link : the Fixing of Multiplicity* London: Le Groupe Bagnolet Working Paper 14.

Bowen, H. K., Clark, K. B., Holloway, C.A. and Wheelwright, S.C. (1994*) The Perpetual Enterprise Machine*, New York: Oxford University Press.

Boynton, A. and Zmud, R. (1984) "An Assessment of Critical Success Factors" *Sloan Management Review*, No. 2: pp. 17-27.

Brickley J.A., Smith, Jr C.W. and Zimmerman, J.L. (1996) *Organisational Architecture: a managerial economics approach*, Homewood, Il: Irwin.

Bridges, W. (1994) *Jobshift*, Reading, Mass: Addison-Wesley.

Brooks, F. P. Jr. (1975) *The Mythical Man-Month: Essays on Software Engineering*, Reading, Mass: Addison-Wesley Publishing Company.

Broomé, S. and Persson, E. (1999) "Fångad i honungsfällan," *Dagens Nyheter*, July 19, p. A13. (Caught in the honey trap, in Swedish)

Brown, S. and Eisenhardt, K. (1997) "The Art of Continuous Change : Linking Complexity Theory and Time-paced Evolution in Relentlessly Shifting Organizations", *Administrative Science Quarterly*, vol 42: 1-34

Brown, S. and Eisenhardt, K. (1998) *Competing on the Edge*, Boston: HBS Press.

Brunsson, N. (1982) "The Irrationality of Action and Action Irrationality: Decisions, Ideologies and Organizational Practise." *Journal of Management Studies*. 19: 29-44.

Bryman, A., Bresnen, M., Beardsworth, A. D., Ford, J., and Keil, T. (1987) "The concept of the temporary system: the case of the construction project," *Research in the Sociology of Organizations,* Vol. 5, pp. 253-283.

Burke, R. (1992) *Project Management: Planning and Control,* 2nd Edition. Chichester, UK: Wiley.

Burns, T. and Stalker, G.M. (1961) *The Management of Innovation,* London: Tavistock Publications.

Butler, A.J. Jr. (1973) "Project Management: A Study in Organizational Conflict", *Academy of Management Journal,* 16(1):84-101.

Cash, J, McFarlane, W. and McKenney, J. (1992) *Corporate Information Systems Management,* Boston: Irwin.

Casson, M. (1990) *Enterprise and Competitiveness,* Oxford: Clarendon Press

Chakhravarty, B.(1997) "A new strategic framework for coping with turbulence" *Sloan Management Review,* winter: 69-82

Charue-Duboc, F. and Midler, C. (1998) "Beyond Advanced Project Management: Renewing Engineering Practices and Organisations". In: Lundin, R. A. and Midler, C. (eds) *Projects as Arenas for Renewal and Learning Processes,* Dordrecht: Kluwer 169-177.

Chaslin, F. (1985) *Les Paris de François Mitterand,* Paris: Gallimard.

Chiesa, V. (1995) "Globalizing R&D Around Centres of Excellence." *Long Range Planning* 28(6):19-28.

Child, J. (1984) *Organization: A Guide to Problems and Practice* (2nd ed). London: Harper & Row.

Clark, K. (1997) "Manufacturing's hidden asset: temp workers", *Fortune,* November 10, pp. 28-29.

Clark, K. B. and Fujimoto, T. (1991) *Product Development Performance,* Boston: Harvard Business School Press.

Clark, P. (1990) "Chronological Code and Organizational Analysis." in *The Theory and Philosophy of Organizations: Critical Issues and New Perspectives,* edited by J. Hassard and D. Pym. London: Routledge.

Clegg, S. (1989) *Frameworks of Power,* London: Sage Publications.

Cleland, D.I. and Gareis, R. (1994) *Global Project Management Handbook,* New York, NY: McGraw-Hill.

Cleland, D.I. and King, W.R. (1972) *Systems Analysis and Project Management,* New York, NY: McGraw-Hill.

Cohendet, P. and Llerena, P. (1990) "Nature de l'information, evaluation et organisation de l'entreprise" (Information, performance and the organization of the firm), *Revue d'Economie Industrielle,* No.51: 141-65.

Conlon, D. E. and Garland, H. (1993) "The Role of Project Completion Information in Resource Allocation Decisions", *Academy of Management Journal* 36 402-413.

Coombs, R. and Hull, R. (1997) *The Wider Context of Business Process Analysis,* BPRC Centre, http://bprc.warwick.ac.uk/umistl.html

Cooper, R.G. (1993) *Winning at new products : accelerating the process from idea to launch (2nd ed.)* Reading, MA: Addison-Wesley.

Cooper, R.G. and Kleinschmidt, E.J. (1987) "What Makes a New Product a Winner: Success Factors at the Project Level", *R&D Management,* 17(3):175-189.

Cova, B. (1990), "Appel d'offres : du mieux disant au mieux coopérant", *Revue Française de Gestion*, mars-avril-mai 1990, p 61-72.

Cova, B. and Holstius (1990), "Le cycle marketing du projet. Fondements pour un marketing de projets", *Revue Française de Marketing*, N°127-128, 1990/23.

Cova, B. and Hoskins, S. (1997), "A twin track networking approach to project marketing", *European Management Journal*, Vol 15, octobre 1997, p 546-556.

Cova, B. and Salle, R. (1997), "Appels d'offres et marketing dans la grande industrie", *Encyclopédie de Gestion*, Simon Y. and Joffre P. (eds), Economica, p 155-170.

Cova, B., Mazet, F. and Salle, R. (1994), "From competitive tendering to strategic marketing : an inductive approach for theory-building", *Journal of Strategic Marketing*, Vol 2, p 29-47.

Cova, B., Mazet, F. and Salle, R. (1996), "Project negociations : an episode in the relationship", *in* Ghauri P. and Usunier JC. (eds) *International Business Negotiations*, Pergamon, p 253-271.

Crowston, K. (1997) "A Coordination Theory Approach to Organizational Process Design." *Organization Science* 8(2):157-175

Cusumano, M.A, and Nobeoka, K (1998) *Thinking Beyond Lean,* New York: Free Press.

D'Aveni, R. (1994) *Hypercompetition : Managing the Dynamic of Strategic Maneuvering*, New York : Free Press

Daft, R.L. and R.H. Lengel. (1986) "Organizational Information Requirements, Media Richness and Structural Design." *Management Science* 32(5):554-571.

Davenport, T.H. (1993) *Process Innovation: Reengineering Work through Information Technology,* Boston: Harvard Business School Press.

Dawes, P. L., Dowling, G.R. and Patterson, P.G. (1992) "Criteria used to select management consultants", *Industrial Marketing Management.* vol. 21: 187-193.

Davis-Blake, A. and Uzzi, B. (1993) "Determinants of employment externalization: the case of temporary workers and independent contractors," *Administrative Science Quarterly*, Vol. 29, pp. 195-223.

Day, E. and Barksdale, H.C. Jr. (1992) "How firms select professional services," *Industrial Marketing Management.* vol. 21: 85-91.

De Cotiis, T.A. and Dyer, L. (1979) "Defining and Measuring Project Performance" *Research Management*, No. 22: pp. 17-22.

De Wit, A. (1985) "Cost-Effective Owner Project Management - the Challange for the Future" Vriethoff, W., Visser, J. and Boerma, H. (eds): *Project Management Clarity for the 90's*, Proceedings of the 8th INTERNET World Congress, Rotterdam 1985, Elsevier Science Publishers, North Holland.

DeBrentani, U. (1989) "Success and failure in new industrial services", *Journal of Product Innovation Management.* vol. 21: 85-91.

DeFillippi, R. J. and Arthur, M. B. (1998) "Paradox in project-based enterprise: the case of film making," *California Management Review*, Vol. 40, No. 2, pp. 125-139.

Delamarter, R.T. (1986) *Big Blue – IBM's Use and Abuse of Power,* New York: Dodd, Mead and Company

DiMaggio, P. and Powell, W. (1984) "The Iron Cage Revisited: Institutional Isomorphism and Collective Rationality in Organizational Fields", *American Sociological Review*, 48(2):147-160.

Dinsmore, P.C. (1984) *Human Factors in Project Management*, New York, NY: AMACOM.

Dobler, D. W. and Burt, D.N. (1996) *Purchasing and supply management*, 6th ed., New York: McGraw-Hill, pp. 408-422 and 700.

Dougherty, D. (1996) "Organizing for Innovation." in *Handbook of Organization Studies*, edited by S. R. Clegg, C. Hardy, and W. R. Nord. London: Sage.

Dougherty, D. and Hardy, C. (1996), "Sustained product innovation in large, mature organizations : overcoming innovation-to- organization problems" *Academy of management journal*, vol 39: 1120-1153

Drummond, H. (1996) *Escalation in decision-making: the tragedy of Taurus*, Oxford: Oxford University Press.

Duncan, W.R. (1996) *A Guide to the Project Management Body of Knowledge*, Newtown Square: Project Management Institute.

Durlabhji, S. and Marks, N.E. (Eds) (1993) *Japanese Business: cultural perspectives*, New York: State University of New York Press.

Eisenhardt, K. M. and Tabrizi, B. N. (1995) "Accelerating Adaptive Processes : Product Innovation in the Global Computer Industry", *Administrative Science Quarterly*, 40, 84-110

Ekstedt, E., Lundin, R.A., Söderholm, A. and Wirdenius, H. (1999) *Neo-Industrial Organising – Renewal by action and knowledge formation in a project-intensive economy*, London: Routledge.

Elton, E. and Gruber, M. (1995) *Modern Portfolio Theory and Investment Analysis*, New York: John Wiley & Sons.

Engwall, M. (1992) "Project Management and Ambiguity: Findings from a Comparative Case Study", In I. Hägg and E. Segelod (Eds.) *Issues in Empirical Investment Research*, Amsterdam: Elsevier Science, pp. 173-197.

Engwall, M. (1994) "Legitimacy and Successful Project Management: Findings from a Case Study of the Fenno-Skan Project of Finland and Sweden". Paper presented at the *IRNOP Conference* on "Temporary Organization and Project Management", Lycksele, March 22-25, 1994.

Engwall, M. (1999), *Jakten på det effektiva projektet* (Hunting for the effective project), Stockholm: Nerenius & Santérus.

Eriksson, J. (1997) *Drivkrafter bakom projekt. Förekomsten av projekt ur ett institutionellt och populationsekologiskt perspektiv* (Driving Forces behind Projects. The Prevalence of Projects from an Institutional and Population Ecology Perspective, in Swedish, unpublished MBA thesis, University of Umeå.

Eskerod, P. (1997) *Nye perspektiver på fordeling af menneskelige ressourcer i et projektorganiseret multi-projekt-miljö.* (New Perspectives on Allocation of Human Resources in a Multi-project Context Managed by Projects) Sönderborg. Handelshöjskole Syd, nr 36.

Eskerod, P. and Östergren, K. (1998) "Bureaucratizing Projects? – on the standardization trend", in Hartman, F., Jergeas, G. and Thomas, J. (eds) *IRNOP III Proceedings – The Nature and Role of Projects in the Next 20 years: Research, Issues and Problems*, Calgary: University of Calgary.

Espejo, R. and Harnden, R. (1989) *The Viable Systems Model*, Chichester: Wiley.

Evaristo, R. and van Fenema, P.C. (1999) "A Typology of Project Management: Emergence and Evolution of New Forms." *International Journal of Project Management* 17(5):275-281.

Fahey, L. and Narayanan, V.K. (1989) "Linking Changes in Revealed Causal Maps and Environmental Change: An Empirical Study." *Journal of Management Studies.* 26: 361-378.

Farrell, J.Jr. (1996) *Portfolio Management Theory: and Application*, New Jersey: McGraw Hill College Div.

Farson, R. (1997) *Management of the Absurd*, New York, NY: Touchstone.

Faulkner, R. R. and Anderson, A. B. (1987) "Short-term projects and emergent careers: evidence from Hollywood," *American Journal of Sociology*, Vol. 92, No. 4, pp. 879-909.

Fazio, P., Moselhi, O., Theberge, P. and Revay, S. (1988) "Design Impact of Construction Fast Track", *Construction Management and Economics* 6.

Ferris, W. P. (1997) "Fear, stress and second-guessing in leadership decision-making: Using interior monologues to teach leadership". http://blue.temple.edu/~eastern/ferris.html. October 9, 1997.

Festinger, L. (1957) *A Theory of Cognitive Dissonance*, Evanston, Ill: Row Peterson.

Fishman, K.D. (1981) *The Computer Establishment,* New York: Harper & Row, Publishers.

Ford, D. (1990) "The Development of Buyer-Seller Relationships in Industrial Markets", in Ford, D. (ed.) *Understanding Business Markets - interaction, relationships, networks,* London: Academic Press Limited.

Ford, L.R. and Fulkerson, D.R. (1962) *Flows in Network,* The Rand Corporation: Princeton University Press

Ford, R.C. and Randolph, W.A. (1992) "Cross-functional Structures: A Review and Integration of Matrix Organization and Project Management", *Journal of Management*, 18(2):267-294.

Forsström, B. (1997) *The Great Wall: On Finnish expatriates in Asia and the interaction between Chinese and Finns,* Åbo: Företagsekonomiska institutionen, Åbo Akademi

Foucault, M. (1977) *Discipline and Punish: The Birth of the Prison*, Harmondsworth: Penguin.

Frame, J.D. (1994) *The New Project Management: Tools for an Age of Rapid Change, Corporate Reengineering and other business realities*, San Francisco, CA: Jossey-Bass.

Frame, J.D. (1995) *Managing Projects in Organizations: How to make the best use of time, techniques and people*, 2nd Edition. San Francisco, CA: Jossey-Bass. (1st Edition, 1987).

Freeman R E. (1984) *Strategic Management: a stakeholder approach*, Boston, MA: Pitman.

Friis Olsen, R. and Ellram L.M. (1997) "A Portfolio Approach to Supplier Relationships". *Industrial Marketing Management* no 26, pp 101-133.

Frisby, W. and Getz, D. (1989) "Festival Management: A Case Study Perspective", *Journal of Travel Research*, Summer, pp. 7-11.

Fritz, W. (1992) *Marktorientierte Unternehmensführung und Unternehmenserfolg, Grundlagen und Ergebnisse einer empirischen Untersuchung* (Market oriented leadership and corporate success - Basics and results of an empirical analysis), Schäffer-Poeschel 1st Ed.

Fukuyama, F. (1995) *Trust: The Social Virtues and the Creation of Prosperity*, London: Hamish Hamilton

Gabarro, J.J. (1990) "The Development of Working Relationships." in *Intellectual Teamwork: Social and Technological Foundations of Cooperative Work*, edited by J. Galegher, R. E. Kraut, and C. Egido. Hillsdale, New Jersey: Lawrence Erlbaum Associates.

Gaddis, P (1959) "The Project Manager", *Harvard Business Review* May-June, 89-97.

Gaillard, J.M. (1997) *Marketing et Gestion de la Recherche et Developpement* (Marketing and research and development management), Paris: Economica

Galbraith, J.R. (1973) *Designing Complex Organizations*, Reading, Massachusetts: Addison-Wesley.

Galbraith, J.R. (1993) *Competing with Flexible Lateral Organisations*, New York: Addison-Wesley OD.

Gardiner. P. and Rothwell, R. (1985) "Tough Customers: Good Designs", *Design Studies* 6.

Gardiner, P.D. and Stewart, K. (2000) "Revisiting the golden triangle of time, cost and quality: the role of NPV in project control, success and failure", *International Journal of Project Management,* Vol. 18, (to appear).

Gareis, R. (Ed.) (1990) *Handbook of management by projects*, Vienna: MANZ.

Garel, G. and Kessler, A. (1998) "New Car Development Projects and Supplier Partnership" In: Lundin, R. A. and Midler, C. (eds) *Projects as Arenas for Renewal and Learning Processes,* Dordrecht: Kluwer 219-230.

Garfinkel, H. (1967) *Studies in Ethnomethodology*, Englewood Cliffs, NJ: Prentice Hall.

Garsten, C. (1999) "Betwixt and between: temporary employees as liminal subjects in flexible organization," *Organization Studies,* Vol. 20, No. 4, pp. 601-617.

Geaney, M. (1997) "The right skills for the job", *Computing Canada*, Vol. 21(24), pp. 52.

Gemmill, G., Wilemon, D. (1994) "The hidden side of leadership in technical team management". *Research – Technology Management*, Vol. 37(6), 25-32.

Gemünden, H.G. (1990) "Erfolgsfaktoren des Projektmanagements- eine kritische Bestandsaufnahme der empirischen Untersuchungen" (Success factors of project management - a critical review of the empirical status quo), *Projekt Management*, No. 1,2: pp.4-15.

Gephart, R.P. Jr. (1978) "Status Degradation and Organizational Succession: An Ethnomethodological Approach." *Administrative Science Quarterly.* 23: 553-580.

Gephart, R.P. Jr. (1992) "Sensemaking, Communicative Distortion and the Logic of Public Inquiry Legitimation", *Industrial and Environmental Crisis Quarterly*, 6:115-135.

Gephart, R.P. Jr. (1993) "The Textual Approach: Risk and Blame in Disaster Sensemaking", *Academy of Management Journal,* 36(6):1465-1514.

Getz, D. (1989) "Special events - Defining the product", *Tourism management*, Vol. 10:2, pp. 125-137.

Getz, D. (1991) *Festivals, Special Events, and Tourism,* New York: Van Nostrand Reinhold.

Getz, D. (1993) "Case study: Marketing the Calgary Exhibition and Stamphede", *Festival Management and Event Tourism,* Vol. 1:4, pp. 147-156.

Getz, D. (1997a), *Event Management & Event Tourism*, New York: Cognizant Communication Corporation.

Getz, D. (1997b) "The Impacts of Mega-events on Tourism: Strategies for Destinations", *The Impact of Mega-events, Papers of the Talk at the Top Conference, 7-8 July 1997*, Östersund: Mitthögskolan.

Giard, V. and Midler, C. (1993) *Pilotages de Projet et Entreprises*, Paris: Economica.

Gioia, D.A. (1986) "Conclusion: The State of the Art in Organizational Social Cognition -- A Personal View", In Sims, H.P. and Gioia, D.A. (eds.) *The Thinking Organization: Dynamics of Organizational Social Cognition*, San Francisco: Jossey Bass.

Globerson, S. (1994) "Impact of various work-breakdown structures on project conceptualization." *International Journal of Project Management* 12(3):165-171.

Goodman, R.A. (1981) *Temporary systems: professional development, manpower utilization, task effectiveness, and innovation*, New York: Praeger,

Goodman R.A. and Goodman, L.P. (1976) "Theater as a temporary system", *California Management Review*, Vol. 15, No. 2, pp. 103-108.

Granovetter, M. (1995) *Getting a job: a study of contacts and career*, Chicago: University of Chicago Press.

Grant, R.M. (1996) "Toward a Knowledge-Based Theory of the Firm." *Strategic Management Journal* 17(Winter):109-122.

Greer, C. R., Youngblood, S. A. and Gray, D. A. (1999) "Human resources management outsourcing: the make or buy decision," *Academy of Management Executive*, Vol. 13, No. 3, pp. 85-96.

Gummesson, E. (1994) "Making Relationship Marketing Operational", *International Journal of Service Industry Management*, Vol. 5, No. 5, pp. 5-20.

Gustafsson, M. (1996) *The power of trust*, Åbo: Åbo Akademis Tryckeri

Gustafsson, M. (1999) *Om visshet i affärer*, (On certainty in business) Åbo: Åbo Akademis Tryckeri

Haas, R.W. (1995) *Business marketing: a managerial approach*, 6th ed., Cincinnati, OH: South-Western College Publishing, p. 26.

Hadjikhani, A. (1996), "Project marketing and the management of discontinuity", *International Business review*, (53), pp 319-336.

Hage, J., M. Aiken, and C.B. Marrett. (1971) "Organization Structure and Communications." *American Sociological Review* 36(October):860-871.

Hall, C. M. (1992) *Hallmark Tourist Events: Impacts, Management and Planning*, London: Belhaven Press.

Hall, E.T. (1976) *Beyond Culture*, New York: Doubleday.

Hall, P. (1980) *Great Planning Disasters*, London: Weidenfield and Nicholson.

Hamel, G. and Prahalad, C.K. (1990), "The core competence of the corporation", *Harvard Business Review*, may-june 1990.

Handy, C. (1996) *Beyond certainty*, Boston: Harvard Business School Press.

Hardy, C. (1994) *Managing Strategic Action: Mobilizing Change*, London, UK: Sage Publications.

Harris, T.A. (1973) *I'm OK - You're OK*, England: Pan Books.

Hartman, F. (1995) "Self Managing Projects". Paper presented at the *Project Management Institute Canadian Conference* in Ottawa.

Hartman, F. (1996) "The Serious Business of Having Fun on Projects". Presented at the *Project Management Institute Canadian Conference* in Calgary.

Hartman, F. (1998) *Don't park your brain outside: A practical guide to outperforming the competition with S.M.A.R.T.© Management*, University of Calgary. Work in progress.

Hartman, F. (2000) *Don't Park Your Brain Outside,* Newtown PA: Project Management Institute.

Hartman, F., Ashrafi, R. and Jergeas, G. (1998) "Project Management in the Live Entertainment Industry; What is Different?" *International Journal of Project Management* 16: 269-281.

Harvey, D. (1990) *The Condition of Post Modernity*, Oxford, UK: Blackwell.

Harvey, M.G. and Rupert, J.P. (1988) "Selecting an industrial advertising agency", *Industrial Marketing Management*. vol. 17: 119-127.

Haugen, R. (1997) *Modern Investment Theory*, New Jersey

Hauschildt, J. (1991) "Zur Messung des Innovationserfolgs" (The measurement of innovation success), *ZfB,* No. 4: pp.451-476.

Hedberg, B. L. T. (1981) "How organizations learn and unlean," in *Handbook of Organizational Design*, Oxford: Oxford University Press.

Hellgren, B. and Stjernberg, T. (1995) "Design and implementation in major investments - a project network approach", *Scandinavian Journal of Management*, Vol. 11, No. 4, pp. 377-394.

Herzberg, F. Mausner, B and Snyderman, B. (1959) *The Motivation to Work*, New York.

Heydebrand, W. V. (1989): "New organizational forms," *Work and Occupations*, Vol. 16, No. 3, pp. 323-357.

Higgins, J.C. and Watts, K.M. (1986) "Some Perspectives on the Use of Management Science Techniques in R&D Management." *R&D Management.* 16(4): 291-296.

Hill, R.E. (1975) "Interpersonal Compatibility and Workgroup Performance", *Journal of Applied Behavioral Science*, 11(2):210-219.

Hill, R.E. (1977) "Managing Interpersonal Conflict in Project Teams", *Sloan Management Review*, 18:45-61.

Hill, R.E. (1983) "Managing the Human Side of Project Teams", In D.I. Cleland and W.R. King (Eds), *Project Management Handbook*, New York, NY: Van Nostrand Reinhold, pp. 581-604.

Hobday, M. (1998) "Product Complexity, Innovation and Industrial Organisation", *Research Policy* 26:689-710.

Hobday, M. (1999) "Innovation in complex products and systems: limits of the project-based organization, " Working Paper, SPRU, *University of Sussex.*

Hofstede, G. (1991) *Cultures and Organisations: software of the mind*, London: McGraw-Hill.

Hollis, M. (1996) *Reason in action - essays in the philosophy of social science,* Cambridge: Cambridge University Press

Huber, G.P. (1991) "Organisational Learning: The contributing Processes and the Literatures", *Organizational Science*, Vol. 2, No. 1 pp. 88-115.

Huey, J. (1994) "Waking up to the new economy," *Fortune*, June:36-48.

Humphrey, W.S. (1990) *Managing the Software Process*, New York, NY: Addison Wesley.

Hunt, B. and Targett, D. (1995) *The Japanese Advantage? Competitive IT strategies, past, present and future*, Oxford: Butterworth-Heinmann.

Hutchins, E. (1991) "Organizing Work by Adaptation." *Organization Science* 2(1):14-39.

Iansiti, M. and Clark, K. (1994) "Integration and dynamic capability : Evidence from product development in automobiles and mainframe computers", *Industrial Corporate and Change*, vol 3: 557-605

IMP Group (1982) *International marketing and purchasing of industrial goods*, London: John Wiley and Sons, pp. 10-27.

International Business review, special issue on Project Marketing and System Selling, 5, (1996), edited by Günter, B. and Bonnacorsi, A.

Jackson, R.W. and Cooper, P.D. (1988) "Unique aspects of marketing industrial services," *Industrial Marketing Management*. vol. 17: 111-118.

Jackson, R.W., Neidell, L.A. and Lunsford, D.A. (1995) "An empirical investigation of the differences in goods and services as perceived by organizational buyers", *Industrial Marketing Management*. vol. 24: 99-108.

Janik, A. (1996) *Kunskapsbegreppet i praktisk filosofi,* (The concept of knowledge in practical philosophy) translation Birgit Häggkvist, Stockholm: Symposium

Janis, I.L. (1972) *Victims of Groupthink: A Psychological Study of Foreign-Policy Decisions and Fiascoes,* Boston, MA: Houghton Mifflin.

Johanson, J. and Associates (1994) *Internationalization, Relationships and Networks,* Stockholm: Almqvist & Wiksell International.

Johanson, J. and Håkansson, H. (1993), "The network as a governance structure Interfirm cooperation beyond markets ans hierarchies", in Grabher G. (eds), *The Embedded Firm The Socio-Economics of Industrial Networks,* London Routledge, p 35-51.

Jolivet, F. and Navarre, C. (1996) "Large-scale Projects, Self-organizing and Meta-rules: Towards new Forms of Management." *International Journal of Project Management* 14(5):265-271.

Jones, C. (1996) "Careers in Project Networks : the Case of the Film Industry" In: M. B. Arthur and D. M. Rousseau (eds.) *The Boundaryless Career : A New Employment Principle for a New Organizational Era,* New York: Oxford University Press 58-75

Jones, C. and DeFillippi, R.J. (1997) "Back to the future in film: combining industry- and self-knowledge to meet career challenges of the 21st century," *Academy of Management Executive*, Vol. 10, No. 4, pp. 89-103.

Jöreskog, K. and Sörbom, D. (1989) *LISREL 7 User's Reference Guide* Scientific Software, Inc.

Keller, R.T. (1995) "Transformational" leaders make a difference. *Research-Technology Management*, Vol. 38(3), pp. 41-44.

Kerzner, H. (1994) *Project Management a Systems Approach to Planning Scheduling and Controlling*, 3rd Edition. New York: Van Nostrand Reinhold. (1st Edition, 1979)

Kesseler, A. (1998) *The creative supplier, A new model for strategy, innovation and customer relationships in concurrent design and engineering processes : the case of the automotive industry*, These de l'Ecole polytechnique, Paris

Kezsbom, D.S. (1992) "Reopening Pandora's box: Sources of project conflict in the 90's". *Industrial Engineering*, Vol. 24(5), pp. 54-59.

Kezsbom, D.S. (1994) "Team-based organizations and the changing role of the project manager". *AACE Transactions, now American Association of Cost Engineers Transactions*, HF 1.1 – 1.5.

Kezsbom, D.S., Donnelly, R. G. (1994) "Overcoming the responsibility – authority gap: An investigation of effective project team leadership for a new decade". *Cost Engineering*, Vol. 36(5), pp. 33-41.

Kharbanda, O.P. and Stallworthy, E.A. (1983) *How to Learn from Project Disasters, True-Life Stories with a Moral for Management.* Aldershot, UK: Gower.

Kharbanda, O.P. and Pinto. J.K. (1996) *What made Gertie gallop? : lessons from project failures* New York : Van Nostrand Reinhold.

Kidd, J.B. (1975) "Scoring rules for subjective estimates", *JORS*, Vol. 26, No. 1ii pp. 186-195.

Kidd, J.B. (1987) "A comparison between the VERT program and other methods of project duration estimating", *Omega*, Vol. 15, No. 2 pp. 129-134.

Kidd, J.B. (1990) "Project Management software - are we being over persuaded?", *Int J Project Management,* Vol. 8, No. 2 pp. 109-116.

Kidd, J.B. (1998) "Knowledge Creation in Japanese Manufacturing Companies in Italy: reflections upon organisational learning", *Management Learning*, forthcoming, Spring 1998.

Kidd, J.B. and Kanda, M. (1997) *The Management of Strategic Planning: A comparison of British and Japanese production managers.* Presentation to 10th Annual Association of Japanese Business Studies conference "Making Global Partnerships Work", Washington, DC.

Kidder, T. (1981) *The Soul of a New Machine.* Boston: Little Brown & Company.

Kidder, T. (1982) *The Soul of a New Machine,* Harmondsworth: Penguin.

Knight, K. (1976) "Matrix Organizations: A Review", *Journal of Management Studies*, 17(2):111-130.

Knott, T. (1996) *No Business as Usual,* London: B. P. Education.

Kogut, B. and Zander, U. (1992) "Knowledge of the firm, combinative capabilities, and the replication of technology," *Organization Science*, Vol. 3, No. 3, pp. 383-397.

Kopp, R. (1994) *The Rice-paper Ceiling*, Berkley, CA: Stone Bridge Press.

Krauss, R.M. and Fussell, S.R. (1990) "Mutual Knowledge and Communicative Effectiveness." in *Intellectual Teamwork: Social and Technological Foundations of Cooperative Work*, edited by J. Galegher, R. E. Kraut, and C. Egido. Hillsdale, New Jersey: Lawrence Erlbaum Associates.

Kreps, D.M. (1990) "Corporate culture and economic theory," In Alt, J. E. and Shepsle, K. A. *Perspectives on Positive Political Economy*, Cambridge: Cambridge University Press.

Kuhn, T. S. (1962) *The Structure of Scientific Revolutions,* Chicago: University of Chicago Press.

Kumar, K. and van Dissel, G.H. (1996) "Sustainable Collaboration: Managing Conflict and Co-operation in Inter-Organizational Systems." *MIS Quarterly* 20(3).

Kumar, K. and Willcocks, L.P. (1996) "Offshore Outsourcing: A Country Too Far?" in *European Conference on Information Systems*, Lisbon, Portugal.

Lagerspetz, O. (1996) *The tacit demand - a study in trust*, Åbo: Åbo Akademis tryckeri

Laigle, L. (1998) "Co-operative Buyer-Supplier Relationships in Development Projects in the Car Industry", In: R. A. Lundin and C. Midler (eds) *Projects as Arenas for Renewal and Learning Processes,* Dordrecht: Kluwer 207-218.

Larson, M. (1997) *Evenemangsmarknadsföring - organisering, styrning och samverkan vid marknadsföringen av VM i friidrott 1995* (Marketing events – organising the marketing of the World Championships in Athletics 1995), Östersund: Tryckeribolaget Östersund AB.

Law, J. and Callon, M. (1992) "The Life and Death of an Aircraft: A Network Analysis of Technical Change", In: W. E. Bijker and J. Law (eds*.) Shaping Technology/Building Society,* Cambridge: MIT Press 21-52.

Lechler, T. (1997) *Erfolgsfaktoren des Projektmanagements* (Success factors of project management), Frankfurt am Main: Peter Lang.

Leiter, K. (1980) *A Primer of Ethnomethodology*, New York: Oxford University Press.

Lester, A. (1982) *Project Planning and Control*, London: Buttersworth Scientific.

Levene, Ralph (1999) *Educating the Project Manager – a European View*, Philadelphia, PA: Proceedings of the 30th Annual Project Management Institute, 1999 Seminars and Symposium, (CD)

Levering, R., Katz, M. and Moskowitz, M. (1984) *The Computer Entrepreneurs*, New York: North American Library

Levin, C. (1996) "Misslyckade projekt och framgångsrika organisationer (Failed projects and successful organizations)," in I. Sahlin (Ed.) *Projektets paradoxer*, Lund: Studentlitteratur.

Lewis, J. P., Bloom, R. (1993) "Building wining teams". *Transportation and Distribution*, Vol. 34(10), pp. 32-35.

Liberatore, M.J. and Titus, G.J. (1983) "The Practise of Management Science in R&D Project Management", *Management Science*, 29(8):962-974.

Lindgren, M. and Packendorff, J. (1997) "Work as Project, Project as Work: An Individual Perspective on the 'Temporarization' of Work Life", 14th Nordic Conference on Business Studies, Programme and Abstracts pp 375 - 378, Bodö, Norway: SIB.

Lindkvist L., Söderlund, J. and Tell, F. (1998) "Managing product development projects: on the significance of fountains and deadlines," *Organization Studies*, Vol. 19, No. 6, pp. 931-951.

Link, A.N. and Zmud, R.W. (1986) "Organizational Structure and R&D Efficiency", *R&D Management*, 16(4):317-323.

Lock, D. (1992) *Project Management,* 5th Edition. Aldershot, UK: Gower (1st edition 1977).

Lock, D. (2000) "Project Appraisal", in Turner, J.R., (ed), *The Gower Handbook of Project Management, 3rd edition,* Aldershot: Gower.

Lundin R. A. and Söderholm, A. (1998) "Managing the black boxes of the project environment" in *Project Management Handbook*, (J. Pinto Ed.,) pp. 41-54, San Francisco, CA: Jossey-Bass Publishers.

Lundin, R.A. (1995) "Editorial: Temporary organizing and project management," *Scandinavian Journal of Management*, Vol. 11, No. 4, pp. 315-318.

Lundin, R.A. (1998) "Temporära organisationer – några perspektivbyten," (Temporary organizations – some perspective changes, in Swedish) in B. Czarniawska (Ed.) *Organisationsteori på svenska*, Stockholm: Liber.

Lundin, R.A. (1999) "If Projects Are So Damned Good, How Come Everything Ain't Projects", in Artto, K., Kähkönen, K. and Koskinen, K. (eds) *Managing Business by Projects*, pp. 189-201, Helsinki: PMI of Finland and NORDNET.

Lundin, R.A. and Söderholm, A. (1995) "A Theory of the Temporary Organization", *Scandinavian Journal of Management*, Vol. 11, No. 4, pp. 437-455.

Lundin, R.A. and Söderholm, A. (1995) "Project Man – Postulates in an Ontology for Temporary Organizations", Umeå Business School: Working paper.

Lundin, R.A. and Söderholm, A. (1998) "Conceptualizing a Projectified society: Discussion of an Eco-institutionalized Approach to a Theory on Temporary Organizations." In Lundin R. and Midler C. (Eds.), *Projects as arenas for learning and renewal processes*, Boston: Kluwer Academic Publishers.

Lundin, R.A. and Midler, C. (eds) (1998) *Projects as Arenas for Renewal and Learning Processes*, Norwell, MA: Kluwer Academic Publishers.

Lundin, R.A. and Midler, C. (1998), "Evolution of project as empirical trend and theoretical focus", in Lundin R.A. and Midler C. (eds), *Projects as arenas for renewal and learning processes*, Norwell, MA: Kluwer.

Lynn, G., Morone, J. and Paulson, A. (1996) "Marketing Discontinuous Innovation : The Probe and Learn process", *California Management Review*, vol 38: 8-37

Løwendahl, B. R. (1995) "Organizing the Lillehammer Olympic winter games," *Scandinavian Journal of Management*, Vol. 11, No. 4, pp. 347-362.

Malone, T.W., Crowston, K., Lee, J. and Pentland, B. (1999) "Tools for Inventing Organizations: Towards a Handbook of Organizational Processes." *Management Science* 45(3):425-443.

Manheim, M. (1993) "Integrating Global Organizations through Task/Team Support Systems." in *Global Networks: Computers and International Communication*, edited by L. M. Harasim. Cambridge, Massachusetts: The MIT Press.

Manz, C.C., Mossholder, K.W. and Luthans, F. (1987) "An Integrated Perspective of Self-control in Organizations." *Administration & Society* 19(1):3-24.

March, J.G. (1994) *A Primer on decision making*, New York: Free Press.

March, J.G. (1991) "Exploration and exploitation in organizational learning". *Organization Science* 2/1, pp 1-13.

March, J.G. and Simon, H.A. (1958) *Organizations*, New York: John Wiley.

Mayer, R.C., Davis, J.H. and Schoorman, F.D. (1995) "An integrative model of organizational trust", *Academy of Management Review*, Vol. 20, pp. 709-734.

Mayfield, T.L. and Crompton, J.L. (1995) "The Status of the Marketing Concept Among Festival Organizers", *Journal of Travel Research*, Spring, pp. 14-22.

McCleary, K. (1995) "Applying internal marketing techniques for better festival organization and management", *Festival Management and Event Tourism*, Vol. 3:1, pp. 1-7.

McDonald, P. (1988) "The Los Angeles Olympic organizing committee: developing organizational culture in the short run, in Jones, M. O., Moore, M. D., and Snyder, R. C. (Ed.) *Inside organizations – understanding the human dimension*, Newbury Park: Sage Publications.

Meadows, C.J. (1996) "Globalizing Software Development." *Journal of Global Information Development* 4(1):5-14.

Medsker, G., Williams, L. and Holahan, P. (1994) "A Review of Current Practices for Evaluating Causal Models in Organizational Behavior and Human Resource Management Research", *Journal of Management*, No. 2: pp.439 - 464.

Mehari, M.A. (2000) "Re-examining project appraisal and control: developing a focus on wealth creation", *International Journal of Project Management,* Vol. 18, (to appear).

Meridith JR and Mantel Jr S.J. (1995) *Project Management: a managerial approach - 3rd edition*, New York: Wiley.

Meyer, A.D. (1982) "How Ideologies Supplant Formal Structures and Shape Responses to the Environment." *Journal of Management Studies.* 19: 45-61.

Meyer, A.D., Tsui, A.S. and Hinings, C.R. (1993) "Configurational Approaches to Organizational Analysis." *Academy of Management Journal* 36(6):1175-1195.

Meyer, J.W. and Rowan, B. (1977) "Institutionalized Organizations: Formal Structure as Myth and Ceremony", *American Journal of Sociology*, Vol. 83, No. 2, pp. 340-362.

Meyerson, D., Weick, K.E., and Kramer, R.M. (1996) "Swift trust and temporary groups," In R.H. Kramer and T.R. Tyler (Eds.), *Trust in Organizations*, Thousand Oaks: Sage.

Midler, C. (1993) *L'auto qui n'existait pas* (The car that wasn't existing), Paris: InterEditions.

Midler, C. (1995) "Projectification of the Firm : the Renault Case", *Scandinavian Journal of Management* 11 363-375.

Miles, M.B. (1964) "On temporary systems," In M. B. Miles (ed.), *Innovation in Education*, New York: Teachers College Press.

Miller, R., Hobday, M., Leroux-Demers, T. and Olleros, X. (1995) "Innovation in Complex Systems Industries; the Case of Flight Simulation", *Industrial and Corporate Change* 4.

Mills, R.W. (1994) *Strategic Value Analysis,* Henley-on-Thames: Mars Business Associates.

Mills, R.W. and Turner, J.R. (1995) "Projects for shareholder value", in Turner, JR, (ed), *The Commercial Project Manager*, London: McGraw-Hill.

Mintzberg, H. (1979) *The Structuring of Organizations*, Englewood Cliffs, N.J.: Prentice-Hall.

Mintzberg, H. (1983) *Structure in fives*, Englewood Cliffs: Prentice-Hall.

Mirvis, P.H. and Hall, D.T. (1994) "Psychological success and the boundaryless career," *Journal of Organizational Behavior*, Vol. 15, pp. 365-380.

Mischel, W. (1981) "Personality and Cognition: Something Borrowed, Something New?", In N. Cantor and J.F. Kihlstrom (Eds.), *Personality, Cognition and Social Interaction*, Hillsdale, NJ: Erlbaum.

Mitchell R.K, Agle B.R, Wood D.J. (1997) "Towards a Theory of Stakeholder Identification and Salience: defining the principle of who and what really counts", *Academy of Management Review*, 22 (4) pp 853 - 886.

Moody, F. (1995) *I Sing the Dance Electronic*, New York: Penguin Books

Morgan, G. (1997) *Images of organization*, Thousand Oaks.

Morley, E. and Silver, A. (1977) "A film director's approach to managing creativity," *Harvard Business Review*, March-April, pp. 59-70.

Morrill, J.M. (1996) "The last boy scout: The proud and the foolish". *Journal of Systems Management*, Vol. 47(1), pp. 23.

Morris, P.W.G. (1994) *The Management of Projects*, London: Thomas Telford.

Morris, P.W.G. and Hough, G.H. (1987) *The Anatomy of Major Projects. A Study of the Reality of Project Management*, Chichester, UK: John Wiley.

Moss Kanter, R. (1983) *The Change Masters: Corporate Entrepreneurs at Work*, New York: Simon & Schuster.

Mulaik, S., James, L., Van Alastine, J., Bennet, N., Lind, S. and Stilwell, D. (1989) "Evaluation of Goodness-of-Fit Indices for Structural Equation Models" *Psychological Bulletin*, No. 3: pp.430-445.

Murphy, D., Baker, N. and Fisher, D. (1974) *Determinants of Project Success*, Boston: Boston College, National Aeronautics and Space Administration.

Naisbitt, J. and Aburdene, P. (1990) *Megatrends 2000: ten new directions for the 1990's*, New York, NY: Avon Books,

Nakhla, M. and Soler, L-G (1996) "Pilotage de Projet et Contrats Internes", *Revue Française de Gestion* 110 17-29.

Nam, C.H. and Tatum, C.B. (1997), "Leaders and Champions for Construction innovation", *Construction Management and Economics*, 15.

Nathan, P. (1991) *Project Planning and Control Systems: An Investigation into their Application and Implications of Usage in the UK Construction Industry*, Henley- The Management College and Brunel University, UK (Unpublished dissertation).

National Audit Office (1989) *Department of social Security Operational Strategy*, Report by Comptroller and Auditor General, HMSO.

National Audit Office (1990) *New Building for the British Library*, London: H.M.S.O.

Navarre, C. (1992), "De la bataille pour mieux produire à la bataille pour mieux concevoir", *Gestion 2000*, n°6, Louvain, pp. 13-30.

Nelson, R. E. and Winter, S. G. (1982) *An Evolutionary Theory of Economic Change*, Harvard.

Newell, A. and Simon, H. A. (1972) *Human Problem Solving*, Englewood Cliffs, NJ: Prentice Hall

Nonaka, I. (1994) "A Dynamic theory of Organizational Knowledge Creation", *Organization Science* 5 14-37.

Nonaka, I. and Takeuchi, H. (1995) *The Knowledge-creating Company*, Oxford: Oxford University Press.

Norbäck, L-E. (1978) *Relationer mellan samarbetande företag* (Relationships between co-operating firms), Göteborg: BAS ekonomiska förening.

Oliver, N. and Wilkinson, B. (1992) *The Japanisation of British Industry: new developments in the 1990s*, Oxford: Blackwell.

Ouchi, W.G. (1980) "Markets Bureaucracies and Clans" *Administrative Science Quarterly*, Vol. 25 No. 1, pp. 129-141

Ouchi, W.G. (1979) "A Conceptual Framework for the Design of Organizational Control Mechanisms" *Management Science*, Vol. 25, No. 9, pp. 833-848.

Ozanne, M.R. (1997) "Managing strategic partnerships for the virtual enterprise", *Fortune*, September 29, pp. Special Section S1-S48.

Packendorff, J. (1993a) "Datorstödd projektadministration -- om användningen av datoriserade projektplaneringsmodeller i repetitiva projekt", (Computer aided project administration – about the use of computerized planning models in repetitive projects) *Handelshögskolan i Umeå Publikationer*, No. 135.

Packendorff, J. (1993b) *Projektorganisation och projektorganisering: Projektet som plan och temporär organisation* (Project organisation and project organising: The project as plan and temporary organisation), Umeå Business School, FE-publikationer 1993: No. 145.

Packendorff, J. (1994) "Temporary Organizing: Integrating Organization Theory and Project Management". Paper presented at *IRNOP Conference* on "Temporary Organizations and Project Management" at Lycksele, March 22-25, 1994.

Packendorff, J. (1995) "Inquiring into the temporary organization: New directions for project management research", *Scandinavian Journal of Management*, Vol. 11, No. 4, pp. 319-333.

Palisi, B.J. (1970) "Some suggestions about the transitory-permanence dimension of organization," *The British Journal of Sociology*, Vol. 21, pp. 200-206.

Payne, J. H. (1995) "Management of Multiple Simultaneous projects: A State of the Art Review." *International Journal of Project Management*, Vol. 13, No 3, pp 163-168.

Pearl, J. (1988) *Probability Reasoning in Intelligent Systems: networks of plausible inference*, San Mateo, CA: Morgan Kaufman.

Pelz, D.C. and Andrews, F.M. (1976) *Scientists in Organizations,* Institute for Social Scientists, University of Michigan, Ann Arbor, Michigan,

Perrow, C. (1986) *Complex Organizations - a Critical Essay,* New York: McGraw-Hill,

Persson, B. (Ed.) (1979) *Surviving Failures: Patterns and Cases of Project Mismanagement,* Stockholm: Almqvist & Wiksell International.

Peters T. (1992) *Liberation Management – Necessary Disorganization for the Nanosecond Nineties*, New York, NY: Ballantine Books.

Peters, T. (1992) *Liberation management: necessary disorganization for the nanosecond nineties*, New York: Alfred A. Knopf, pp. 125-225.

Pinto, J.K. (1986) *Project Implementation: A Determination Of Its Critical Success Factors, Moderators And Their Relative Importance Across The Project Life Cycle,* Pittsburgh: Dissertation at the University of Pittsburgh.

Pinto, J.K. (1999) "Managing Information Systems Projects: Regaining Control of a Runaway Train", in Artto, K., Kähkönen, K. and Koskinen, K. (eds) *Managing Business by Projects*, pp. 30-43, Helsinki: PMI of Finland and NORDNET.

Pinto, J.K. and Prescott, J. (1990) "Planning and tactical factors in the project implementation process," *Journal of Management Studies*, Vol. 27, No. 3, pp. 305-327.

Pinto, J.K. and Rouhiainen, P. (1998) "Toward a Theory of Customer-Based Project Success", Paper presented at the 14th World Congress on Project Management, Ljubljana, Slovenia, June.

Pinto, J. K., and Slevin, D. P. (1987) "Critical factors in successful project implementation". *IEEE Transactions on Engineering Management, EM-34*, February, pp. 22-27.

Pinto, J.K. and Slevin, D. (1988a) "The Project Champion: Key to Implementation Success" *Project Management Journal,* No.1: pp.15-20.

Pinto, J.K. and Slevin, D.P. (1988b) "Project Success: Definitions and Measurement Techniques", *Project Management Journal*, Vol. 19, No. 1, pp. 67-72.

Porter, M.E. (1985) *Competitive Advantage,* New York: Free Press.

Powell, W.W. , Koput, K.W. and Smith-Doerr, L. (1996) "Interorganizational Collaboration and the Locus of Learning: Networks of Innovation in Biotechnology", *Administrative Science Quarterly* 41 116-145.

Project Management Institute Standards Committee (1987) *Project Management Body of Knowledge* (PMBOK). Drexel Hill, PA: Project Management Institute.

Pucik, V. (1997) *Competitive Collaboration and Learning: the next round.*,Presentation to the LMVH conference "Partnership and Joint Ventures in Asia", Euro-Asia Centre, INSEAD, Fontainebleau.

Rajkumar, T. and Dawley, D. (1997) "Problems and Issues in Offshore Development of Software." in *Information Systems Sourcing: Theory and Practice*, edited by L. Willcocks and M. Lacity. Oxford: Oxford University Press.

Ranson, S., Hinings, B. and Greenwood, R. (1980) "The Structuring of Organizational Structures", *Administrative Science Quarterly,* 25:1-17.

Richman, L. (1994) "The new work force builds itself," *Fortune,* May:46-58.

Ritz, G.J. (1990) *Total Engineering Project Management*, New York, NY: McGraw-Hill.

Roberts, W. (1997) *Protect you Achilles Heel: Crafting Armour for the new Age at work*, Kansas City: Universal Press.

Roche, M. (1994) "Mega-events and Urban Policy", *Annals of Tourism Research*, Vol. 21, No. 1, pp. 1-19.

Romanelli, E. and Tushman, M. (1994) "Organizational transformation as punctuated equilibrium : an empirical test " *Academy of Management Journal,* vol 5: 1141-1166

Romberg, D. (1998) "Project Management Tools Cannot Guarantee Success", *Computing Canada* (November 9)

Rosenau, M. D. Jr. (1992) Successful Project Management. New York: Van Nostrand Reinhold.

Rothwell, R., Freeman, C., Horsley, A., Jervis, V., Robertson, A.B. and Townsend, J. (1974) "SAPPHO updated - project SAPPHO phase II" *Research Policy,* No.3: pp.258-291.

Russell-Hodge, J. and Hunnam, P. (1998) "Learning about Culture Through Projects in Aid Programmes", In: R. A. Lundin and C. Midler (eds) *Projects as Arenas for Renewal and Learning Processes,* Dordrecht: Kluwer 47-58.

SAF (1997) "Labor statistics," Published Report. Stockholm: *SAF.*

Sahlin, I. (1996) "Vad är ett projekt? (What is a project?)" in Sahlin, I. (red), *Projektets paradoxer* (Paradoxes of the project), Lund: Studentlitteratur.

Sahlin, I. (1996), (Ed.) *Projektets paradoxer*, Lund: Studentlitteratur. ("Paradoxes of the project")

Sahlin-Andersson, K. (1986) *Beslutsprocessens komplexitet* (The complexity of the decision process), Lund: Doxa Ab.

Sahlin-Andersson, K. (1989) *Oklarhetens strategi – organisering av projektarbete* (The strategy of unclearness - organising project work), Lund: Studentlitteratur.

Sahlin-Andersson, K. (1991) *Ostyriga projekt - att styra och avstyra stora kommunala satsningar* (Uncontrollable projects - to control and prevent large municipal ventures), Ds 1991:50.

Sahlin-Andersson, K. (1992) "The Use of Ambiguity -- The Organizing of an Extraordinary Project", In I. Hägg and E. Segelod (Eds.) *Issues in Empirical Investment Research*, Amsterdam: Elsevier Science, pp. 143-158.

Saia, R. (1997) "Harvesting project leaders". *Computerworld*, Vol. 31(29), pp. 81.

Salter, S.B. and Niswander, F. (1995) "Cultural Influences on The Development of Accounting Systems Internationally", *J. Int. Business Studies*, Vol. 26, No. 2 pp. 379-398.

Sanchez, R. and Mahone, J.T. (1996) "Modularity, Flexibility, and Knowledge Management in Product and Organization Design." *Strategic Management Journal* 17(Winter):77-91.

Sanderson, S.W. (1992) "Design for Manufacturability in an Environment of Continuous Change", In: Susman, G. I. (ed.) (1992*) Integrating Design and Manufacturing for Competitive Advantage,* New York: OUP

Santo, B. (1997) "Managing Electrical Engineers by feel and by metrics". *Electrical Engineering Times*, no. 966, pp. 113-114.

Sapolsky, H.M. (1972) *The Polaris System Development. Bureaucratic and Programmatic Success in Government*, Cambridge, MA: Harvard University Press.

Saxenian, A. (1996) "Beyond boundaries: open labor markets and learning in Silicon Valley," in Arthur, M.B. and Rousseau, D.M. (Eds.) *The boundaryless career: a new employment principle for a new organizational era*, New York: Oxford University Press.

Sayles, L.R and Chandler, M.K. (1993) *Managing Large Systems,* New Brunswick: Transaction Publishers.

Schelle, H. (1990) "Operations Research and Project Management: Past Present and Future", In H. Reschke and H. Schelle (Eds), *Dimensions of Project Management. Fundamentals, Techniques, Organization, Applications*. Berlin, Heidelberg: Springer, pp.111-120.

Schutz, A. (1967) *The Phenomenology of the Social World*, Evanston, Ill: Northwestern University Press.

Schön, D. (1997), "Apprentissage organisationnel et épistémologie de la pratique", in Reynaud B. (eds) *Les limites de la rationalité*, La découverte,

Scott, W.G., T.R. Mitchell, and N.S. Peery. (1981) "Organizational Governance." in *Handbook of Organizational Design*, edited by P. C. Nystrom and W. H. Starbuck. New York: Oxford University Press.

Scudder, G.D., Schroeder, R.G., Van de Ven, A.H., Seiler, G.R., and Wiseman, R.M. (1989) "Managing Complex Innovations: the Case of Defence Contracting", In A.H. Van de Ven, H.L. Angle, M. S. Poole (eds.) *Research on the Management of Innovation,* Grand Rapids: Ballinger.

Senge, P. M. (1990) *The fifth discipline: The art and practice of the learning organization*, New York: Doubleday.

Sharpe, W., Alexander, G. J. and J. Bailey, (1995) *Investments*. New Jersey.

Shenhar, A.J. (1993) "From Low- to High-tech Project Management", *R&D Management*, 23(3):199-214.

Shenhar, A.J. (1995) "Contingent Project Management: A Classical Concept in a New Arena". Paper presented at the *Academy of Management Meetings* in Vancouver, BC.

Shenhar, A.J. and Dvir, D. (1996) "Toward a typological theory of project management," *Research Policy*, Vol. 25, pp. 607-632.

Shenhar, A.J., Levy, O. and Dvir, D. (1997) "Mapping the Dimensions of Project Success", *Project Management Journal*, Vol. 28, No. 2, pp. 5-13.

Shibagaki, K, Trevor, M. and Abo, T. (eds) (1989) *Japanese and European Management: their international adaptability*, Tokyo: University of Tokyo Press.

Simon, H. (1997, original 1947) *Administrative Behavior*, New York: The Free Press.

Simon, H.A. (1957) *Models of Man, Social and Rational: Mathematical Essays on Rational Human Behavior in Social Settings*, New York: Wiley.

Simon, H.A. (1969) *The Sciences of the Artificial*, Cambridge, Massachusetts: MIT Press.

Slack, N., Chambers, S. Harland, C. Harrison, A. and Johnston R. (1995) *Operations Management*, London: Pitman Publishing.

Slevin, D.P. and Pinto, J.K. (1986) "The Project Implementation Profile: New Tool For Project Managers" *Project Management Journal*, No. 4: pp.57-70.

Slevin D.P. and Pinto, J.K. (1987) "Balancing Strategy and Tactics in Project Implementation", *Sloan Management Review,* Fall 33-41.

Smith, M.A., Mitra, S. and Narasimhan, S. (1996) "Offshore Outsourcing of Software Development and Maintenance: A Frame-work for Issues." *Information and Management* 31(3):165-.

Sobel, R. (1981) *IBM: Colossus in Transition*, New York: Truman Talley Books. Times Books

Solomon, C.M. (1995) "Global Teams: The Ultimate Collaboration." *Personnel Journal* (September):49-58.

Soni, K., Lilien, G.L. and Wilson, D.T. (1993) "Industrial Innovation and Firm Performance: A Re-Conceptualization and Exploratory Structural Equation Analysis" *International Journal of Research in Marketing*, No.10: pp.365-680.

Staehle, W. (1986) *Management, Eine verhaltenswissenschaftliche Perspektive* (Management: A behavioral perspective), München: Vahlen.

Stalk, G. and Hout, T.M. (1990) *Competing against Time,* New York: Free Press.

Starbuck, W.H. (1983) "Organizations as Action Generators", *American Sociological Review*, 48:91-102.

Steffensen, S.K. and Dirks, D. (1997) *Between Efficiency and Effectiveness: technological change, restructuring, and human resource management in Japanese firms,* Presentation to the XIVth Euro-Asia Management Studies Association Conference, Metz, France.

Stewart, K. L. and Deibert, M. S. (1993) "A Marketing Study of Festivals and Special Events to Attract Tourism and Business", *Journal of Professional Services Marketing*, Vol. 8:2, pp. 215-222.

Stinchcombe, A.L. (1985a) "Project Administration in the North Sea", In A.L. Stinchcombe and C.A. Heimer (Eds), *Organization Theory and Project Management. Administering Uncertainty in Norwegian Offshore Oil*, Oslo: Norwegian University Press, pp. 25-120.

Stinchcombe, A.L. (1985b) "Authority and the Management of Engineering on Large Projects", In A.L. Stinchcombe and C.A. Heimer (Eds), *Organization*

Theory and Project Management. Administering Uncertainty in Norwegian Offshore Oil. Oslo: Norwegian University Press, pp. 225-256.

Stinchcombe, A.L. and Heimer C.A. (1985) *Organizational Theory and Project Management,* Oslo: Norwegian University Press.

Stockholm Cultural Capital (1999) *Stockholm 98: EU's cultural capital*, Official Report, Stockholm: The municipality of Stockholm.

Stuckenbruck, L.C. (Ed.) (1982) *The Implementation of Project Management: The Professional's Handbook,* Reading, MA: Addison-Wesley.

Suarez, J.G. (1993) "Managing fear in the work place". Http://www.tql-navy.org/tqlpub/manfear.txt. October 9, 1997.

Sverlinger, P-O. M. (1996) *Organisatorisk samordning vid projektering - en studie ur ett konsultföretagsperspektiv* (Organisational co-ordination in planning projects – a study from the perspective of a consultant firm), Institutionen för byggnadsekonomi och byggnadsorganisation, Chalmers tekniska högskola, Göteborg.

Söderholm, A. (1991) *Organiseringens* logik (The logic of organising), Studier i företagsekonomi, Umeå universitet.

Söderlund, J. and Andersson, N. (1998) "A framework for analyzing project dyads: the case of discontinuity, uncertainty and trust," in R. A. Lundin and Midler, C. (Eds.), *Projects as arenas for learning and renewal processes,* Boston: Kluwer Academic Publishers.

Taylor, J. and Wacker, W. (1997) *The 500 Year Delta – What happens after what comes next,* New York, NY: Harper Business Press.

Thamhain, H.J. (1987) "The New Project Management Software and Its Impact on Management Style", *Project Management Journal,* 18(3):50-54.

Thamhain, H.J. (1996) "Best practices for controlling technology-based projects". *Project Management Journal*, Vol. 27(4), pp. 37-48.

Thamhain, H.J. and Wilemon, D.L. (1975) "Conflict Management in Project Life Cycles", *Sloan Management Review*, 16(3):31-50.

Thompson, J.D. (1967) *Organizations in action*, New York: McGraw-Hill.

Thorelli, H.B. (1986) "Networks: Between Markets and Hierarchies", *Strategic Management Journal*, Vol. 7.

Thorngate, W. (1980) "Efficient Decision Heuristics." *Behavioral Science.* 25: 219-225.

Townley, B. (1995) *Reframing Human Resource Management: Power, Ethics and the Subject at Work*, London: Sage Publications.

Trompenaars F. (1993) *Riding the Waves of Culture: understanding cultural diversity in business*, London: Economist Books.

Trägårdh, B. (1997) *Samverkan och samexistens - om relationer mellan operativa chefer* (Co-operation and co-existance - on relationships between operative managers), Göteborg: BAS ekonomiska förening.

Turnbull, P.W. and Gibbs, M.L. (1987) "Marketing bank services to corporate customers", *International Journal of Bank Marketing.* vol. 14-4: 7-19.

Turner, J.R. (1993) *The Handbook of Project-Based Management: Improving the Processes for Achieving Strategic Objectives*, London: McGraw-Hill.

Turner, J.R. (1999) *The Handbook of Project-based Management, 2nd edition,* London: McGraw-Hill.

Turner, J.R. (2000) "Project Success and Strategy", in Turner, J.R., (ed), *The Gower Handbook of Project Management, 3rd edition,* Aldershot: Gower.

Tushman, M. and Andersen, P. (1986) "Technological discontinuities and organizational environments" *Administrative Science Quarterly,* vol 31: 439-465.

Tushman, M.L. and O'Reilly, C.A. III (1997) *Winning through Innovation,* Boston, MA: Harvard Business School Press.

Tushman, M.L. and Nadler, D.A. (1978) "Information Processing as an Integrating Concept in Organizational Design." *Academy of Management Journal* 3:613-624.

Twyford, J. (1999) "Project Managers, Profession or Trade", in Artto, K., Kähkönen, K. and Koskinen, K. (eds) *Managing Business by Projects,* pp. 121-135, Helsinki: PMI of Finland and NORDNET.

Tyre, M. and Orlikowski, W. (1994) "Windows of opportunity: temporal patterns of technological adaptation in organizations," *Organization Science,* Vol. 5, No. 1, pp. 98-118.

Usunier, J-C. (1993) *International marketing: a cultural approach,* London: Prentice Hall, pp 102-105.

Utterback, J. (1994) *Mastering the Dynamics of Innovation : How Companies Can Seize Opportunities in the Face of Technological Change* Boston, MA: Harvard Business School Press.

Walsh, J.P. (1995) "Managerial and Organizational Cognition: Notes From A Trip Down Memory Lane", *Organization Science,* 6(3):280-321.

Walton, M. (1997) *Car: A Drama of the American Workplace,* New York: W. W. Norton.

Van de Ven, A.H., Delbecq, A.L. and Koenig, R. Jr. (1976) "Determinants of Coordination Modes Within Organizations." *American Sociological Review* 41(April):322-338.

van Fenema, P.C. (1997) "Coordination & Control of Globally Distributed Software Development Projects: The GOLDD Case." in *International Conference on Information Systems (ICIS),* edited by J. I. DeGross. Atlanta, GA.

van Fenema, P.C. and Kumar, K. (2000) "Towards a Comprehensive Theory of Organizational Coordination and Control." Working Paper, Rotterdam School of Management. (forthcoming)

Van Seters, D. A. and Field, R. H. G. (1990) "The evolution of leadership theory". *Journal of Organizational Change Management,* Vol. 3(3), pp. 29-45.

Wateridge, J.F. (1995) "IT Projects: a basis for success", *International Journal of Project Management,* Vol. 13, No. 3, pp 169-172.

Wateridge, J.F. (1996) "Delivering successful IS/IT projects: 8 key elements from success criteria to implementation via management, methodologies and teams", Ph.D. thesis, Henley Management College and Brunel University.

Wateridge, J.F. (1998) "How can IS/IT project be measured for success", *International Journal of Project Management,* Vol. 16, No.1, pp 59-64.

Vaughan, D. (1996) *The Challenger Launch Decision: Risky Technology, Culture and Deviance at NASA,* Chicago: University of Chicago Press

Webster, (1994) "We Don't Do Projects", In Cleland, D.I. and Gareis, R. (Eds), *Global Project Management Handbook.*

Weick, K.E. (1979) *The Social Psychology of Organizing*, New York, NY: Random House.

Weick, K.E. (1993) "The Collapse of Sensemaking in Organizations: The Mann Gulch Disaster." *Administrative Science Quarterly* 38:628-652.

Weick, K.E. (1995) *Sensemaking in Organizations*, London: Sage Publications.

Weick, K.E. (1996) "Enactment and the boundaryless career: organizing as we work," in Arthur, M. B. and Rousseau, D. M. (Eds.) *The boundaryless career: a new employment principle for a new organizational era*, New York: Oxford University Press.

Weick, K.E. and Roberts, K. (1993) "Collective Mind in Organizations: Heedful Interelating on Flight Decks." *Administrative Science Quarterly* 38:357-381.

Welch, L.S. (1985) "The international marketing of technology", *International Marketing Review*. vol. 2-1: 41-53.

Wellins, R.S., R. Wilson, and A.J. Katz. (1990) *Self-directed Teams: A Study of Current Practice*, Pittsburgh: DDI.

Wheelwright, S. C. and Clark, K.B. (1992) "Creating Project Plans to Focus For Product Development" *Harvard Business Review*, March-April, pp70- 82.

Wheelwright, S.C. and Clark, K.B. (1992) *Revolutionizing Product Development*, New York: Free Press.

Wheiler, K. (1987) "Referrals between professional service providers", *Industrial Marketing Management*. vol. 16: 191-200.

Whipp, R. and Clark, P. (1986) *Innovation and the Auto Industry*, London: Frances Pinter.

Whittington, R., Pettigrew, A., Peck, S., Fenton, E. and Conyon, M. (1999) "Change and complementarities in the new competitive landscape: a European study", *Organization Science*, forthcoming.

Whittington, R., Pettigrew, A., Peck, S., Fenton, E. and Conyon, M. (*forthcoming*) "Change and Complementarities in the New Competitive Landscape: A European Panel Study 1992-1996", *Organization Science*

Wideman, M. and Shenhar, A.J. (1996) "Improving Project Management: Linking Success Criteria to Project Type". Paper presented at the *Project Management Institute Canadian Conference* in Calgary.

Wilemon, D.L. and Baker, B.N. (1983) "Some Major Research Findings Regarding the Human Element in Project Management", In D.I. Cleland and W.R. King (Eds), *Handbook of Project Management*. New York, NY: Van Nostrand Reinhold, pp. 623-641.

Wilensky, H.L. (1967) *Organizational Intelligence: Knowledge and Policy in Government and Industry*, New York, NY: Basic Books.

Wiley, N. (1988) "The Micro-macro Problem in Social Theory", *Sociological Theory*, 6:254-261.

Williamson, O.E. (1975) *Markets and Hierarchies: analysis and antitrust implications*, New York: Free Press.

Williamson O.E. (1995) *The Economic Institutions of Capitalism*, New York: Free Press.

Willman, P. and Winch, G. M. (1985) *Innovation and Management Control*, Cambridge: CUP.

Wilson, T.L. and Smith, F.E. (1996) "Business services 1982-1992: growth, industry characteristics, financial performance", *Industrial Marketing Management.* vol. 25: 163-171.

Winch, G.M. (1994) *Managing Production; Engineering Change and Stability,* Oxford: OUP.

Winch, G.M. (1996a) "The Renaissance of Project Management", *Financial Times* 9/8/96.

Winch, G.M. (1996b) *The Channel Tunnel; le Projet du Siècle,* London: Le Groupe Bagnolet Working Paper 11.

Winch, G.M. (1998), "Zephyrs of creative destruction: notes on the innovation problem in construction",

Winch, G.M., Usmani, A. and Edkins, A. (1998) "Towards Total Project Quality: A Gap Analysis Approach", *Construction Management and Economics* 16 193-207.

Winkler, D. A. (1996) "Building business breakthroughs". *Chief Executive (U.S.),* no. 115, pp. 58-62.

Wittgenstein, L. (1992 orig. 1969) *Om visshet,* (On certainty) translation Lars Hertzberg Stockholm: Thales,

Wittgenstein, L. (1996 orig. 1953) *Filosofiska undersökningar,* (Philosophical investigations) translation Anders Wedberg, Stockholm: Thales

Volberda, H.W. (1997) "Toward the Flexible Form: How to Remain Vital in Hypercompetitive Environments." *Organization Science* 7(4):359-374.

Womack, J. P. and Jones, D. T. (1996) *Lean Thinking,* New York: Simon and Schuster.

Womack, J. P., Jones, D. T., and Roos, D. (1990*) The Machine that Changed the World,* New York: Rawson Associates.

von Hippel, E. (1990) "Task Partitioning: An Innovation Process Variable." *Research Policy* 19(5):407-418.

von Hippel, E. (1994) "'Sticky Information' and the Locus of Problem Solving: Implications for Innovation." *Management Science* 40(4):429-439.

von Hippel, E. (1998) "Economics of Product Development by Users: The impact of 'Sticky' Local Information." *Management Science* 44(5):629-644.

Woods, J.C. and Randall, M.R. (1989) "The Net Present Value of future investment opportunities: its impact on shareholder wealth and implications for capital budgeting theory", *Financial Management,* Vol. 1, pp 85-92.

Woodside, A.G., Wilson, E.J. and Milner, P. (1992) "Buying and marketing CPA services", *Industrial Marketing Management.* vol. 21: 265-272.

Woodward, J. (1965) *Industrial organization: theory and practice,* New York: Oxford University Press.

Yorke, D.A. (1990) "Developing an interactive approach to the marketing of professional services", in *Understanding business markets: interaction, relationships, networks,* Ford, D., ed., London: Academic Press, pp. 347-358.

Zielasek, G. (1995) *Projektmanagement für den Praktiker, Erfolgreich durch Aktivierung aller Unternehmensebenen* (Project management for the practitioner: Successful by activating all firm levels), Heidelberg: Springer.